UNINVITED GUESTS

UNINVITED GUESTS

A Documented History Of UFO Sightings, Alien Encounters & Coverups

RICHARD HALL

AURORA PRESS

P.O. Box 573
Santa Fe, New Mexico 87504

First published in 1988 by:
Aurora Press
P.O. Box 573
Santa Fe, N.M. 87504

ISBN: 0-943358-32-9
Library of Congress Catalogue No: 88-0704-77

DEDICATION

This work is dedicated to the three people whose friendship and intellectual stimulation have most influenced both my UFO studies and, in many respects, my life:

Maj. Donald E. Keyhoe (USMC, Ret.), who took me as a raw recruit and trained me in investigative journalism, entrusted me with considerable responsibility at NICAP, and treated me like a son.

Isabel L. Davis, late companion, supporter, and peerless proponent of good English-language usage and rigorous intellectual discipline, always with love and understanding.

Dr. James E. McDonald, late professor of meteorology and senior physicist at the Institute of Atmospheric Physics, University of Arizona, my role model as a true scientist and also a treasured friend; a truly "sweet man," so termed by a New York *Times* reporter in conversation with me upon learning of McDonald's untimely death.

DEDICATION

ACKNOWLEDGMENTS

An article in *International UFO Reporter*, July-August 1985, published by the Center for UFO Studies, was based on an earlier, condensed version of Chapter 4, "Bodies in the Morgue." The chapter has since been revised and updated.

I would like to thank Ted Bloecher for reviewing Chapter 3, Len Stringfield for reviewing Chapter 4, and Budd Hopkins for reviewing Chapter 5, though I remain personally responsible for the content of each.

Thanks to my good friend Dr. Peter Rank for a critical reading of the complete manuscript and for editorial suggestions; and to Edith Ortanez for the original typing of the manuscript.

Most of all, I wish to thank my brother, William H. Hall, for his invaluable help and support, and for editorial and computer services in the production of the final manuscript.

ABOUT THE AUTHOR

RICHARD HALL resides in Brentwood, Maryland. He has been a writer-editor in the Washington, D.C., area for over 25 years, including extensive work on scientific publications. He is former Assistant Director and Acting Director of the National Investigations Committee on Aerial Phenomena (NICAP), and in that capacity was editor of the 200,000-word documentary report *The UFO Evidence* and consultant to the University of Colorado UFO Project, sponsored by the Air Force Office of Scientific Research.

Hall currently is Director of Publications for the Mutual UFO Network (MUFON), Consulting Editor to the J. Allen Hynek Center for UFO Studies (CUFOS), and a National Board Member of the Fund for UFO Research. The views presented in this book are his own, and do not necessarily represent the opinions of the organizations with which he is affiliated.

His UFO-related publication credits include a 1968 *Encyclopedia Britannica Book of the Year* article; the introduction and epilogue in the 1968 Prentice-Hall book *Mysteries of the Skies: UFOs in Perspective*; and several articles and a major appendix with by-line in the 1980 Doubleday *Encyclopedia of UFOs*.

Why did the Central Intelligence Agency run a security clearance on the author without his knowledge or consent? In 1965, Richard Hall, then Acting Director of NICAP, a civilian UFO group in Washington, D.C., was questioned by a CIA agent and given a direct telephone line to his office, using it once to report some high quality UFO sightings, as requested. Many years later he learned of the security clearance, and recently used the Freedom of Information and Privacy Acts to request CIA files mentioning him by name. Some previously known documents were obtained after an appeal, but the

CIA refused to release the security clearance "paper trail." (See Government Documents in Appendix.)

When the author was in charge of NICAP, the major civilian UFO group of the 1960s, the State Department called to make an appointment for an Argentine "newsman" and an interpreter. The "newsman" turned out to be a military intelligence officer who requested — and was granted — a long, private conference to exchange information. (See Chapter 11.)

Because of his unique background and experience in the UFO field, Hall has participated in major news conferences at the National Press Club; has been interviewed by TV networks, the Canadian Broadcasting Corporation, the Voice of America, French and Italian National TV, and hundreds of daily newspapers, radio and TV stations; and twice has been a guest on the nationally syndicated Larry King show.

Due to his career in and around Washington, D.C., Hall also has interacted with Members of Congress, Administration officials, employees of national intelligence agencies, the Washington press corps, international agencies such as the United Nations, and foreign diplomatic missions in the U.S. Thus, his views on the UFO subject are drawn from a broad background of knowledge and experience.

TABLE OF CONTENTS

PART II — DISCOVERY

PART III — EVALUATING THE UNKNOWN

FOREWORD

Forty years have now passed since the first "flying saucer" sightings, signalling the birth of the UFO phenomenon as it has come to be recognized. During this same period, the world and our perception of it have changed beyond the measure of all previous human history. Science and the accompanying transformations of technology have brought us machines that have taken people to the Moon and back, an almost instantaneous world communications system, and computers that control a global inundation of information. At the same time, we have created a "star wars" world of fearful weapons and an uncontrolled exploitation of planetary resources that threaten not only the ecological balance, but also the very life of planet Earth itself.

The discovery of DNA and molecular biology have placed us at the threshold of a genetically engineered "brave new world" of unfathomable implications. Beginning with radar and the advent of radio astronomy, the eyes of astronomers have now been opened to virtually the entire electromagnetic spectrum from gamma rays to the radio signals from the echo of the "Big Bang" that likely formed the universe as we now know it. It is also during this 40-year span of time that scientists and philosophers have begun to seriously pose the questions . . . "Are we alone in the universe?" and, if not, "Where are they?".

This latter question, reputed to have been asked by physicist Enrico Fermi at a Los Alamos gathering of Manhattan Project scientists, neatly characterizes one of the primary observations regarding extraterrestrial life, intelligent or otherwise

. . . it has not made its existence overwhelmingly obvious to us! Fermi's question was made in the context of the mainstream of contemporary Western thought regarding our place in the universe, namely that we likely are a typical, random sample of what we might expect to find in the cosmos. Usually called the Cosmological Principle, this idea derives from the many lessons learned since the Copernican revolution that there is nothing we know of to single out the Earth, our Solar System, Milky Way galaxy, or even our Local Group of galaxies as being unique or in any preferred place in the cosmos. We simply are not in the center of any system, and furthermore, contemporary cosmologies suggest that the concept of a spatial center of the universe has no meaning. Therefore, life is a natural, inevitable consequence of the evolution of the universe and must be quite a common occurrence out there among the 200 billion stars in the Milky Way. And the Milky Way is but one of trillions of known galaxies. So . . . Where are they?

At present, I would suggest that the spectrum of opinion in the scientific community can readily be separated into three groups. The majority opinion might be called the "Main Stream." In this view, there likely are tens of thousands of advanced, intelligent life forms in our Galaxy alone. We probably would find ourselves to be at the average level of consciousness in the scheme of things. But, due to the great distances and time scales involved, interstellar space travel is difficult, rare, and limited in any case by the speed of light. The islands of life are marooned on their worlds of origin, and so must be content to explore the universe by observation and by interstellar communication. The search for radio signals from extraterrestrials in the form of intentional messages or "leakage" radiation has apparently yielded negative results to date . . . and I speak as a radio astronomer who has taken some interest in this matter.

A second approach, which I will characterize as the "Loners" group, looks at the same data but comes to the conclusion that we may actually be virtually the only advanced technical civilization in the Galaxy! The nucleus of this group was formed by astronomers Michael Hart, Michael Papagiannis, and Ben Zuckerman who organized a 1979 conference on "Extraterrestrials: Where are they?" (Hart and Zuckerman, 1982).* Their answer to this question is that life on planetary worlds is in a far more precarious position than previously supposed. Hart's work has suggested the liquid-water-based life of Earth is delicately balanced between the runaway greenhouse effects that have produced the desert world of Venus and the runaway glaciation of Mars. Though life may readily form on other worlds, it is repeatedly snuffed out by instabilities within solar systems or from without by being close to stars exploding in deadly supernovae.

These statistics would seem to show that the 4 billion year history of liquid-water-based life on planet Earth is so unlikely that we are lucky to be the only ones to survive this long in the history of the Galaxy. This view is further reinforced by space colonization scenarios which suggest that, if expansionist intelligent life forms that had begun interstellar voyaging were common in our Milky Way, then, even at space colony velocities well below the speed of light, the whole Galaxy should have been colonized long ago in time scales of a few hundred million years. Though this time sounds astronomically great, it is quite modest when compared with the 10 billion year age of our Galaxy.

The third group, probably the farthest from the Main Stream, would aspire to discover the "Galactic Club." Their answer to Fermi's question is that they *are* here, but have not chosen to make their presence known. Variants of the Galactic Club hypothesis have been called the "zoo theory" or the "quarantine theory" in which case we are under extraterrestrial scrutiny as a rare example of an emergent technical civilization. After all, in the 4 billion year history of Earth's ecosystem, agriculture was invented only a few thousand years ago. In this view, we are rapidly emerging to join the Galactic

---

*Hart, Michael H. and Zuckerman, Ben (Eds.). *Extraterrestrials: Where are They?* (New York: Pergamon Press, 1982).

Club or "Overmind," however you might conceive of it. Somehow, this always reminds me of Charles Fort's words . . . "I think we're property."

Of the three groups of opinion presented here, it is only among some members of the Galactic Club that the UFO evidence is taken as data worthy of serious scientific consideration. This lack of attention is most unfortunate because, as Richard Hall says in his introduction to Chapter 10, "The data of reported UFO sightings contain either the makings of the greatest scientific revolution of all time, or of the most pervasive delusion in human history." I strongly concur, and might reiterate that there *is* a real UFO phenomenon (or phenomena) and, regardless of whether its origins lie in outer space or inner space, the potential magnitude of its implications makes thorough investigation imperative.

Dick Hall, whom I have known as a friend and colleague for 20 years, is one of the pioneering scientific researchers who hold the Galactic Club view of our place in the cosmos of life. The present work is the culmination of a lifetime of careful, open-minded questioning in an area that has been studiously avoided by many who are unwilling to explore beyond the narrow boundaries of their prejudices. "This is not a book of answers, because nobody on any side of the issue really *knows* what UFOs are. Instead, it is a book of questions starting with . . . What *if* UFOs are real? What might they mean for Humankind?" [quoted from the Introduction].

Reading this book will take the reader through a stimulating intellectual exploration of the ideas and data that relate to the contemporary UFO mystery in all of its bewildering complexity. The potential significance is awe inspiring and I am left with the feeling of standing right at the threshold.

John B. Carlson, PhD
Assistant Professor of Astronomy & Anthropology
University of Maryland
College Park, Maryland
April 1988

PROLOGUE

STATE OF THE ART

Have human beings been abducted on board alien craft and subjected to physical examinations or testing by small humanoid beings? Does the U.S. Government have in storage crashed "saucers" and preserved alien bodies?

Twenty years ago, or even ten, both of these notions would have been considered crackpot by all serious researchers, but times have changed and strange new evidence has emerged. These two startling questions dominate UFO research in the 1980s. The major UFO groups of past decades have dwindled to mere shells of their former selves, but new groups and alliances have been formed.

Today UFO investigation and research is led by three complementary groups in the United States (with counterparts overseas): The J. Allen Hynek Center for UFO Studies[1] with prominent scientists on its board; the Mutual UFO Network[2] an independent, grass roots membership organization with a widespread investigative network that is shared with CUFOS; and the Fund for UFO Research[3] which channels tax-exempt contributions into worthwhile research and public education projects. The three organizations have overlapping directorates and interests, and cooperate closely.

Another specialized research group, recently revitalized and expanding its scope, is Citizens Against UFO Secrecy[4] which concentrates on Freedom of Information Act lawsuits and other legal activities designed to pry loose "hidden" cases and historical documents from various Government agencies, including the Central Intelligence Agency.

The "strangeness" of UFO sightings has increased with time. No longer are "routine" UFO fly-by reports of much interest. Instead, attention is focused on physical evidence cases (CE II, in Dr. Hynek's terminology) and reported encounters with humanoid beings (CE III), better known as "Close Encounters of the Third Kind." A large computer catalogue of UFO sightings (UFOCAT), initially compiled by Dr. David R. Saunders, now is operated by CUFOS. Efforts are underway to develop computer bulletin boards and other computer systems to track UFO patterns.

MUFON and other groups continue to investigate and compile reports on sightings, and to generate catalogues and other documents, but how much new information can be derived from additional "ordinary" sightings that would expedite the search for the meaning of UFOs?

Increasing emphasis has been given to the world-wide reports of humanoid beings observed in association with UFO landings or other encounters. Preeminent among researchers in this area have been Ted Bloecher and David Webb, who served as co-chairmen of the MUFON Humanoid Study Group. The two compiled a computer catalogue of humanoid reports, containing over 2,000 entries. If UFOs are spaceships, or something even stranger than that, Bloecher and Webb feel that the key to the puzzle lies in the careful study of the humanoid reports.

A perplexing spin-off of humanoid cases began to emerge in the 1960s and mushroomed in the 1970's: witness reports (many obtained under hypnotic regression but some from conscious recall) that they had been forcibly abducted by seemingly alien humanoids, examined or probed, then released.

In most cases, according to the stories, the aliens more or less successfully induced amnesia in their captives before releasing them. However, vague memories or troubling dreams — or awareness of an unaccounted-for period of time — led them to seek help in removing the apparent memory block. Often partial memory blocks remain even after hypnosis, but details of the stories that have emerged are startlingly similar, sometimes identical. There is no doubt that the events are psychologically real for the "victims." The question remains: Are they physically real as well?

At the same time that abduction reports began coming to the fore, veteran UFO researcher Leonard Stringfield had begun to re-examine the long-standing rumors that flying saucers had crashed during the 1950s, and the craft along with dead humanoid bodies had been spirited away by military units for study — usually, according to the rumors, to Wright-Patterson AFB, Ohio. Stringfield and his scientifically oriented colleagues, including the writer, had been skeptical of the stories, in particular of the lack of *first-hand* witnesses. The stories always were second- or third-hand.

A revival of the rumors caused Stringfield to review the question in a 1977 book[5] updating his investigations of the entire UFO subject. To his surprise, the book touched off a flurry of new claims, but this time Stringfield was able to locate and meet face-to-face first-hand witnesses who said *they were there* ... they had personally observed or participated in the recovery of apparent spacecraft and humanoid bodies, either at the crash site or during the arrival of the "remains" at a military facility.

The only catch was that the witnesses, almost uniformly fearing reprisals from authorities (some have reported threats and intimidation), were only willing to give information if their identities were totally protected. Impressively, the key witnesses were doctors, bank officials, law enforcement personnel, and other professionals holding responsible positions. Their stories sketched a picture of UFO crashes beginning in the late 1940s, peaking in the 1950s, and continuing sporadically well into the 1970s.

An important implication of the information provided to Stringfield was that U.S. Government teams, after the earliest crashes which leaked out to the public, were so well organized that they quickly blanketed new crash sites, gathered up all the evidence, and covered up the truth by any means necessary — including harsh intimidation of personnel who participated in the recoveries. If true, then clearly the Government long has had absolute physical proof of alien visitors and the entire public UFO program has been a sham; truly a Cosmic Watergate.

Oddly, the two scenarios — abductions and crash/retrievals — depict "spacemen" in ways that, on the face of it, seem inconsistent. The alien abductors, though often described as similar both to the humanoids seen worldwide and to the alleged corpses in military custody, seem superhuman in their powers or abilities. Theirs is an almost magical "technology," according to the abductees, involving manipulations of matter and energy far beyond even our most advanced science. Yet, the crashes seem to imply an all-too-human fallibility and vulnerability.

Several possible explanations come to mind. First, it is possible that either or both of the scenarios is untrue — that the "abductions" are a psychological aberration of some kind, or that the "crashes" somehow are an elaborate hoax, or both. Alternatively, if both are true, it is possible that we (private researchers) are missing a key piece of the puzzle, which may or may not be known to presumed Government investigators. Something that would explain why "super-scientists" from elsewhere sometimes have accidents, albeit ones that tend to give the game away.

Perhaps some of the multitude of electromagnetic radiation we daily shower into the atmosphere interferes with their propulsion system. Or, perhaps the picture given to abductees is distorted, deliberately by the supposed aliens or accidentally by the human mind filter of someone trying to grasp and recount things beyond his or her ken. Only careful, empirical investigation may supply us the answers.

The case for UFOs, anyway, is independent of these presently dominant, spectacular themes. Even if there are no bodies and abductions are not physically real occurrences, a large body of well-attested reports exists describing craft-like objects that often interact with human beings at close range, display extraordinary performance, and cause an array of physical and physiological effects. It is these underlying "hard-core" UFO reports that establish UFOs as a genuine scientific mystery in the first place. Except for them, we would have no basis for taking abduction reports or retrieval reports serious-ly. But we do have them, and therefore we must take a close — if cautious — look at the evidence suggesting direct inter-vention in human affairs by humanoid beings from elsewhere.

NOTES

1. CUFOS, 2457 W. Peterson, Chicago, IL 60659
2. MUFON, 103 Oldtowne Road, Seguin, TX 78155
3. Fund for UFO Research, Box 277, Mt.Rainier, MD 20712
4. CAUS, P.O. Box 218, Coventry, CT 06238
5. *Situation Red: The UFO Siege* (N.Y.: Doubleday, 1977)

INTRODUCTION

The idea that UFOs are extraterrestrial in origin — so-called "nuts and bolts" craft carrying intelligent beings from some other planet in space — has dominated all thinking on the subject since 1948. In that year, the Air Technical Intelligence Center of the U.S. Air Force drew this conclusion in a Top Secret report that travelled through channels all the way to General Hoyt S. Vandenberg, Air Force Commander, who rejected the conclusion because it lacked "proof."

Capt. Edward J. Ruppelt, chief of the Project Blue Book UFO investigation in the 1950s, later was to ask, "What constitutes proof?" He reported that the rebuff from on high sent Air Force intelligence units scurrying to explain away all UFO reports for several years thereafter . . . until insistent reports from pilots and scientists forced the Air Force to reopen the investigation.

The extraterrestrial hypothesis (ETH) was first publicly aired in 1949 by Major Donald E. Keyhoe, USMC (Ret). Taking his cue from personal contacts in the Pentagon who funnelled information to him, Keyhoe contributed a bombshell article in *TRUE* magazine, reputedly the most widely read magazine article ever up until that time. This was followed by an expanded version in the 1950 book *Flying Saucers Are Real*.

Because of his military and aviation background, Keyhoe's views — that extraterrestrial beings were observing the earth, apparently attracted by the series of A-bomb explosions that began in 1945 — carried a lot of weight. He remains to this day the foremost proponent of the ETH, but he is not alone.

Over 35 years of sightings since then have convinced a majority of Americans that UFOs are real and probably extraterrestrial, according to Gallup polls (May 1966 and December 1973).

The lack of absolute proof during this same period, however, has led a number of UFO theorists to believe that the ETH is simplistic; that if UFOs were extraterrestrial, it would have become obvious by now through direct contact or strong scientific evidence. The elusiveness of UFOs, their constant failure to leave behind totally convincing evidence, suggests to these theorists that something more than "mere" spaceships must be involved.

More to the point, they argue, the content of UFO reports has become increasingly bizarre: stories of alien creatures abducting humans and subjecting them to physical examinations have multiplied since the 1960s. The beings, who sometimes appear more like apparitions than solid entities, display almost magical powers, including levitation, telepathy, movement through solid matter, and cause electrical malfunctions.

Moreover, even if the abduction reports are imaginary, why would intelligent beings repeatedly hover over installations and then dart away, for no apparent purpose? Why would they buzz human vehicles, take soil samples, and all the other repetitive actions year after year without doing *something* to remove all doubt about their nature and purpose? Why do they continue to dazzle us with exotic displays but not make open contact or communicate something definite to us?

Faced with a phantasmagoria of magic machines and ghost-like beings whose actions defy rational explanation, these theorists reject the ETH and suggest instead that UFOs must be something else entirely: psychic projections collectively created by Humankind to suit its own psychological needs (something on the order of Carl Jung's "collective unconscious"); time travellers; beings from a parallel universe; or even angels or demons. A few analysts think the UFOs and associated humanoid beings may be illusions or staged events orchestrated by some pervasive background intelligence.

Most of these ideas, obviously including the ETH, have been treated many times in science fiction literature. Now some UFO researchers are considering them as possible truth. One purpose of this book is to examine the various theories to see which make the most sense. The dynamic tension between ETH advocates and "other" theorists has led to a new look at the evidence to see who may be right.

A deep and compelling human curiosity to know the "why" of it causes us to overlook the fact that we really don't know the "what" of it very well yet. Which of the bewildering mass of reports constitute valid evidence that any theory must take into account? Spectacular new cases are reported by credible witnesses each year, but science largely ignores them and private investigators lack adequate resources to conduct thorough investigations in many cases. The "body of data" remains largely (but not totally) anecdotal, unconfirmed by instrumental studies or systematic evaluation of the oft-reported physical and physiological evidence.

Until a comprehensive scientific investigation is undertaken, we must work with what evidence we have. The following discussions are based on the premise that UFOs are *not* all explainable as mistaken observations, but instead are *something* real and unexplained. The "nuts and bolts" theory, other variants on the extraterrestrial theme, and non-ETH theories all are weighed against cases cited from the UFO literature. Summaries of the reports are included in the Case Book Appendix with sources for each case, and chapter-end bibliographies are provided for serious researchers.

This is not a book of answers, because nobody on any side of the issue really *knows* what UFOs are. Instead, it is a book of questions starting with . . . What *if* UFOs are real? What might they mean for Humankind?

Strict scientific procedure does not allow something to be called a "theory" or "hypothesis" unless its truth or falsity can be tested by further investigation and study. Some of the notions discussed are testable, while others are not . . . or their credibility might only be determined by such complex chains of evidence and reason that the argument would not be totally convincing. Therefore, the discussions frankly contain outright speculation at times about what UFOs *might* mean.

If UFOs do represent "nuts and bolts" craft piloted by sentient beings from other civilizations in space, then no particular interpretation of their meaning for us necessarily follows. They could be moral, peaceful, advanced beings whose visitations might bode well for Humankind, or they could be something so different from us that meaningful interaction with them would be impossible. If we don't resemble their concept of "intelligent life" or "worthy lifeforms," we may be in danger of accidental or deliberate harm as mere objects or specimens from their viewpoint.

On the other hand, if UFOs are something even more marvelous than visitors from another planet — for example, human-like or human time travellers, or beings from some other realm presently unknown to science — recognition of this could profoundly alter our understanding of the universe and our outlook on life.

The analyses and speculations that follow are intended to encourage thought and discussion about the ideas advanced. The concepts explored here need to be critically examined and measured continuously against the still-unfolding UFO manifestation. Only careful sifting of evidence and increased scientific investigation are likely to provide the ultimate answers.

Meanwhile, we need to know what has been credibly reported, what possible explanations there are, and what it all might mean. If this book contributes toward obtaining a better understanding of the UFO mystery, and of its potential significance, I will have achieved my main purposes.

Richard H. Hall
Brentwood, Maryland
April 1988

PART I
CONFRONTATION

"Tyger! Tyger! burning bright
In the forests of the night;
What immortal hand or eye
Could frame thy fearful symmetry?"

WILLIAM BLAKE

CHAPTER 1

CLOSE ENCOUNTERS OF THE VEHICULAR KIND

At some indefinable point, UFOs "came down from the skies" and began interacting with human beings in a much more direct and intimate fashion than they had in the early years. During the 1940s and 1950s, "fly-bys" were common — disc-shaped or elliptical objects seen flying past — but skeptics always assumed the reported images were only aircraft or balloons distorted by light reflection or some other aspect of the viewing conditions. Even though radar sometimes seemed to confirm the presence of an unexplained object, radar has its vagaries too.

Furthermore, so the scientists said, UFOs didn't behave as extraterrestrial visitors would. Their actions seemed purposeless; they remained too remote and aloof. Now, 40 years later, the reverse is believed. The alleged interactions of UFOs and alien beings with humans are *too* intrusive, too intimate to be credible as the acts of intelligent beings from space.

Like the story of Goldilocks and the Three Bears, one saucer is too cool, and the other saucer is too hot. No one has defined exactly what behavior would be "just right" in order to be acceptable. The problem is that one person's preconceptions about how UFOs (if extraterrestrial) ought to behave may be another person's anathema.

It is past time for scientists to shed their preconceptions — and their misconceptions — and to study the now overwhelming data indicating that UFOs are *something* real, something of potentially vital importance as the following cases suggest. Scientists, in general, are abysmally ignorant of 40 years of extremely close-range and detailed encounters with UFOs by a cross section of humanity world wide. Scientists, however, cannot take the whole rap for failure to study UFOs; they need the political backing and resulting sources of funds, the legitimization of the problem, in order to lend their skills to a solution. But UFOs are sticky politically too, so it becomes a question of who will have the courage to stand up and be counted. A handful of scientists have had the courage to say that UFOs are a problem demanding the attention of society.

Both scientists and other opinion-makers have been prone to accept, without investigation, the stereotype of UFOs as vague reports of lights seen fleetingly in the sky by careless observers. According to the skeptics, UFO witnesses irrationally convert this weak data into evidence of "spaceships" or "saviors from space." To the contrary, the innumerable close encounter cases compel attention because of the *proximity* and the *immediacy* of the phenomenon. Rather than vague lights, witnesses have reported structured objects seen at close range, and with astounding frequency.

A major category of UFO reports comprises cases in which craft-like objects have engaged in what can only be described as *confrontations* with automobiles and aircraft. Common features include interference with the vehicle's motive power, forcible alteration of the vehicle's course, and even blocking of roadways. The typically frightened witnesses, whose thoughts were on anything but "spaceships" or "saviors from space," describe events that are terrifyingly unfamiliar to their experience . No known natural phenomenon and no human technology fits the description of the reported phenomena.

In one extreme case a young pilot and his plane disappeared without a trace after radioing that his aircraft was besieged by a UFO that seemed to be "playing games" with him. (Aircraft accidents or disappearances have been linked to UFO sightings in a handful of cases.)

At 6:19 p.m. on Saturday, October 21, 1978, Frederick Valentich, 20, took off from a Melbourne, Australia, airport in a single engine Cessna 182 bound for King Island in the Bass Strait. At 7:06 p.m. he informed the tower that what he took to be an aircraft was in his vicinity, something with four bright lights, but air traffic control replied in the negative. Minutes later he reported that he could now see a long shape; then . . . "It's coming for me right now . . . It's got green light and [is] sort of metallic; it's all shiny [on] the outside . . . It is not an aircraft."

Valentich radioed that he was orbiting and the UFO was hovering above him. Then his engine began running rough, "idling and coughing." Through the open microphone the controllers heard a scraping metallic sound, but no further transmission from the young pilot. Despite an extensive search over a several day period, no trace of plane or pilot has ever been found.

Australian investigators later located more than a dozen witnesses who saw a mysterious green light over the strait in the direction where the aircraft was and at about the same time. The pilot's father, who was asked to identify his son's voice on the tape of the radio transmissions, maintains that the Australian government has released a censored transcript of the tape. Be that as it may, the information that is publicly known describes a typical UFO that *confronted* an aircraft and could not be identified as anything conventional. Whether the UFO somehow destroyed the aircraft, or even abducted it, remains purely conjecture.

Bright illumination, malfunction of the vehicle, and the confrontational character of the UFO encounter are frequent and common occurrences, not rarities. A green light beam also figures significantly into the widely reported helicopter-UFO encounter near Mansfield, Ohio, on October 18, 1973. A green beam of light emanated from a structured UFO that rapidly approached and hovered above an Army Reserve helicopter, illuminating the interior of the cabin. Various anomalies were experienced; the craft apparently was lifted upward (loss of pilot control) and the radio failed to function. Finally the UFO broke off contact with a "bump" felt by the crew and disappeared. The pilot then regained control and continued on to their destination.

At least two similar aircraft encounters since then involving *loss of vehicle control* are on record. (For additional details of these and other reports, see Case Book Appendix.) A young pilot flying near Mexico City on May 3, 1975, was confronted by three classic "flying saucer" discs with domes. His controls all failed and the Piper aircraft was *pulled or lifted*. Airport radar confirmed the objects near his plane.

On May 5, 1977, near Tabio, Colombia, a white disc-shaped UFO hovered near an aircraft and the controls failed. "The whole aircraft seemed to be locked into this machine, or being controlled by somebody else," the pilot said. The pilot's vision faded as if he were in a dense fog (another recurring feature) and he had to be guided down to a landing by other pilots as his vision slowly returned.

As far as is known, aircraft encounters are less frequent (or less frequently reported) than automobile encounters in which the vehicle has been forcibly diverted from its course or stopped altogether, often by a UFO literally blocking the road. In other cases the UFO has abruptly approached a car travelling along the highway and interfered with its progress, with electromagnetic (E-M) interference in the car's electrical system a common feature.

In March 1985, during a flurry of other sightings in the area, a 45-year-old industrialist driving between Aculeo Lake and Santiago, Chile, at 9:30 p.m. was suddenly confronted by a strange phenomenon. A powerful light fell on the car and illuminated the road ". . . shaking the vehicle in an unusual and strong way . . . the radio began to buzz with interfering noise and the . . . motor stopped."

At first, the man thought he was caught in an earthquake. Leaning out the window, he looked up and saw ". . . a huge object with a diameter of approximately 30 meters hovering over his car and illuminating it with a strong stream of light so brilliant . . . that it caused pain to his eyes."

The encounter lasted 15 minutes; then the radio began functioning normally and the man started the car and fled the scene. Formerly a total UFO skeptic, he was in a state of shock for several weeks, not even telling his wife about the experience.

On October 20, 1986, near Edmonton, Queensland, Australia, a 41-year-old woman driving home at about 9:30 p.m. suddenly began experiencing difficulty in controlling her car, which was pulling to the right side of the road. After a while the dashboard lights and headlights faded, a buzzing sound was heard, and the engine lost power.

Above the road ahead she could see a bright, oval, blue-green light. Although she had her "foot flat to the floor" on the gas pedal, the motor seemed to be only idling and the car moved forward at a very slow speed. This continued for about 4 km., as the UFO traveled roughly parallel to the road.

As the car passed over a one-lane bridge, the UFO suddenly took off. Immediately, the car lights came back on, the buzzing sound stopped, and she regained control of the steering. The incident had lasted about 8-10 minutes. The car had been functioning normally before the encounter, and functioned normally afterwards.

The road-blocking cases, the UFO that "just happened to be sitting there," have led some observers to suggest that these are also staged confrontations rather than accidental encounters.

Near Vicksburg, Michigan, shortly after 2:00 a.m. on March 31, 1966, a worker was driving home from a late night work shift. As he topped a hill he saw lights on the road ahead and assumed there had been an accident. He slowed the car and approached cautiously. When his headlights passed *beneath* what he had thought was an ambulance and he saw the curved undersurface of an object hovering a few feet above the roadway, bobbing gently, he jammed on the brakes and stopped, puzzled. No police, no ambulance driver, no other car.

Multi-colored body lights on the superstructure of the disc-like object blinked randomly, then a white *beam of light* like a searchlight fell on him. Suddenly overwhelmed with fear, he began backing away, but his car was buffeted as if by a strong blast of wind and the UFO now appeared behind him. His engine stalled and he could hear a low hum like a swarm of bees. Finally the UFO rose abruptly and sped off at a steep angle to the east.

The UFO in this and many similar cases can only be interpreted as a *craft*. The body lights, light beam, sound, and car buffeting all suggest the presence of a technological object capable of hovering and moving at high speed. Had it been a helicopter, the witness would have been deafened by the noise.

Two more recent cases involving UFOs on or near the road illustrate the variety of features in vehicle encounter cases. A woman driving near Auburn, Massachusetts, in the early evening of January 5, 1979, noticed three red-glowing triangular objects flying over woods to her left. Shortly afterwards as she rounded a corner, she was confronted by three glowing red UFOs over the road directly in front of the car. Her AM and Citizen's Band (CB) radios both went off, and the car slowed smoothly to a stop while still in third gear (standard transmission) with the engine still running. She was totally *paralyzed*. Though her foot remained on the accelerator, the car sat motionless.

She had a clear view of the closest UFO only about 30 feet away and felt heat on her face, and a pungent odor (like a "sweet skunk smell") filled the car. Her face felt hot and

flushed and her eyes watered. When another car approached
from behind, the UFOs accelerated straight up, one at a time,
and moved away to the northwest at low altitude. Immediately, the AM and CB radios came on and the paralysis ended.
When she arrived home some time after 8:00 p.m., her mother
noticed her flushed face, like mild sunburn, and a dazed look.
Next day she had a mild rash and some skin peeling around
her eyes and nose, but the condition healed quickly. No aftereffects were found on the car, a 1970 Ford Maverick.

On February 8, 1979, at Liverpool Creek, Queensland,
Australia, a banana farmer driving on the Bruce Highway
about 9:00 p.m. saw a dimly lighted UFO sitting on the edge
of the road. As he approached, it rose vertically and when
about 1 meter off the road and 10 meters away, there was a
blinding flash of light. All of the car lights and the engine
failed. A little later the lights came back on and the engine
was started without difficulty. No aftereffects were found on
the car. Immediately after the flash and the car failure, the
man felt as if he had just awakened from a nightmare. Such
psychological reactions bear watching in relation to more
bizarre UFO-related events to be examined in ensuing chapters.

The very fact that the E-M effects cease as the UFO departs seems to establish a causal relationship of some kind.
Clearly it suggests a distance relationship (unless we wish to
invoke a UFO pilot throwing a switch).

Early on the morning of August 4, 1965, Don Tenopir,
a Nebraska truck driver, was hauling a load of peanuts north
and was situated about 25-30 miles south of Abilene, Kansas,
at about 1:30 a.m. Suddenly a domed disc (sort of hat shaped)
whizzed over his truck from behind, and his truck headlights
went out. The engine, a GMC diesel, did not fail. The UFO
settled on the road ahead, forcing him to jam on his brakes.
Then the object moved ahead a little and his headlights came
back on. In their beam, he could see the UFO hovering about
2 feet above the roadway. It was orange colored, about 15 feet

in diameter, and had what looked like square windows around the top. Tenopir started to converse with another driver who stopped after seeing the same thing, but both fled as the UFO took off in a shower of sparks.

On October 15, 1966, a forester who had been camping near Split Rock Pond, N.J., and was driving home in the early morning, saw a disc-shaped object following his car and illuminating the surrounding area. Each time the UFO neared the car the headlights and engine failed. Each time the UFO retreated the engine and lights worked again. The E-M effects seemed to be associated with the illumination from the UFO.

An even more striking case linking E-M effects with distance from a UFO occurred about 6:40 a.m. on March 4, 1969, near Atlanta, Missouri. A City Marshal and rural mail carrier found his mail truck being paralleled by a large red object that was emitting a strong beam of white light down onto the ground; the beam was tapered toward the bottom, and within it, debris seemed to be magnified in size. The witness also felt strong heat.

After a while the UFO turned in front of him, and each time he pulled near the cone of light his engine and CB radio quit. Then as he coasted and the UFO eased off a few feet, he heard static on his radio, let out the clutch, and the engine restarted. The case bears a remarkable resemblance in many respects — particularly the cone-shaped, tapered light beam illuminating the ground — to another incident of cat-and-mouse pursuit along a highway near Ravenna, Ohio, April 17, 1966 (see Case Book). During the Missouri incident, the light from the UFO was so brilliant that the witness pulled down his sun visor and shielded his eyes with his hand.

On August 13, 1975, near Haderslev, Denmark, a police officer driving home in his police car about 10:50 p.m. suddenly found himself engulfed in a bright bluish-white light and, at the same moment, his *headlights went out and the engine failed.* He coasted the car to the side of the road and stopped, *shielding his eyes from the dazzling light* with his arm. He grabbed for the microphone of his radio and tried to call the police station, but the *radio was dead* too.

The temperature in the car was rising, and it felt like heat from the sun "on a warm summer day." (The American City Marshal in the previous case had compared the heat to ". . . sitting out in the sun on a hot summer day.")

Looking up, he saw the beam of light, *shaped like a cone,* begin rising. He watched it retract into an opening in the bottom of a circular object about 10 meters in diameter, hovering about 20 meters overhead. On its underside he could see two dome-like protrusions. Instinctively, he activated a special camera mounted on the patrol car and snapped three pictures. He stepped out of the car, and seconds later the UFO rose vertically at high speed and accelerated out of sight, with no sound. As the UFO departed, *the patrol car lights came back on and the engine could be started normally.* The radio was now functioning, so he reported the encounter to the police station.

Developing the film the next day, the officer found that a light source had been captured on it, so he turned over the film to the Danish Air Force. There is no follow-up report on whatever analysis was conducted.

TABLE 1
Representative UFO Vehicle Encounter Cases
[C-Car, A-Aircraft, T-Truck, B-Boat, V-Van)

DATE/LOCATION	VEHICLE	E-M EFFECTS	LEVITATION	SOUND	STEERING LOSS	PHYSIOLOGICAL EFFECTS	BRILLIANT LIGHT	HEAT	PHYSICAL TRACES	ALTERED SURROUNDINGS	ABDUCTION
10/1/48 Fargo, N.Dak.	A										

cont'd

DATE/LOCATION	VEHICLE	E-M EFFECTS	LEVITATION	SOUND	STEERING LOSS	PHYSIOLOGICAL EFFECTS	BRILLIANT LIGHT	HEAT	PHYSICAL TRACES	ALTERED SURROUNDINGS	ABDUCTION
10/15/48 Japan	A										
11/18/48 Andrews AFB, Md.	A										
11/23/48 Fursten-Feldbruck, Germany	A										
7/9/51 Dearing, Ga.	A										
10/21/51 Battle Creek, Mich.	A										
5/5/58 Pan de Azucar, Uruguay	A							•			
6/29/64 Lavonia, Ga.	C	•		•		•			•		
5/28/65 Bougainville Reef, Australia	A										
8/4/65 Abilene, Kans.	T	•		•							
9/65 Brabant, Belgium	C		•		•	•					
9/3/65 Damon, Texas	C					•	•	•			
3/31/66 Vicksburg, Mich.	C	?		•			•				
10/15/66 Split Rock Pond, N.J.	C	•				•	•				

cont'd

DATE/LOCATION	VEHICLE	E-M EFFECTS	LEVITATION	SOUND	STEERING LOSS	PHYSIOLOGICAL EFFECTS	BRILLIANT LIGHT	HEAT	PHYSICAL TRACES	ALTERED SURROUNDINGS	ABDUCTION
11/2/67 Ririe, Idaho	C				•		•				
2/18/69 Craigmyle, Alta, Canada	C		•								
3/4/69 Atlanta, Mo.	T	•					•	•			
5/24/71 Blackfoot Indian Res, Alta, Canada	C		•		•						
8/1/71 Queensland, Australia	C		?						•		
10/18/73 Mansfield, Ohio	A	•	•		•		•				
1/24/74 Aische-en-Refail, Belgium	C	•				•					
2/14/74 Ely, Nevada	T	•	•		•				•		
5/31/74 Rhodesia	C	•	•		•		•			•	
7/74 Bridgewater, Tasmania	C				•						
10/27/74 Aveley, England	C	•	•							•	•
2/19/75 Orbak, Denmark	C	•				•	•	•	•		
5/3/75 Mexico City, Mexico	A		•		•						

cont'd

43

DATE/LOCATION	VEHICLE	E-M EFFECTS	LEVITATION	SOUND	STEERING LOSS	PHYSIOLOGICAL EFFECTS	BRILLIANT LIGHT	HEAT	PHYSICAL TRACES	ALTERED SURROUNDINGS	ABDUCTION
8/13/75 Haderslev, Denmark	C	•					•	•			
1/6/76 Bethel, Minn.	C					•	•				
1/6/76 Stanford, Ky.	C		?		•	•	•			•	•
3/22/76 Nemingha, N.S.W., Australia	C	•					•				
9/19/76 Tehran, Iran	A	•				•					
1/21/77 St. Bernard Parish, La.	B	•			•		•			•	
5/5/77 Tabio, Colombia	A	•			•		•			•	
6/16/77 Middelburg, S. Africa	V	•		•			•				
3/29/78 Indianapolis, Ind.	T	•			•		•			•	
9/17/78 Torrita di Siena, Italy	C	•		•			•		•		
9/23/78 Buenos Aires, Argentina	C		•		•		•	•			
10/21/78 Bass Strait, Australia	A	•									

cont'd

DATE/LOCATION	VEHICLE	E-M EFFECTS	LEVITATION	SOUND	STEERING LOSS	PHYSIOLOGICAL EFFECTS	BRILLIANT LIGHT	HEAT	PHYSICAL TRACES	ALTERED SURROUNDINGS	ABDUCTION
11/78 Trier, W. Germany	C										•
12/27/78 Torriglia, Italy	C				•	•	•				
1/5/79 Auburn, Mass.	C	•			•	•		•			
2/5/79 Lawitta, Tas., Australia	C	•				•	•				
2/8/79 Queensland, Australia	C	•					•				
7/25/79 Canoga Park, Calif.	C										•
4/2/80 Pudasjarvi, Finland	C					•				•	•
8/22/80 East Texas	C	•	•	•		•				•	•
12/29/80 Huffman, Tex.	C			•		•	•	•			
6/12/81 Alice, Tex.	T	•	•					•			
7/31/81 Lieksa, Finland	B					•					
3/85 Santiago, Chile	C	•					•				
10/20/86 Edmonton, Queensland, Australia	C	•		•	•						

cont'd

DATE/LOCATION	VEHICLE	E-M EFFECTS	LEVITATION	SOUND	STEERING LOSS	PHYSIOLOGICAL EFFECTS	BRILLIANT LIGHT	HEAT	PHYSICAL TRACES	ALTERED SURROUNDINGS	ABDUCTION
11/17/86 Fork Yukon, Alaska	A	•					•	•			
TOTALS 53 cases (19 countries) — Car - 31, Aircraft - 14, Other - 8		28	13	9	16	19	24	11	5	8	6

Table 1 provides a representative sample of more than 50 vehicle encounter cases in 40 years, including some additional features such as "levitation" to be taken up later. What conclusions can we draw from these reports?

First of all, as pointed out over 25 years ago by Aime Michel and Lex Mebane (see Michel in chapter bibliography), machines do not hallucinate. The distinctive electromagnetic failures of vehicles associated with nearby UFOs indicate the presence of something real that apparently is radiating some form of energy. The same energy fields, presumably, are responsible for physiological effects, heat, and other common elements of the events. With sufficient data, and with scientists motivated to study the phenomena, it should be possible to determine something about the mechanisms involved. If, as some scientists insist, UFOs are an unrecognized natural phenomenon, then its "assaults" on human beings should make it a proper matter for immediate scientific study.

The most serious problem with the natural phenomenon theory, however, is the craft-like appearance of the UFOs: smooth, metal-like curved surfaces, domes or turrets, pulsating body lights, porthole-like apertures, and all the rest. Past suggestions that UFOs could be plasma akin to ball lightning, or ice cometoids, are patently absurd when applied to structured object cases. The theorizers conveniently discard those aspects of the data that contradict their theories. (see Chapter 6.)

Neither plasma nor ice would be likely to have a dark, elongated form with a dome, and the wherewithal to swing a green beam of light around into the cabin of a helicopter, or to display "body lights" and persist in pacing vehicles for long periods of time. The UFO light beams are by themselves an indicator that the UFO proper is a carrier or platform for light energy, among other things.

From the human standpoint, the encounters are not something that was desired. The "wishful thinking hypothesis" is strongly refuted by the manifest terror of the witnesses. Human beings going about their ordinary day-to-day business have suddenly found themselves accosted and thwarted by some strange *machine* that seemed to be directed at them personally. The confrontational nature of the incidents is their salient feature. Wishful thinking or a desire for "saviors from space" does not enter into it. The incidents are abrupt, unexpected, and frightening, leaving the witnesses deeply concerned about the nature of the apparent craft that has toyed with them.

The personalized nature of close encounters of all types is one of the most puzzling features about UFOs, and perhaps the single most significant feature. Although similar encounters have occurred to small groups of people and vehicles, mass encounters are virtually unknown. This selectivity factor suggests that UFOs, whatever they are, by choice or by design of nature interact intimately with human beings only when they are isolated from larger numbers of other people.

The general tenor of vehicle confrontation cases is reminiscent of an all too common human experience. A motorist returning home late at night nears an intersection, and suddenly a truck or car lurches into his path with a squeal of tires and blinding headlights, nearly colliding with him and forcing him off the road. The other vehicle then speeds away and disappears. The driver cannot prove a thing. He cannot say with certainty that the other vehicle was a Ford pickup or a Plymouth sedan, but he *knows* that he has had a close encounter with another vehicle.

BIBLIOGRAPHY

Basterfield, Keith. "Two Vehicle Effect Cases from Australia," *MUFON UFO Journal*, No. 142, Dec. 1979.

Chalker, William C. "Valentich-Bass Strait (Australia) Affair," in *Encyclopedia of UFOs* (N.Y.: Doubleday, 1980).

_____. "The UFO Mystery in Australia," in *MUFON 1987 International UFO Symposium Proceedings* (Seguin, Texas: MUFON, 1987). Oct. 20, 1986, vehicle control loss and E-M effects case, p. 176.

Friedman, Stanton T. "Electromagnetic Effects of UFOs," in *Encyclopedia of UFOs* (N.Y.: Doubleday, 1980).

Fuller, Curtis. "The Flying Saucers — Fact or Fiction," *FLYING*, July 1950. Round-up of UFO sightings by professional pilots.

Hall, Richard H. "Special Evidence," Section VIII, *The UFO Evidence* (Washington, D.C.: NICAP, 1964). Includes table and discussion of E-M effect cases.

_____. "1967: The Overlooked UFO Wave and the Colorado Project," in *1978 MUFON UFO Symposium Proceedings* (Seguin, Texas: MUFON, 1978). Special study of UFOs displaying structural features, including 39 vehicle encounter cases.

_____. "Portage County (Ohio) Police Chase," in *Encyclopedia of UFOs* (N.Y.: Doubleday, 1980). Summary of Apr. 17, 1966, Ravenna, Ohio, "cat-and-mouse" case involving cone-shaped beam of light.

Huneeus, J. Antonio, "Historical Survey of UFO Cases in Chile," in *MUFON 1987 International UFO Symposium Proceedings* (Seguin, Tex.: MUFON, 1987). March 1985 Chilean vehicle illumination and E-M effects case, p. 200-201.

Keyhoe, Donald E. and Lore, Gordon I. R., Jr. Section III, "Vehicle Pacings and Encounters" and Section IV, "Close-Range Sightings and Structural Details," *UFOs: A New Look* (Washington, D.C.: NICAP, 1969).

McCampbell, James M. "Horses Under the Hood," in *Thesis-Antithesis*, Proceedings of Joint Symposium by AIAA and World Futures Society (Los Angeles, Calif: AIAA, 1975). Electromagnetic radiation theory to explain E-M and other UFO effects.

Michel, Aime. *Flying Saucers and the Straight Line Mystery* (N.Y.: Criterion, 1958). Includes accounts of E-M effects on vehicles during 1954 European and 1957 U.S. UFO sighting waves.

Zeidman, Jennie. *A Helicopter-UFO Encounter Over Ohio* (Evanston, Ill: Center for UFO Studies, Mar. 1979). Investigation report on Oct. 18, 1973 case.

CHAPTER 2

MAGIC TECHNOLOGY

Arthur C. Clarke, a UFO skeptic, once observed that if we were to encounter an advanced alien technology it might appear to us as magic. The "data" of UFO reports includes magic-like happenings that, if true, defy immediate scientific understanding. Because the reports do trample on scientific dignities, many scientists reject them, assuming there must be some madness afoot in the world that causes otherwise sane people to hallucinate or fabricate the accounts.

The nub of the matter is simply this: either the reports are untrue (mistakes of some kind), or we are faced with a "magic technology." The display strongly suggests that UFOs are not any known natural phenomenon because we know of nothing that can produce the range of effects reported in association with UFO sightings. That leaves extraterrestrial technology or something even stranger, which for want of a better label we will call "paranormal forces."

Electromagnetic (E-M) effects on vehicles and electric systems are a well-established feature of many UFO reports, including frequent engine, headlight, or radio failure while a UFO is observed in close proximity. Other features are manifest radiation sickness, levitation and "control" of vehicles, paralysis, altered appearance of the surroundings, and amnesia or "mental blackouts" of witnesses. These reports, when well-attested, are part of the data that any theory must attempt to encompass in some way.

On September 23, 1978, Carlos Acevedo, 38, and Miguel Angel Moya, 28, both Chileans, were finishing out the last

1,000 km of a gruelling road rally sponsored by the Argentine Automobile Club. Due to problems with their Citroen they were no longer in competition, but pride urged them on to complete the race.

About 2:00 a.m. they stopped for gas in Viedam, Rio Negro Province, Argentina, where they filled the 50-liter main tank and a reserve 40-liter tank. After a short break, they left at 2:30 a.m., bound for Bahia Blanca. Around 3:00 a.m. they were in the vicinity of Salina de Piedra, about 30 km north of the Rio Negro river with Acevedo driving, when a very bright yellow light appeared in the rear view mirror. The light rapidly increased in size as if approaching at high speed (they were traveling at about 100 km/h.) Thinking it must be a high performance car gaining on them, Acevedo slowed and pulled to the right to let it pass.

The light quickly filled the rear view mirror, and the interior of the car was suddenly flooded with light and heat. "I couldn't see any farther than the hood of the car," Acevedo later said. "Its color was yellowish with a violet tint. At that moment the car seemed to go out of control. I looked through the window and saw that we were about two meters off the ground. I immediately thought that we had hit something, flying into the air, and started getting ready for the moment when the car would hit the road again."

Instead of crashing back to earth the car continued its ascent, totally out of Acevedo's control. Out the window he could see nothing but the brilliant light; he couldn't even see Moya seated beside him or the dashboard of the car.

Moya, meanwhile, felt paralyzed by the light. "My first thought was also that we had hit something and I was frightened by the possibility of turning over, but when I noticed that the car seemed to float in the air and didn't come down, I was even more scared. It was truly a situation which I couldn't comprehend . . . I was seeing everything as if through a yellow fog, as if I were at a distance, someplace else."

At this point the two lost all conception of time, until they felt a bump and saw that the car was once again on the road. It seemed as if about a minute had passed, but they couldn't really tell. Then the light intensity diminished and they could see again. To the west they saw something like a yellow cone of light receding, its glow illuminating the surrounding area. The light sort of rolled up like a curtain, from bottom to top, leaving an oval shape that continued west and disappeared in the distance.

"I was stunned," Moya said. "My hands were shaking, and I felt something pressing against my chest. It was difficult to breathe." The car was sitting on the opposite side of the road, on an embankment. Acevedo's legs felt like they were "asleep" and he felt a tingling sensation. He stepped out to check for damage, then climbed back in and resumed driving north on Route 3.

About 15 minutes later they arrived at Pedro Luro in Buenos Aires Province, about 123 km north of the Rio Negro, and stopped at a service station. There they discovered that something was wrong. The distances didn't add up — the odometer showed only about half the distance they had covered — and the time didn't make sense either. They apparently had lost a little over an hour of time that they couldn't account for. They were also astonished to discover that their reserve tank, which had not been used at all, was completely empty.

Confused and apprehensive about these discoveries, they reported the incident to Inspector Daniel Osimi of the Pedro Luro police department, who assigned Corporal J. Garcia to accompany the shaken men to Bahia Blanca. Both police officers told investigators that the men were rational and coherent, but obviously frightened. The service station attendant, who had witnessed their puzzlement, said that others in a nearby town had seen a bright yellowish light headed west early the same morning. There were no observable aftereffects on the car.

The incident bears all the hallmarks of an abduction case as developed by Budd Hopkins in his book *Missing Time* (see Chapter 5 Bibliography). No follow-up report has been received to indicate whether the men subsequently recalled an encounter fitting the abduction scenario — confrontation with alien beings.

An extremely strange and complex case in Rhodesia on May 31, 1974, contains all the same features ... and more. (For additional details, see Case Book Appendix.) A young couple driving from Salisbury, Rhodesia, to Durban, South Africa, found their car "taken over" by a UFO and levitated above the highway for a long distance. They experienced abnormal silence as well as visually altered surroundings, and amnesia. In a dry area of Rhodesia, they "saw" lush tropical foliage! They *did* recall seeing alien humanoid beings.

Witnesses in a July 22, 1982 sighting in Katy, Texas, also experienced an abnormal lack of environmental sounds as they observed a boomerang-shaped UFO. The object, however, emitted a hum.

On February 14, 1974, two brothers were driving a rental truck in the vicinity of Ely, Nevada, when two UFOs of different types appeared on a lonely stretch of desert highway. A blast of wind shook the truck, the lights and engine failed, and steering control was lost. "We felt that we were in a vacuum of some kind and isolated from the rest of the world," they told investigators. The truck was floating in the air just off the highway. After the UFOs departed, the truck was found to be totally disabled, and the entire rear end ultimately had to be replaced.

These totally "interrupted journeys" with complete loss of vehicle control, and the psychological/visual alterations in the surroundings, escalate vehicle confrontation cases to a new level of strangeness. Almost as if putting on a display of magic technology, the UFOs somehow levitate heavy masses, manipulate the vehicle controls, and induce abnormal states (or perceptions) of the environment: reduced vision as if in a dense luminous fog, abnormal silence, feelings of isolation or "vacuum," and altered appearance of the terrain.

Whether these witnesses are describing phenomena due to sensory deprivation as a byproduct of the forces that induce E-M effects is purely speculative. An alternative speculation is that intelligent beings operating the UFOs are conducting psychological tests or "freezing" the humans for some kind of *in vito* study. The true nature of what is going on — what portion of the events may be attributed to objectively real happenings and what to psychological or subjective perceptions — is a thread that runs throughout the high strangeness cases, becoming particularly acute in attempted analysis of abduction reports.

Another report of envelopment in fog-like light, abnormal silence, and a sense of isolation is of special interest because it occurred to three vehicles and their drivers simultaneously. About 9:30 p.m. on March 29, 1978, a caravan of trucks was travelling on I-70 in the vicinity of Indianapolis, Indiana, and three drivers were talking back and forth on their CB radios. All at once, as if someone had turned on a giant light bulb, a bright blue light enveloped the three trucks. The drivers were *not able to see out beyond the hoods* of their trucks. Everything went quiet — all noise, all the road sounds ceased.

The truck engines sputtered as if about to fail for an estimated 3-5 seconds, and the CB radios failed. Then, as if a giant light bulb were turned off, the light vanished, the CB's resumed working, and the road noise became normal again. Once again, the engines were running smoothly.

The three drivers were incredulous. The rear driver impulsively shouted on the CB, "Hey, UFO, if you have your ears on, I want to go with you!" Almost as suddenly as before, the strange blue light enveloped the trucks again, cutting off visibility, this time for about 15 seconds. The engines sputtered and, jerking and jumping, the trucks were slowed to 5-10 m.p.h. While in the bath of blue light, the drivers said *they felt like there was no one else in the world*. Everything was restful and quiet. Then the light disappeared and everything returned to normal.

Other drivers outside the light also witnessed the phenomenon. A woman across the highway said on the CB, "It looked like a big bright blue lampshade over the three trucks."

Above the roughly dome-shaped region of light, stretching vertically upwards, was a long, narrow spout of light.

One of the drivers, interviewed by a MUFON investigator, said his truck clock began losing about an hour a day after the event, whereas before it had worked perfectly. His battery had been drained of power and took about 1-1/2 hours to regain full charge.

Light engulfment, strange silence, heat, and a particularly unusual E-M (or gravity) effect also stunned two Louisiana hunters who were engaged in poaching nutria for their pelts. About 8:45 p.m. on January 21, 1977, Robert M. was plying his trade along a canal in St. Bernard Parish, when he noticed a star-like object moving toward him. When a brilliant light engulfed him he thought at first it was a Wildlife and Fisheries helicopter, but there was no sound. To the contrary, *total silence* prevailed: no wind, no frogs croaking, no bird sounds. Robert felt warmth from the light. Then a glowing object shot away and things returned to normal.

Robert spotted the campfire of a friend, Irwin M., and stopped to tell him what had happened. Irwin joined him in the boat, powered by a 25 h.p. Evinrude, and they proceeded with their nutria hunting. Suddenly the light (or a twin) approached again and hovered about 65 feet above the boat. Again, silence prevailed. Robert's hair was standing on end ("It stood out like wire") and everything felt warm. They were petrified.

Most intriguing of all, they were aware that the engine was still running but the boat was standing still, as if something were holding them. Irwin described it as like being held by "strong gravity forces." A later search at the site found no roots or impediments that could have held up the boat's motion. In fact, the canal had been dredged recently to permit large fishing boats to use it.

The UFO was roundish and about 20 feet in diameter. Its surface had a textured pattern like connecting diamonds or squares. When it departed, the boat lurched forward throwing both men down — as if the force gripping them had suddenly been turned off. They watched the UFO retreat and stop near an oil refinery at 9:05 p.m. An oil company guard also saw it. The UFO moved again and hovered in a new spot, where the men could see a beam of light shining downward from it. After about 30 minutes it disappeared.

Another light engulfment case on the other side of the world has intriguing similarities to these cases. If the primary witness could be located, it would be of exceptional interest. An Australian couple returning from a holiday on March 22, 1976, found themselves in the small settlement of Nemingha, New South Wales, about 5:45 a.m. studying a road map to determine the best route home. A small white car approached and they stepped out intending to ask the driver for directions.

Suddenly a bright greenish-yellow light descended from above and completely enveloped the small car. The light then disappeared, and the car drifted to the wrong side of the road, covered by a thick white haze. The car stopped, its lights out. The couple then saw a woman emerge from the car and wipe a white substance off the windshield with a cloth. The car lights came back on, and the woman threw the cloth away, whereupon it burst into flames. The woman got back into the car and drove off before the startled couple could react. As the car passed, they noticed that it was covered with a thick white substance.

Attempts to locate the woman in the car have not been successful. Her report of what she witnessed and experienced inside the affected car would be invaluable.

What these cases have in common is indications of a *directedness* to the UFO phenomenon. The UFO was not merely passing within the perceptual field of the witness. Instead, as in most vehicle confrontation cases, it approached the witness(es) directly and interfered with or disrupted the normal performance of the vehicle, while inducing perceptual anomalies or paranormal events. Unlike the truckers case, which is exceptional in many ways, the incidents typically occur in isolated locations or during hours when few vehicles are on the road.

The driver is not always alone; in fact, all of the cases reported here involve at least two witnesses who experienced or observed the anomalous events. No one knows why these particular vehicles, or their drivers, were singled out for attention — if indeed they were — or what attracted the UFO to the scene. The events could be random encounters, but if so, the exact nature of the transaction between luminous UFO and isolated vehicle remains to be explained. The seeming "cone of silence," levitation, and altered surroundings certainly are features not attributable to any known natural phenomenon.

BIBLIOGRAPHY

Chalker, Bill. "A Road Hazard Down Under?" Report for UFO Investigation Centre, Lane Cove, NSW, Australia. (Mar. 22, 1976 Australian case.)

Hall, Richard H. "Special Evidence," Section VIII, *The UFO Evidence* (Washington, D.C.: NICAP, 1964). Includes E-M and physiological effects cases.

McCampbell, James M. "Electrical Interference," Ch. 5 and "Physiological Effects," Ch. 6, *UFOlogy: New Insights from Science and Common Sense* (Belmont, Calif: Jaymac, 1973).

Peters, Ted. "Warm Light Stops Everything!" *MUFON UFO Journal*, No. 111, Feb. 1977. (Jan. 21, 1977, Louisiana case.)

Roncoroni, Guillermo C. "The Rally Incident: A Teleportation?" *MUFON UFO Journal*, No. 140, Oct. 1979. (Sept. 23, 1978, Argentine car levitation case.)

Tucker, Charles L. "Truckers Engulfed by 'UFO' Light." *MUFON UFO Journal*, No. 126, May 1978. (Mar. 29, 1978, Indianapolis, Indiana case.)

CHAPTER 3

THE HUMANOIDS

"They had strange-looking eyes that seemed to look right through you," said William Blackburn. "Their skin was reddish-orange and they wore tight-fitting shiny suits to the neck."

The General Electric Company draftsman in Waynesboro, Virginia, was confirming to the author — in a roundabout way — the details of a story printed in the Waynesboro *News-Virginian* on January 23, 1965. After the story was printed, Blackburn had been approached by Government agents from an agency he refused to identify and "sternly warned" not to talk about his experience. Local residents had seen a car bearing U.S. Government license plates in town, which stood out like a sore thumb. Apparently fearful about his livelihood, Blackburn clammed up.

Before the visit by mysterious agents, however, he had told the story to two colleagues at the Waynesboro GE plant. With their help, and that of Dallas Kersey who ran the local Richmond *Times-Dispatch* bureau, it was possible to piece together most of the facts. By nodding his affirmation or dissent, and by annotating a copy of the newspaper story, Blackburn confirmed important details.

On January 19, after work, Blackburn drove to the Augusta Archery Range (Augusta County, Virginia) to prepare for an archery match scheduled for that evening. Due to snowy, inclement weather, no one else showed up. Shortly after his arrival at 5:40 p.m., Blackburn was chopping wood, moving back and forth near the east side of the clubhouse and out toward the flagpole adjacent to the south parking area.

After about 35 minutes, a glint of light attracted his attention to a pyramid-shaped or conical object estimated to be over 200 feet in diameter. (Apparently influenced by his archery avocation, he gave all estimates in yards, here converted to feet.) The UFO descended to approximately 3,000 feet and positioned itself about 15 degrees to the left of the flagpole and at about 40 degrees elevation, in a southerly direction. As he was watching this, a smaller object — about 60 feet in diameter — landed to his left.

As a draftsman experienced and well-informed on metal finishing, Blackburn said: "I never saw metal polished like that in *my* life. I bet you couldn't see that thing at 5,000 feet on a clear day!" His implication was that the finish was so mirror-like that it would blend in with its surroundings. He could not tell whether the landed object had come from the huge object overhead. Even the smaller object was huge by most comparisons, covering almost all of the available cleared area next to the clubhouse. Whatever it was, the thing had landed within 50 feet of him.

As he stood gaping in astonishment, an opening appeared in the landed craft, "like someone took a slice of pie from it," and three humanoid beings *floated* toward him, their feet never touching the ground. They were about 3 feet tall, but otherwise human-like. As they approached to within 35 feet, Blackburn froze, with double-edged axe in hand (perhaps paralyzed, but he refused comment on this point).

The humanoids uttered unintelligible sounds as if attempting to communicate. Blackburn observed that their shoe soles were several inches thick (holding his fingers apart to demonstrate), and that "the one on the right" had an abnormally long finger on its left hand. Moments later, the beings turned around and floated back to their craft, re-entering the door. The opening then closed, seeming to "mold itself to the ship" and leaving no indication of a door after it closed. Both UFOs then departed quickly. No tracks or traces were visible in the snow after their departure.

Considering that Blackburn is a draftsman accustomed to details and to structural materials, the features he reported are intriguing. The surface of the UFO was like highly polished metal or glass. Except for a slight sound when the opening appeared in the craft and the unintelligible utterances, no sound was heard. On top of the landed craft was a bubble or oval shape that Blackburn said was "... quite strange ... you felt quite strange when you looked at it." Questioned on this point, he refused to elaborate. Nor would he augment the sketchy published description of the humanoids except to confirm, indirectly, its general accuracy.

Blackburn's engineer colleagues had listened to him as he — white faced and perspiring — first recounted the experience. Through lengthy conversations and later correspondence with them, it was possible for me to gain a strong sense of confidence that something very strange had happened. Blackburn was no hoaxer, and his visible distress had concerned them. Formerly skeptical or disinterested in UFO reports, they were shaken by his story and by the apparent Government awareness of such events.

On the following Tuesday, January 26, a local high school boy and some friends reported seeing a small humanoid in the Brands Flats area, across the highway from the archery range. They reported it to the police and a search party, including a photographer, scoured the area. In the vicinity of a deserted barn, one of the party was knocked down and slightly injured by "something." In the ensuing panic the photographer took a picture of that "something" near the barn before fleeing. It was felt that a humanoid may have been photographed.

According to Dallas Kersey, unidentified Government agents also visited the high school boy and probably the others in the party. Due to the pressures of other affairs, this incident was never properly investigated. The implication is that the possible humanoid photograph was confiscated. At any rate, nothing further was ever heard about it.

Blackburn's story, bizarre as it may sound, is fairly typical of world-wide humanoid reports of a particular type.

Although it is difficult to present a "representative" sample
of the wide variety of humanoid types and behaviors, *Table
2* includes a sampling of typical cases. It must be stressed,
however, that the sample represents only about 1% of the
cases on record.

TABLE 2
Representative Sample of Humanoid Reports

DATE LOCATION TYPE	DESCRIPTION	ACTIONS	OTHER FEATURES	SOURCE
8/25/52 Pittsburg, Kans. A	Head and shoulders plus other figures visible through windows of UFO.	Considerable activity noted, partly obscured as if by window shade.	Low-hovering UFO emitting throbbing sound; vegetation disturbed.	USAF; Project Blue Book Spec. Rpt. #14
9/10/54 Mourieras, France. C	One, avg. height.	Approached and touched witness.	Hum or buzz as UFO took off vertically.	Michel, p. 40
9/10/54 Quarouble, France. C	Two, abt 3½ ft tall, wide shoulders, small legs, helmet.	Witness ran toward beings, then paralyzed.	Blinded & paralyzed by light from UFO; physical traces found on railroad ties.	Michel, p. 44
9/26/54 Chabeuil (Drome), France. C.	One, abt 3 ft tall, helmet.	Moved toward witness, who fled.	UFO emitted whistling sound on departure; crushed foliage at landing site.	Michel, p. 82
11/4/54 Pontal, Brazil. B.	Three, small, white clothing, dark skin, "skull caps."	Emerged from UFO, gathered foliage and water.	UFO rose vertically, no sound.	Bowen, p. 92
5/25/55 Branch Hills, Ohio. E.	Three, 3½ ft tall, grayish, forehead folds, wide slit mouth, lopsided chests.	Standing by road as witness car passed.	No UFO visible; odor like alfalfa and almonds.	Davis & Bloecher, p. 138

cont'd

DATE LOCATION TYPE	DESCRIPTION	ACTIONS	OTHER FEATURES	SOURCE
7/3/55 Stockton, Ga. E	Four, 3½-4 ft tall, large eyes, wide shoulders, long arms, tapered chin.	Standing in road, one holding "stick," as witness car passed.	No UFO visible.	Davis & Bloecher, p. 149
8/21/55 Kelly, Ky. C	Three (?), abt 3 ft tall, large wide eyes, large ears, broad shoulders, long arms.	Repeated approaches to house, rapid locomotion on "all fours," floating.	Luminosity of beings noted at times.	Davis & Bloecher, Ch. I-V
11/7/57 House, Miss. B	Three, 4½ ft tall, gray clothing, dark hair, "pasty white" faces.	UFO blocked road, beings approached witness making unintelligible sounds.	UFO took off "straight up."	Michel, p. 272
12/16/57 Old Saybrook, Conn. A	Two, 3½-4 ft tall, robot-like motions, square heads.	Moving past windows of low-hovering elliptical UFO.	UFO glowed over entire surface, tilted up sharply and shot away; no sound.	NICAP (1), Sect. VII
6/26/59 Boianai, Papua, New Guinea, A	Four, luminous figures on top of low-hovering UFO.	One raised arms in apparent response to wave from witnesses.	UFO wobbled in apparent response to flashlight signals.	NICAP (1), Sect. VII
4/24/64 Socorro, N.M. C	Two, 4 ft tall, white clothing.	Standing next to landed UFO, turned in direction of witness, vanished into UFO.	Loud roar during vertical take-off, then silence; foliage scorched, imprints at site.	Bowen, p. 130
9/4/64 Cisco Grove, Calif. C	Four, two humanoids, two robots.	Treed witness, tried to dislodge him from tree.	All-night encounter during which witness blacked out when robot emitted vapor.	NICAP (2) (See Case Book, Appendix)

cont'd

DATE LOCATION TYPE	DESCRIPTION	ACTIONS	OTHER FEATURES	SOURCE
1/19/65 Brands Flats, Va. B	Three, 3 ft tall, shiny clothing, penetrating eyes.	Floated out of landed UFO, approached witness, made unintelligible sounds.	Large UFO overhead; both with mirror-like surfaces.	Personal files
11/2/67 Ririe, Idaho. B	Two, 3 ft tall, wrinkled faces, large ears, small eyes, wearing backpacks.	Stopped car, one floated down, entered car, made unintelligible sounds.	Small disc with dome hovered above car, bathed area in green light.	NICAP (1), Sect. VII
12/8/67 Idaho Falls, Idaho. A	Two, details obscured by glare, in dome of low-hovering UFO.	UFO tilted down and rotated, bring figures into view.	Description almost identical to case in Blenheim, N.Z., 7/13/59, same source	NICAP (1), Sect. VII
1/7/70 Heinole, Finland. B	One, 2 ft tall, white face, gray coveralls, conical headgear.	Emerged from light beam beneath low-hovering UFO; black box emitted blinding light ray.	Witness paralyzed, physiological aftereffects.	*Inforespace*, Brussels, Belgium No. 22, Aug. 1975
10/11/73 Pascagoula, Miss. G	Three, robot-like beings, pointed ears, wrinkled skin.	Floated out of hovering UFO, abducted two witnesses on board.	Examination by X-ray-like device, witnesses returned to ground.	Blum, Ch. 1-3.
10/17/73 Danielsville, Ga. B	Two, 4-4½ ft tall, silver suits, white hair, reddish faces.	Appeared beneath UFO blocking the road.	Witness took gun in hand, UFO took off with "whooshing" sound.	Webb (1), p. 12.
11/4/73 Goffstown, N.H. D	Two, 4½-5 ft tall, luminous, dark oval eyes, large pointed ears, silver suits.	Confronted outside house, one w/flashlight-like object, 2nd picking up things from ground.	Witness had seen round silver UFO 5 hrs. earlier.	Fowler, p. 322.

con't

DATE LOCATION TYPE	DESCRIPTION	ACTIONS	OTHER FEATURES	SOURCE
2/14/74 Petite-Ile, France. B	Four, 1-1.2 meters tall, white metallic clothing.	Poking on ground, directed light beam on witness.	UFO hovered 50 cm off ground.	Ouranos, No. 14 2nd Q 1975
6/12/77 Crystal Lake, Ill. E	Four, 4 ft tall, slender, silver suits.	Three emerged from alley and retrieved 4th who seemed to be disabled.	Silence enveloped area; no UFO seen.	Bloecher (2), p. 21.
9/17/78 Torrita de Siena, Italy. B	Two, 3-5 ft tall, helmets w/aerial-like protrusions, green clothing.	Floated out of low-hovering UFO, circled car, re-entered UFO.	E-M effects stopped car; UFO took off w/light flash and explosive sound; scorch marks found on road.	MUFON UFO Jnl, No. 153, Nov. 1980.
8/4/79 Canoga Park, Calif. A	Two, large heads	Seen through clear dome of discoid UFO that approached and hovered.	UFO tilted, levelled, moved, tilted opposite direction, flew away to west.	MUFON UFO Jnl, No. 151, Sept. 1980.
10/24/84 (approx) Park Rapids, Minn. C	One, 4 ft tall, large head, large eyes, slender limbs.	After sighting of UFOs, approached farmstead within 25 ft, stood in light for 10 minutes, turned and disappeared into darkness.	UFOs were blue-white and diamond-shaped.	MUFON UFO Jnl, No. 220, Aug. 1986

HUMCAT Types:
- A — Entity seen inside of UFO
- B — Entity seen getting in and/or out of UFO
- C — Entity seen in immediate vicinity of UFO
- D — Entity seen during independent local UFO activity
- E — Entity seen with no record of local UFO activity
- F — Voices heard or messages received during UFO encounter
- G — On-board experience, or dislocation in time or space

Ted Bloecher and Dave Webb of the Mutual UFO Network (MUFON) Humanoid Study Group logged over 2,000 humanoid reports in the HUMCAT computer catalogue, which at this stage mainly serves as a rapid indexing and searching aid. Slightly over 50% of the cases are raw reports only; no in-depth investigation has been conducted of them. However, many humanoid reports *have* been thoroughly investigated and remain totally unexplained. The scope of the reports dictates that they be considered an integral part of the UFO mystery; they are part of the data that need to be explained by any theory.

When and where it all began is unclear ... when humanoid beings were first credibly reported in association with typical UFOs, almost always craft-like objects in the humanoid cases. Scattered reports of 1940s humanoid sightings are on record, but the reports first came to the fore in the mid-1950s. The HUMCAT records show peaks of humanoid sightings coincident with major UFO sighting waves in 1954 (Europe, primarily France and Italy), 1967-68 (the largest volume UFO wave on record), and 1973 (the last major sighting wave as of this writing). Since 1973 the incidence of humanoid sightings has remained relatively high, but this is a possible artifact of investigation reflecting the fact that more attention is being paid to such reports and a central repository for them now exists.

Other than humanoids sighted inside a UFO (HUMCAT Type A), certain recurring patterns of behavior have been noted:

- Standing near craft, flight when observed (the famous Socorro, N.M. case of April 24, 1964, is an example).

- Sample gathering (plants, rocks, water ...).

- Approaching witness, no physical contact (the Blackburn case cited above is an example)

- Approaching or stopping vehicles and interacting, sometimes forcibly, with the occupants.

The behavior patterns are listed here in ascending order of aggressiveness and direct confrontation/interaction with humans.

The possibility of human misperception of familiar or known objects (and beings) is reduced to nil in humanoid reports. Taken at face value, the reports describe craft displaying "magic technology" and strange nonhuman beings obviously of types not known on earth. If the reports are valid, then UFOs must be intelligently guided craft not from this earth — or at least not from any realm that we know about.

An example of aggressive behavior occurred during the 1967 UFO sighting wave; a "high strangeness" case, but an investigated case that seems to be reliable. Two Indian youths, Guy Tossie and Will Begay, were driving near Ririe, Idaho, about 9:30 p.m. November 2. Suddenly there was a blinding flash of light ahead and a small, domed UFO appeared, with two small humanoid beings visible in it. The car was stopped without brakes being applied (loss of vehicle control) and the area was bathed in a vivid green light. One of the humanoids floated down and forced his way into the car, which was then moved off the highway in some manner. Tossie bolted out of the car and fled in terror to the nearest farmhouse.

As Begay cowered in fear, the being, about 3 feet tall with large ears, wrinkled or creased face, small eyes, and slit-like mouth, *uttered unintelligible sounds*. Then it left the car and *floated* back up to the UFO, which ascended in a zig-zag path. (For further description, see Case Book Appendix). The investigator later learned that another man in the vicinity had a similar encounter that night, but refused to elaborate on it and insisted on remaining anonymous.

The beings in this case appeared not to be wearing helmets or headgear, but did have something like packs on their backs (which could have been "life support systems" or even "levitation devices"). Many humanoid reports depict beings whose heads are encased in transparent domes resembling divers' helmets.

An analogous case in which aggressiveness was displayed took place on August 21, 1955, in Kelly, Kentucky, and is well-documented by Isabel Davis. The beings besieged a rural house for hours, constantly approaching it and even climbing on the roof, despite a hostile reception (including shotgun blasts) by the terrified residents. An ability to float or levitate again was evident. Although these creatures also were just over 3 feet tall, they had very large, almost elephant-like protruding ears, large widely spaced eyes, long arms with taloned hands, and spindly legs. To call them "humanoid" might be stretching the meaning of the word. Except for bilateral symmetry, they were distinctly nonhuman in appearance and behavior; for example, using their arms for locomotion on "all fours" at times.

The perplexing variety of humanoid forms observed is an impediment to wider acceptance of the reports as valid observations. One might expect some variation of forms, but the collection of humanoid reports comprises a veritable circus menagerie of types. Still, most are roughly humanoid and some very human-like. Three basic types can be discerned, with considerable variation within type:

- Diminutive: typically 3-4 feet tall, disproportionately large heads, slender bodies, often clothed in "coveralls," and sometimes with transparent helmets. (Humanoid form.)

- Average: about 5-6 feet tall, human-like in appearance and behavior, in fact sometimes indistinguishable from humans except for the association with UFOs. (Human form.)

- Giant: perhaps 8-12 feet tall with oversize, often grotesque features. (Monster form.)

The "monsters" are not a well-established type, but have been reported and must be considered. Also, other cases do not fit neatly into these categories (for example, see 1955 cases in *Table 2.*) Clearly, a lot of work remains to be done in deriving a definitive model or models of UFO-associated entities, and reliable data are hard to come by. With over half of the cases sketchy and uninvestigated, any speculation about the meaning of the observations has to be highly tentative.

A fourth category of entity sightings indicates that some of the beings associated with UFOs probably are not purely biological beings. A number of reports suggest that some of the "humanoids" are robots or androids. The creatures in the widely reported October 11, 1973, Pascagoula, Mississippi, case, for example, appeared to be robots, as did — distinctly — two of the entities in the September 4, 1964, Cisco Grove, California, case (see Case Book Appendix). In other instances the beings walked with a stiff-legged gait or turned their heads in a mechanical fashion.

In many other cases, however, the humanoids definitely appeared to be biological, with facial features, eyes, muscula-ture, and hands visible. A good guess would be that biological entities and robots both are involved, probably operating together as has been reported in a few cases.

Some researchers argue that the variety of forms indicates multiple origins, which may be the case but does not logically follow from the skimpy information presently at hand. Beings from a single planetary culture easily could display the general similarities with differences in detail, and could be employing the services of robots and/or androids. Astronomical and related biological arguments about the unlikelihood of multi-ple alien races finding us, wanting to come here, and being able to come here, also would militate against this possibility ... except that astronomical arguments are suspect because *no one* is supposed to be able to, or to want to, come here. The paucity of information available to us does not allow any answer, nor even any reasonable speculation.

A potentially fertile field of investigation and research for now is analysis of the reported behavior (activities, reactions, locomotions ...) of the humanoids, which has not yet been attempted systematically or on a large scale. When HUMCAT is further developed, pattern studies will be facilitated.

With the data presently on hand, the straightforward in-terpretation would be that alien humanoids, scientist-like, literally are studying the earth environment, human beings included. However, some analysts feel that after 35 years of sample gathering and other study the humanoids, wherever from, would have all the information they need. But, the exotic richness of lifeforms on earth might not be that easy for scientists from a totally different biosphere (presumably) to catalogue and understand. Also, we inevitably make assumptions without thinking about it that alien psychology would be similar to ours, and that their purposes should be easily decipherable.

More importantly, we tend to assume that their lifespan is about the same as ours and that 35 years is a long time to them as it is to us. Then again we tend to attribute to them some monolithic purpose, when some of the activities we observe could be a sporadic, "spare-time" activity rather than the main "mission." These are totally unknown factors, and we *assume* at our own risk of grossly misinterpreting what is going on.

It would seem to be questionable to assume that the humanoids are single-minded in purpose or psychologically uniform in their attitudes and behavior toward humans; the observed facts (if we accept them as valid) suggest otherwise. In any given case, the interaction that occurs may be dependent on the individual psychology or interests of the particular UFO crew, or the particular mission they happen to be on at the time.

Vehicle confrontation cases like the one in Ririe, Idaho, seem to be deliberate, planned encounters with humans for purposes unknown. The seemingly accidental encounters like the one in Socorro, N.M., are totally different in character, and the landing there could have been for any number of purposes. Intermediate between these two extremes are numerous cases in which the interaction with humans may have been a "target of opportunity," a brief diversion from some other activity to look over a human in the vicinity.

The Ririe, Idaho, case is one of a type that at a minimum suggests that some of the humanoids (whether from the same or different cultures) have no compunction about forcibly intruding in human affairs and terrifying human beings. These may be the Klingons among other groups present, behaving from different cultural imperatives, or they may simply be the rogues of the party out freelancing just for the hell of it. Alternatively, their actions could be one part of an orchestrated "master plan" whose ultimate purpose cannot be inferred from a few particular events. We could be observing a variety of tactics but lacking sufficient information to discern the ultimate strategy.

Broadly speaking, the evidence so far suggests that we are dealing with a variety of beings who may have various outlooks, purposes, or roles to play in some master plan, but a party or parties roughly analogous to a scientific or exploratory expedition. The most commonly mentioned alternative "theory" or speculation is that the bewildering observations indicate some measure of deception, staging, or psychological games by the intelligences behind UFOs to veil their true purposes or intentions from us while they carry out some secret "game plan."

Since there is nothing we could do to interfere in any case, this would seem to be a rather pointless exercise. The one supposition that makes this alternative interpretation somewhat plausible is that we are being carefully prepared or conditioned for an ultimate peaceful contact that would not be possible if it were forced on us suddenly.

Nothing in the humanoid sightings compels us to accept any theory at this point. What it all comes back to is that we have a surplus of premature theory and a lack of adequately investigated data. Until we have far more thorough empirical investigation, we should not become too enamored of our theories.

The main lesson of the humanoid reports is that the entire UFO subject is far more complex and substantial than the skeptics realize and not likely to be unraveled any time soon by amateurs on a spare-time basis. The investigated cases are individually credible, and the reports are made by people from all walks of life world-wide. They deal not with vague lights in the distance, but instead with proximate craft and animate

beings. The proximity factor, by normal common sense interpretation of immediately experienced events, leaves us with a
considerable puzzle.

The only tentative answer we have is that the universe is
populated by more intelligent lifeforms than merely the recognized races of earth. No matter where the origin, human
beings have encountered other humanoid lifeforms whose
purposes and relationship to us remain to be determined.

BIBLIOGRAPHY

Banchs, Roberto E. and Heiden, Richard W., "The Humanoids in Argentina," *Journal of UFO Studies*, v. II, 1980, Center for UFO Studies,
Evanston, Ill.

Bloecher, Ted (1). "A Catalog of Humanoid Reports for 1974" (plus 1973
case supplement) in *1975 MUFON UFO Symposium Proceedings* (Seguin, Texas: MUFON, 1975).

Bloecher, Ted (2). "A Survey of CE III Reports for 1977," in *1978 MUFON
UFO Symposium Proceedings* (Seguin, Texas: MUFON, 1978).

Blum, Ralph. *Beyond Earth: Man's Contact With UFOs* (N.Y.: Bantam,
1974). Chapters 1-3 on Oct. 11, 1973, Pascagoula, Miss., case plus other
humanoid reports.

Bowen, Charles (Ed.). *The Humanoids* (Chicago: Regnery, 1969).

Davis, Isabel and Bloecher, Ted. *Close Encounter at Kelly and Others of 1955*
(Evanston, Ill.: CUFOS, Mar. 1978). Aug. 21, 1955, Kentucky case.

Fowler, Raymond E. *UFOs: Interplanetary Visitors* (N.Y.: Exposition, 1974).
General survey including humanoid reports.

Hendry, Allan. "Kelly/Hopkinsville (Kentucky) Encounters," in *Encyclopedia of UFOs* (N.Y.: Doubleday, 1980). Summary of Aug. 21, 1955, Kentucky case.

Lorenzen, Jim and Lorenzen, Coral. *Encounters With UFO Occupants* (N.Y.:
Berkley, 1976). Survey including U.S. and foreign humanoid reports.

Michel, Aime. *Flying Saucers and the Straight Line Mystery* (N.Y.: Criterion,
1958). Numerous humanoid reports during 1954 French wave and 1957
U.S. wave.

NICAP (1). *UFOs: A New Look* (Washington, D.C., 1969). Chapter on
humanoid reports.

NICAP (2). *Strange Effects From UFOs* (Washington, D.C., 1969). Section II, "The Occupants."

Story, Ronald. "Cisco Grove (California) Encounter," in *Encyclopedia of UFOs* (N.Y.: Doubleday, 1980). Sept. 4, 1964, case with humanoids and robots.

Webb, Dave (1). *1973 — Year of the Humanoids* (Evanston, Ill.: CUFOS, May 1976).

Webb, Dave (2). "Analysis of Humanoid Reports," in *1976 MUFON UFO Symposium Proceedings* (Seguin Texas: MUFON, 1976).

CHAPTER 4

BODIES IN THE MORGUE

The ultimate proof that UFOs are extraterrestrial, of course, would be a captured spacecraft (which would then become an IFO) and/or bodies of the alien astronauts who crashed on Earth. But who would seriously maintain that such an event actually happened?

The *rumors* of such an event date back to 1947, the year in which the term "flying saucers" was coined in the U.S. In July of that year, in Roswell, New Mexico, the local Air Force station issued a press release in which it was stated that fragments of a "flying saucer" had been retrieved after exploding and showering parts down in desert terrain. A rancher found the unusual material — thin but extraordinarily tough pieces of apparent metal — and notified Air Force officials.

This has become known as the "Roswell Incident," and a book by the same name was published by Charles Berlitz and William L. Moore in 1980. Moore, with the assistance of scientist Stanton T. Friedman, has doggedly pursued the case and provided periodic updates of the results of their investigations. The parts, allegedly, were spirited away to Wright-Patterson AFB, Ohio, under the cover story that the retrieved materials were merely fragments of a research balloon. (The story is a complex one, and the reader is referred to the chapter bibliography for sources to make an independent judgment.)

The Fall 1949 issue of *Variety* magazine contained a report on "crashed saucer" rumors by Frank Scully, who later wrote *Behind the Flying Saucers* recounting several instances reported to him of UFO crashes in the Southwest. When some of his sources were later identified as con-men and publicly discredited, Scully was believed to be the victim of a hoax. The pseudoscientific speculations that he incorporated into the story did not help the credibility of his book either.

In hindsight, it appears that Scully — as a popular author — was picking up on the same widespread stories that later investigators have uncovered, but perhaps was somewhat careless in reporting information from questionable sources. *Time* magazine for January 9, 1950, reported rumors of "crashed saucers" and small humanoid bodies in New Mexico, and *Newsweek* for April 17, 1950, contained a similar article. A recently released FBI document obtained under a Freedom of Information Act request is a Special-Agent-in-Charge report to FBI headquarters in Washington, D.C., dated March 22, 1950. It reports the following information obtained from an Air Force investigator:

"Three so-called flying saucers had been recovered in New Mexico ... circular in shape with raised centers, approximately 50 feet in diameter. Each one was occupied by three bodies of human shape but only 3 feet tall, dressed in metallic cloth of a very fine texture." (See Appendix B.)

Was this based on the personal knowledge of the Air Force investigator or merely hearsay? The document indicates his source to be an "informant" whose credentials are not given, and no additional FBI or Air Force documents have been located that would shed further light on the question or on any follow-up investigations.

Similarly an Air Force intelligence message to headquarters dated January 16, 1950, recounts stories going the rounds in the Denver, Colorado, area and reported in a Kansas City newspaper of crashed saucers in the Southwest. The metal allegedly "defied analysis." Bodies were said to be 3 feet tall. The spot intelligence report was filed by the Air Force Office of Special Investigations district office at Offutt AFB, Omaha, Nebraska, which conducted some follow-up investigation and next day downgraded the report from SECRET to CONFIDENTIAL.

These documents do not prove that it really happened; but, along with the news media reports and other sources they do establish the fact that in 1949 and 1950, "crashed saucer" stories were circulating through both journalistic circles and military intelligence channels. The so-called "Scully hoax" soon thereafter succeeded in killing off public interest in the question.

Despite the uniform skepticism by all serious UFO investigators from that time on, the possibility that there are bodies and craft undergoing secret study in Government facilities has been revived in the 1980s — and not without reason. In those days firsthand witnesses (or claimants) were just about impossible to find. The stories always emanated from second- or third-hand sources. Today several dozen firsthand witnesses are known to a handful of UFO investigators.

A leading investigator on this question is Leonard H. Stringfield, a retired public relations executive in Cincinnati, Ohio. A conservative UFOlogist, he too had been skeptical ever since Scully. When he touched on the "crashed saucer" theme in his 1977 book, he was surprised when a number of alleged first-hand witnesses contacted him and he was able to learn their identities and obtain their stories in considerable detail. They included former military intelligence personnel and members of such professions as law enforcement and banking. To Stringfield, the credibility of these sources was clear and his interest in the question was renewed.

The stories were given to him with the understanding that the sources would remain totally anonymous. In 1978 he went public with the information, as fully as possible within the bounds of witness confidentiality, at the MUFON UFO Symposium in Dayton, Ohio. But his refusal to name names embroiled him in controversy. To complicate matters his public appearances stimulated a spate of "crashed saucer" stories from the public — or fragments of stories heard from relatives or friends — and not all of these were plausible sounding or even checkable. Still, he felt an obligation to report publicly on the information he was receiving and he reported the stories, "warts" and all, in a series of articles and monographs.

When flaws were found in some of the stories, Stringfield was accused of failure to investigate and accused of being gullible. Strong hostility to the idea of "crashed saucers" persisted among UFO investigators, and they failed to understand his reason for "going public." In the first place, Stringfield does not have the personal resources to fully investigate every story or case lead presented to him and he did not want to pass personal judgment on them until more complete investigation could be accomplished. Secondly, his main motivation for publishing incomplete or questionable cases has been to air out the stories and encourage the needed investigation in cooperation with others. In that way he hoped to either refute a given report or find substantiation of it rather than let it gather dust in his files.

Instead of cooperation, Stringfield took a lot of flak and was given a lot of grief. Yet, his unquestioned personal integrity probably is one of the reasons that some of the more credible sources have sought him out and confided in him. He also has resisted any temptation to write a trade book capitalizing on the stories, whose inherent interest would make them saleable even without complete documentation. Instead, he has released all possible information through private publications to the UFO research community and not made any profit by doing so.

In addition to Stringfield, Moore, and Friedman, former Army Security Agency employee Todd Zechel has investigated "crashed saucer" stories, which he first heard about from a military source while on active duty. He was able to track down and interview the original sources of a few of the early stories that had been submitted to the National Investigations Committee on Aerial Phenomena. As of this writing, Zechel has notified me that he has been able to obtain substantial firsthand information about a 1950 case in Mexico, opposite Del Rio, Texas (Case B-7 in Stringfield's 1980 monograph) which he planned to make public in 1987.

Raymond E. Fowler, a highly regarded researcher in Massachusetts, also has contributed a potentially important case to the literature. The case is reported in detail in his 1981 book: a 1953 crash near Kingman, Arizona, as described by one of the specialists allegedly called to the scene to analyze the craft.

If we assume for the sake of argument that there is a long-suppressed Government secret, then it would not be surprising for disinformation specialists to appear on the scene to confuse the issue with false stories and attempts to discredit the reporters of valid information. Indeed, obvious attempts have been made to hoax Stringfield into accepting false information as a means of discrediting him, and ridiculous-sounding crash/retrieval stories have been planted in the newspapers and popular newsstand magazines. One such major "plant" that received wide publicity just happened to be released in Cincinnati, Stringfield's home base, linked with personal attacks on him by the same source. As a result of such manipulations, more heat than light has been shed on crash/retrieval reports, and they remain highly controversial even among UFO researchers.

Personalities also enter into it strongly, and there is little or no cooperation among the crash/retrieval investigators. In some instances a selfish desire to break the greatest story in the history of Humankind (which is what it would be if true) causes jealousies and creates ". . . a house divided . . . "

What should we believe? After a lot of soul-searching and reconsideration of the crash/retrieval question, I have been converted from a total skeptic to an advocate of keeping an open mind and carefully sifting the evidence on the *possibility* that there may be something to it after all. First, a summary of some so-far credible reports which — until proven otherwise — tend to support the reality of "crashed saucers" and alien bodies:

July 2, 1947; Roswell, New Mexico. Military intelligence officer, ranchers, and others report various observations, from their perspectives, of a disc-shaped UFO that exploded in mid-air; fragments with unusual characteristics spirited away to Wright-Patterson AFB under cover story of "balloon." Associated rumors of bodies found at separate site 150 miles away. Investigators: William L. Moore and Stanton T. Friedman.

1950; Mexico, across the border from Del Rio, Texas. "Crashed saucer" and alien body retrieval reportedly involving Mexican military forces and U.S. Air Force units. Investigator: Todd Zechel.

1952; New Mexico (crash site); Wright-Patterson AFB, Ohio (viewing site). A retired Air Force Major states that while attending a high-level secret meeting at the airbase he observed, in an underground chamber, an alien body in deep-freeze preservation. The alleged alien was about 4 feet tall with gray skin and a large head. Investigator: Leonard H. Stringfield.

1953; near White Sands, New Mexico. Army helicopter pilot who served as aide to Air Force General states that a "crashed saucer" of ovoid shape (about 18 ft. x 30 ft.) and bodies about 4 ft. tall were retrieved and later stored (at least temporarily) at Langley AFB, Virginia. Investigator: Todd Zechel.

1953; Arizona (crash site); Wright-Patterson AFB (viewing site). Air National Guard Flight Commander reports seeing four alien bodies in crates being offloaded in hangar, packed in dry ice. Bodies approximately 4 ft. tall, large heads. Report coincides in all major particulars with following reference and could very well be an independent confirmation. Investigator: Leonard H. Stringfield.

May 21, 1953; near Kingman, Arizona. A project engineer on Air Force contract with Atomic Energy Commission reports being one of a group of specialists taken to the crash site in a bus with blacked-out windows to study the craft. He observed a supposedly alien body about 4 ft. tall in a nearby tent. Investigator: Raymond E. Fowler.

1966; Wright-Patterson AFB. Businessman and former Army intelligence officer states that he observed nine alien bodies about 4 ft. tall with grayish skin, in deep-freeze conditions in a glass enclosure. Investigator: Leonard H. Stringfield.

1973: Wright-Patterson AFB. Air Force Sergeant, air policeman, called to duty in the middle of the night states that he was led blindfolded to an area where he was instructed to guard three bodies stretched out on a table. The bodies were about 3 ft. tall with large heads and offwhite skin. Investigator: Leonard H. Stringfield.

January 18, 1978; McGuire AFB, New Jersey. Air Force security policeman ("Blue Beret") states that while on security patrol duty, UFOs were observed over adjacent Ft. Dix and encroaching on a deserted runway of the airbase, including an alleged "alien" creature who was shot and fell dead. Claims to have observed a special Blue Beret team take over and cordon off the area, crate and load body on a special plane from Wright-Patterson AFB. Investigators: Leonard H. Stringfield and Richard H. Hall.

Although this meager body of "evidence" falls far short of providing convincing "proof" of anything, it is important to note that the key witnesses appear to be reliable individuals. Other similar reports could be cited, but these are among the more credible core reports. For the most part they come from military intelligence and security personnel trained to work in secrecy and conditioned not to talk about their work in any public forum. They have guardedly told their stories to only one or two persons and insisted on total anonymity. According to their stories, the only reason they have talked at all is to "get it off their chests" or because of a conviction that "the public ought to know." Occasionally a credible-sounding story has come from someone bragging to close friends about being "in the know," not intending for the story to be publicized.

Would-be hoaxers are fairly easy to spot when it comes to crash/retrieval claims. In order to be credible, a person must have been in a job position or profession that would plausibly place him at a crash site or secret storage area, and able to supply military service records or other relevant documentation that would permit verification of key details. In addition, he must be able to pass the usual screening for personal character and reliability. Quite a few crash/retrieval claimants either have failed to pass these tests or are unwilling to risk accidental public disclosure by supplying relevant records (typically on the grounds that they have signed oaths of secrecy and their pensions and/or livelihood are at stake). The claimants in the small sample reported here have substantially passed these tests. Though *complete* documentation is not necessarily available, they have supplied enough information to lend credence to their stories and verification of their professional positions.

Considering the degree of secrecy that would prevail if the reports are true, complete documentation is an elusive goal. The people likely to be in a position to have observed craft and/or bodies normally are tight-lipped by the very nature of their work. The claimants in the core cases tend to fit the sort of picture you would expect.

Partially supporting testimony also has been given by a prominent physical and engineering scientist, Dr. Robert I. Sarbacher. California researcher William Steinmann tracked down and contacted Sarbacher, whose involvement with UFOs was first uncovered by Canadian sources and reported by Stringfield (see June 1982 reference, bibliography). In a letter to Steinmann, Sarbacher confirmed his awareness of crash/retrieval cases.

He has since been interviewed by William Moore, Stanton Friedman, and Jerry Clark. The gist of his story is that in the 1950s, he was made aware of "crashed saucer" information by scientific colleagues who directly participated in the investigations, and he has implicated other prominent scientists by name. He also states that he was personally involved in analysis of physical trace evidence at UFO landing sites. Given Sarbacher's background and credentials (see *Who's Who*), his confirmation of the long-standing rumors cannot be taken lightly despite its hearsay nature.

From a personal standpoint, I have now interviewed several of the claimants face-to-face and others via telephone, and conducted some personal background checking and study of their psychological make-up. In addition, Stringfield has opened some of his files to me in confidence. By these means, I have been able to evaluate many of the stories and to form some impressions about the type of person telling them. Despite the high "noise" level in crash/retrieval claims, there is disturbing evidence of a muted "signal."

If *all* the reports are hoaxes, then someone must explain: (a) why the more credible information has only slowly trickled out over a period of 40 years, often obtained only after extensive detective work; (b) why experienced professionals (as the key witnesses tend to be) would risk their careers by involving themselves; and (c) what conceivable purpose such a hoax could serve.

Perhaps it is an elaborate CIA hoax to trick the Soviet Union into thinking that we have access to a revolutionary propulsion system and other advanced knowledge from an extraterrestrial source. But how many precedents can be found for such a monolithic, long-lasting, single-minded counterintelligence ploy without visible, productive benefit? This clever "trick" has survived half a dozen presidential administrations, almost as many CIA directors, and constant personnel turnover in 40 years, yet has succeeded only in "fooling" a handful of UFO investigators who only recently have begun to consider the reports seriously.

Moreover, Soviet intelligence agencies over the 40-year period could easily observe that the U.S. has not developed any radically new, high-performance technology amounting to a quantum leap, so the game would seem to be pointless. Yet, something of this nature is the only apparent alternative to accepting the better reports as essentially factual, if possibly garbled in some details due to the passage of time or a limited perspective on the incident.

Why, then, would such an astounding development as the retrieval of extraterrestrial hardware be kept secret for so long?

Why wouldn't an immediate announcement be made to the entire world of this dramatic development? Questions like this are naive. Such an announcement, particularly in the 1950s, would have sent shock waves around the world, threatening the survival of our political systems, our beliefs, our religions, the world economy — our very way of life.

In addition, the military implications are obvious. The country that figured out the power source of the alien vehicles would be way ahead of the rest of the world. Considering the Cold War climate of the 1950s, total secrecy could have been justified on these grounds alone.

Craft and bodies would constitute the ultimate proof of alien visitors, but if scientists didn't have answers to the urgent questions raised by their presence (Where do they come from? Why are they here? Are their intentions friendly? Is Earth society in danger?), there are obvious reasons why total secrecy would prevail until some answers could be found.

The answers still may not be known 40 years later; or, perhaps, if they are known they would not be easily digestible.

If crash/retrievals have occurred, what do the alien humanoid bodies look like? In the course of his investigations, Stringfield made contact with a doctor (Doctor "X") who said he had conducted medical tests on alien cadavers at a major Eastern medical facility. Stringfield later visited Doctor "X" at his place of employment, a medical facility in another city, thus verifying his credentials.

Stringfield was also a guest at the home of a colleague of Doctor "X," who said he had also examined an alien tissue sample under a microscope. From these seemingly unimpeachable sources (ruling out a Byzantine hoax cleverly employing established professionals to dupe Stringfield for unknown purposes), he obtained confirmation of key portions of humanoid physiology as pieced together from several alleged eye-witness descriptions.

Doctor "X" declined to answer a number of questions, apparently taking his signals from some higher authority, but confirmed this general description:

- 3-1/2 to 4-1/2 feet tall

- About 40 pounds

- Large head, about proportion of 5-month human fetus

- Heavy brow ridge

- Round eyes without pupils, large and "Oriental" looking

- Apertures rather than ears

- Small indistinct nose

- Small slit-like mouth without lips

- Slender torsos and long thin arms

- Skin tannish or grayish and elastic, reptile-like

- Colorless liquid prevalent in body; no red cells

Though broadly humanoid in general appearance, the bodies had these distinctly nonhuman features: mouths appeared to be nonfunctional, no teeth, no apparent reproductive organs, no human-like internal organs, and generally clone-like in appearance, or possibly androids. The doctor would not answer questions about the brain.

There the matter stands at present: a few partially documented cases, and a larger number of incomplete or hearsay cases that, nevertheless, are known to come from credible sources who profess reluctance to talk openly for fear of reprisals, plus the statements from Dr. "X" and Dr. Sarbacher. Without more complete testimony and documentation, skepticism is fully justified. Yet, Stringfield is not making up the cases reported to him, nor are Friedman, Moore, Zechel, or Fowler.

The core reports, so far, have held up under investigation, but do not amount to totally convincing proof. What we have is a small body of highly credible witnesses (unusually so because of their special training and sensitive positions) who are telling a highly incredible story. In the Hynek matrix, these are High Credibility/High Strangeness reports. At this point we can only seek out new evidence and keep an open mind.

Unlike any other aspect of the UFO subject, investigation of these reports amounts to an attempt to establish the *corpus delecti*. Craft and bodies potentially are the whole ball game. Yet, of all aspects of the UFO subject, this one poses unique problems of "evidence" and "proof." All we know is that, if it really happened, the witnesses in all likelihood *would* be under severe restraints. Most likely they would be unable to do more than relate the basic story in confidence to someone they trusted and then withdraw into silence. The behavior of the core witnesses is at least plausible in relation to what they claim.

The entire question deserves the closest possible scrutiny, with vigorous investigation and public disclosure of hoaxes. However, the ultimate resolution may lie in efforts to encourage the witnesses to go public in unison on the "safety in numbers" principle, perhaps with high-level guarantees of immunity from prosecution, or at least strong legal backing and protection from retaliation. Maybe then the reports can be either verified or laid to rest for once and for all.

POSTSCRIPT

Since this chapter was written, Bill Moore and his colleagues in 1987 released a document held by some to be the possible "smoking gun of UFOlogy" and by others to be an outrageous hoax. Opinion within the UFO research community already was completely polarized on the topic of "crashed saucers," and the so-called MJ-12 story has only aggravated that sharp division of opinion.

The document in question (see Appendix C) purports to be a "TOP SECRET/MAJIC EYES ONLY" briefing paper dated Nov. 18, 1952, for President-Elect Dwight D. Eisenhower, prepared by a group of top scientists and military leaders called "Majestic 12." They are named in the document, and include very prominent persons of that time.

The document came anonymously in December 1984 to Jaime Shandera, a colleague of Moore, in a roll of undeveloped film. Basically, it confirms the Roswell, N.M., case and advises the incoming President on what is known about the craft and bodies. The all-important "Tabs," allegedly consisting of physical analysis and autopsy information, are listed but not included.

For 2-1/2 years, a team consisting of Moore, Shandera, and Stanton Friedman analyzed the document and sought confirmation, including some clever documentary research on the alleged principals and on questions of form and style for contemporary Government records. They could find nothing wrong with the document; in fact, a number of internal clues tended to authenticate it and it was consistent with certain key biographical information.

During their research, they discovered a second document in Government files at the National Archives that makes reference to MJ-12: a July 14, 1954, memo from the office of Gen. Robert Cutler (an Eisenhower aide) to Gen. Nathan Twining (an alleged member of MJ-12) advising him of a change in schedule for an MJ-12 briefing.

On the other hand, the highly regarded group Citizens Against UFO Secrecy (CAUS) has presented a serious critique of the MJ-12 documents, concluding that the case for them is "severely flawed" and that ". . . we do not regard the MSF (Moore-Shandera-Friedman) documents as convincing proof of the MJ-12 group of the Roswell crash. There are too many hard questions which haven't been answered effectively . . . ."

As of this writing (January 1988) I am privy to some of the MSF research data that has not yet been made public, and it tends to give satisfactory answers to most of the objections raised by CAUS. Still, without additional supporting evidence, the authenticity of the supposed Eisenhower briefing document remains open to question.

CAUS is entirely correct to raise questions and express skepticism, and to hold out for more complete documentation. That skepticism, however, should leave room for open-minded reappraisal as the story unfolds. MJ-12, as of this writing, has been neither proved nor disproved, and remains very much an open question.

So far, the MJ-12 controversy has raised the heat level, but shed no further light (unless accepted at face value) on interpretation of the persistent "crashed saucer" stories. The Eisenhower briefing document, if a hoax, displays an incredible detailed insider's knowledge of UFO history and obscure details of Government form and style for that era. That leads me to believe that if it is a hoax, the hoax is being perpetrated by knowledgable persons in the U.S. intelligence community for their own obscure purposes.

BIBLIOGRAPHY

Berlitz, Charles and Moore, William L. *The Roswell Incident* (N.Y.: Grosset and Dunlap, 1980). 1947 crash/retrieval case in New Mexico.

Citizens Against UFO Secrecy. "The MJ-12 Fiasco" in *Just Cause*, No. 13, Sept. 1987.

Fowler, Raymond E. *Casebook of a UFO Investigator* (N.J.: Prentice-Hall, 1981). Chapter 17, "Retrievals of the Third Kind," featuring the 1953 Arizona retrieval case.

Friedman, Stanton T. "MJ-12: The Evidence So Far," in *International UFO Reporter*, v. 12, no. 5, Sept.-Oct. 1987.

Friedman, Stanton T. and Moore, William L. "The Roswell Incident: Beginning of the Cosmic Watergate," in *1981 MUFON UFO Symposium Proceedings* (Seguin, Tex.: MUFON, 1981).

Hall, Richard. "Crashed Discs — Maybe," in *International UFO Reporter*, v. 10, no. 4, July-Aug., 1985.

Maccabee, Bruce S. *The Roswell Incident* book review, *MUFON UFO Journal*, no. 162, Aug. 1981.

_____. "Documents and Supporting Information Related to Crashed Flying Saucers and Operation Majestic Twelve" (Washington, D.C.: Fund for UFO Research, 1987).

Moore, William L. "The Roswell Investigation: New Evidence, New Conclusions," *Frontiers of Science*, v. III, no. 5, July-Aug., 1981.

_____. Crashed Saucers: Evidence in Search of Proof," in *MUFON 1985 UFO Symposium Proceedings* (Seguin, Tex.: MUFON, 1985). Detailed examination of Scully story and update on the Roswell Incident.

Scully, Frank. *Behind the Flying Saucers* (N.Y.: Henry Holt, 1950). The original accounts of alleged crashed saucers and humanoid bodies.

Stringfield, Leonard H. *Situation Red: The UFO Siege* (N.Y.: Doubleday, 1977).

_____. "Retrievals of the Third Kind," in *1978 MUFON UFO Symposium Proceedings* (Seguin, Tex.: MUFON, 1978).

_____. *UFO Crash/Retrieval Syndrome* (Seguin, Tex.: MUFON, Jan. 1980).

_____. *UFO Crash/Retrievals: Amassing the Evidence* (Cincinnati, Ohio: Author, June 1982).

_____. "Fatal Encounter at Ft. Dix-McGuire: A Case Study" in *MUFON 1985 UFO Symposium Proceedings* (Seguin, Tex.: MUFON, 1985).

Zechel, W. Todd. Private communications to the author.

CHAPTER 5

THE INTERVENTIONISTS

Newly emerging information from a broad spectrum of witnesses world-wide suggests a startling conclusion: We are — and have been for decades — biological test subjects for "beings from elsewhere." Sometimes the witnesses have seen a UFO and then experienced a memory lapse or "time loss," and an abduction scenario emerges under hypnotic regression. At other times, and significantly often, the witnesses have immediate or delayed conscious recall of an abduction experience without the use of hypnosis.

Skeptical objections to abduction reports center on the unreliability of hypnosis as a tool for accurate recall of events that allegedly have been repressed from conscious memory. As is well known, hypnotic subjects are notoriously suggestible, usually attempting to "please the hypnotist" by filling in the gaps of recall with unrelated memories or even outright fabrications, though the process may not be an entirely conscious one. This process is known as "confabulation."

"Suggestibility, a state of greatly enhanced receptiveness and responsiveness to suggestions and stimuli, constitutes the central phenomenon of hypnosis," according to the author of the hypnosis entry in the *Encyclopedia Britannica* (1969). "The psychological processes involved are essentially those of vivification of memories, ideas, understandings, emotions . . . so that they are experienced subjectively as deriving from external events rather than from internal processes."

Deliberate or unconscious cues from the hypnotist, or others present, easily can induce a subject to embellish or fabricate details to flesh out otherwise incomplete recall of actual events. Although this line of argument does not invalidate the productive use of hypnotism by skilled professionals, it does show that hypnotism easily can be misused and that "memories" retrieved under hypnosis must be evaluated carefully in the context of all available objective evidence, and not simply taken at face value. Most popular books on UFOs that recount hypnotic regression cases contain examples of fairly obvious cues to witnesses who otherwise are not coming forth with an abduction story. *Caveat emptor.*

Another confounding factor is that many or most professional practitioners of hypnosis are accustomed to using it in a therapeutic, rather than a truth-seeking, mode. In general, a therapist is seeking to relieve his or her patient of unpleasant symptoms. In that context, it often is quite proper and appropriate to cue or "lead" the patient in order to relieve anxieties. A point often overlooked by UFO researchers is that the therapeutic approach carries with it the danger of muddying the subject's memory for recall of actual events.

Hypnosis in the truth-seeking mode most often is employed by police psychologists, in attempts to bring out repressed details bearing on the commission of a crime. Definite success has been obtained in eliciting a key fact, such as a license plate number, that has helped to solve a crime. This form of hypnosis, however, uses the emerging information only as a clue or lead whose factuality is then checked through objective sources such as motor vehicle records. The fact remains that hypnosis can, when properly used, enhance recall of factual information.

Hypnotic regression applied to UFO cases would seem to require a hybrid technique, but something closer to the truth-seeking model since the critical question is the truth or accuracy of the emerging story. However, abduction victims ("abductees") often are badly shaken by their perceived experiences and also need or would benefit by some therapy too.

The credibility of an individual abduction story emerging under hypnosis hinges entirely on the techniques used and the skill of the hypnotist in isolating relevant accurate recall from real but unrelated memories, and in identifying confabulation by the subject. All of this requires psychological sophistication and clinical skills, and is best left to clinical psychologists and psychiatrists. The UFO literature is replete with abduction stories of dubious pedigree, evoked by amateur hypnotists.

By far the most professional application of hypnosis to abduction cases is that of clinical psychologist Aphrodite Clamar, reported in Budd Hopkins' eye-opening book *Missing Time*. The resulting information makes the strongest case to date for the possible objective reality of abductions. Even here, though, there are some examples of a subject possibly being pressured inadvertently into telling an abduction story (notably "Philip Osborne," in chapter 7, who himself had doubts about the disjointed story that was emerging).

The conscious recall cases, especially, should give us pause about discarding all of the hypnotic recall cases merely because hypnosis is tricky. A prime example of a consciously recalled abduction, with multiple witnesses to the initial UFO encounter, is the widely reported Travis Walton case on November 5, 1975 (not recounted here; see chapter bibliography). Another is the case of Staff Sgt. Charles L. Moody on August 13, 1975 in Alamogordo, New Mexico (see Case Book Appendix).

The problematical reliability of hypnosis is not sufficient reason to doubt that abductions may be occurring. Most likely the cases emerging under hypnosis (those that are not totally contaminated by faulty technique) contain some admixture of confabulation, but there also is a good possibility that they contain significant elements of objective "truth." The problem — and it is a serious and difficult one — is to separate the two. The worldwide incidence of abduction stories and the concordance of specific details argue against abductions being purely imaginary. Yet, there is little doubt that imaginary elements are seriously confusing the issue.

Either we really are under the microscopes of alien beings, or we are faced with an hysteria of unprecedented scope that, itself, demands explanation. *Table 3* provides a cross-section of abduction reports.

TABLE 3
Representative UFO Abduction Reports

DATE/ IDENTIFICATION	LOCATION	INITIAL BLACKOUT	EXAM TABLE	X-RAY-LIKE EXAM DEVICE	BODY PROBES	TIME LOSS	TRANSLOCATION	COMMUNICATION/ MESSAGES
1964 Pa. "Osborne"	i		•	?	•			
4/5/69 N.Y. "McMahon"	v		•		?			
Fall 72 Md. "Kilburn"	v	•	•		•	•		
10/11/73 Miss. Hickson	o		•	•				• (later)
10/17/73 Midwest "Price"	i	•	•		•			
10/28/73 Brazil Yanco	o	•			•		•	•
Summer 75 Oreg. Tony & Darryl M.	o	•	•	•		•		•
8/13/75 N. Mex. Moody	o	•	•		•	•		•

con't

DATE/ IDENTIFICATION	LOCATION	INITIAL BLACKOUT	EXAM TABLE	X-RAY-LIKE EXAM DEVICE	BODY PROBES	TIME LOSS	TRANSLOCATION	COMMUNICATION/ MESSAGES
1/21/76 Brazil Reis	v			•	•		•	•
3/18/78 S.C. Hermann	o	•	•	•			•	•
8/30/78 Argentina Freitas	o				•		•	•
11/78 W. Germany Owens	v	•	•		•			•
12/6/78 Italy Zanfretta	v	•	?		?	•	•	
7/25/79 Calif. Shari N.	v	•	•		•	•		
8/4/79 Canada Sarah H.	o	•			•			•
10/6/79 N.J. "Rich"	i	•			•	•		
4/2/80 Finland	v	•	•			•		•
8/22/80 East Texas "Megan Elliot"	v		•		•		•	•
11/19/80 Colorado "Michael" & "Mary"	v	•	•	•		•		•

cont'd

UNINVITED GUESTS

DATE/ IDENTIFICATION	LOCATION	INITIAL BLACKOUT	EXAM TABLE	X-RAY-LIKE EXAM DEVICE	BODY PROBES	TIME LOSS	TRANSLOCATION	COMMUNICATION/ MESSAGES
19 cases (7 countries)	v-9 o-7 i-3	13	14	6	14	8	6	12

CODES — Location at start of experience; v — vehicle, o — outdoors, i — indoors

    • — Reported presence of feature (Not all data points are present in available information)

    ? — Feature suggested but not unambiguous

DEFINITIONS —

Initial Blackout: After sighting UFO and/or beings, subject became unconscious and/or suffered a memory loss

Body Probes: Variety of bodily examinations described, often involving instruments or "needles" to penetrate the skin

Time Loss: After experiencing UFO sighting or other aberrant event, subject was consciously aware of an unaccounted-for period of time

Translocation: After an abduction experience, subject found himself-herself in a different location than at the start

The prototype abduction case is the 1961 Betty and Barney Hill encounter in the White Mountains of New Hampshire, which has been the subject of a book by John Fuller and a made-for-TV documentary that faithfully recounted the broad features of the case. After a close-range sighting during which Barney saw humanoid beings through the windows of a UFO, the couple had troubling dreams. They had experienced a time loss following the sighting and wondered what had happened during the lost hours.

Later, under hypnosis, Barney and Betty both described being forcibly abducted on board a craft by small humanoid beings. Both recounted undergoing bodily probings by the beings, and Betty was shown a star map purportedly showing

94

where they came from. Under hypnosis, she replicated the map. Subsequent research established that the star system it depicted was visible from earth, but not in the particular configuration shown so that she could not have subconsciously recreated it from contemporary star maps. The star system was at the time considered a logical candidate for intelligent life. More recent astronomical information has cast some doubt on that possibility.

A re-reading of the hypnotic regression sessions with the Hill's, conducted by Dr. Benjamin Simon (since deceased), provides a strong example of therapeutic, as opposed to truth-seeking, hypnotic methods. As a psychiatrist, Dr. Benjamin clearly (and properly) was treating the Hill's for their symptoms of anxiety, not trying to establish whether the abduction was objectively real. The distinction has important implications for the accuracy or reliability of the story content. Many details easily could be interpreted as reflections of the subjects' personal fears and concerns rather than actual "interests" or actions of the supposed aliens.

Certainly we cannot accept at face value such things as the "Leader's" sudden fit of pique because Betty could not instantly understand the star map. More likely we are seeing an expression of Betty's own minor feelings of inadequacy for not understanding more about space. Any number of case details suggest that we are seeing individual bits of human psychology superimposed on recall of a real experience of some kind. There are strong indications that personal psychology "colors" abduction stories, but equally certainly the stories are not totally imaginary creations. If they were, it is doubtful that we would find so much convergence of detail.

The abduction stories are puzzling because they do not emanate from a motley crew of psychic cooks and bottle washers as did the "contactee" stories of the 1950s. In those years, a variety of tinkerers and would-be cosmic "priests" presented themselves as the "chosen" of the space people; chosen to bring a message of peace and brotherly love to Earth. The contactees claimed specially privileged liaison with space people, who gave them rides in spaceships and transported them to exotic planets.

The "messages" for Earth, unfortunately, contradicted each other and the contactees each described a different home planet for the spacemen. Both the contactees and, by implication, the spacemen, often were caught in contradictions. Once the United States and the Soviet Union sent men into space, many of the specific claims were proved to be untrue. The golden-haired saviors and platitudinous message-givers of the 1950s bear little resemblance to the modern-day abductees.

The abductees describe a different breed of "spacemen" altogether. The aliens usually are small, hairless, sometimes grotesque humanoid creatures who blatantly intercede in human affairs. The 1950s spacemen always were bound by some "universal code" not to intercede. Unlike the Nordic universalist philosophers depicted as piloting the 1950s spaceships, the modern-day abductors often appear emotionless, with "masklike" faces, and instead of proselytizing for a universal religion, they subject their captives to frightening and sometimes painful physiological probings.

The abductors think nothing of invading a bedroom or stopping a vehicle, kidnapping the terrified and resisting humans, paralyzing them or rendering them unconscious if necessary, and — without explanation — probing their bodies with needles or other instruments. All things considered, the 1950s spacemen were much more gentlemanly and likeable, if stuffy in their views.

Clearly the contactee and abductee reports are fundamentally different in all respects but one: the abductors also occasionally give messages for Earth through the abductees (or the abductees think they do). Some form of communication often occurs between the captors and the captives. When coherent, it is typically a "message" describing their purpose in being here. Frequently the communication is incoherent, or couched in pseudoscientific or mystical jargon, suggesting a possible psychological origin.

The 1950s messages, not surprisingly in the midst of the Cold War era, concerned the threat of atomic destruction. No doubt this very real fear was embedded in the unconscious minds of the idealistic contactees (when not consciously used as an attention-getting ploy), and they conjured up benevolent spacemen to save us from ourselves. Exactly what new cultural compulsion drives the more recent "messages" is unclear, but the overriding theme is biological or medical in nature.

The abductees frequently appear to be unable to articulate the experience they have undergone, and the "messages" may well represent a futile attempt by the subjects to rationalize an incomprehensible event within the framework of their personal experience and understanding. The individual backgrounds of the abductees vary from that of a fundamental religionist like Betty Andreasson (see Fowler reference in bibliography), whose story carries strong religious overtones, to highly educated professionals. In some cases there is suggestive evidence that the subjects' personal medical histories are reflected in their abduction stories.

A number of cases suggest that deep-seated human fears are being triggered into the conscious mind by some sort of frightening experience. But what is that "frightening experience?" The common description is an uninvited and typically frightening physical intervention in their lives by manifestly alien beings. Beyond that, very little can be said. The contactees invariably found their liaisons to be pleasant experiences and flattering to them, and they subsequently made a career of "spreading the faith." The abductees, typically, are terrified and their subsequent lives are disrupted; many afterwards have serious psychological problems and difficulty in adjusting.

The general flavor of abduction reports is conveyed by the following small sample. (Some of these cases are incomplete, not fully investigated, but they agree in many details with thoroughly investigated cases like those in *Missing Time*.)

October 28, 1973; Bahio Blanca, Brazil.

Dionisio Yanca, a young truck driver, stopped to change a flat tire in the early morning. A UFO approached and hovered nearby, disembarking three human-like beings wearing silvery clothing. Yanca blacked out and had no conscious memory of what happened next.

His next conscious memory was of falling — slowly — into a pasture in a state of mental confusion. When later hypnotized, he described being levitated on board a craft which had "technological" instruments. His abductors seemed to communicate among themselves with a humming sound; they communicated to him via a "radio," in Spanish, describing their mission to study humans. One of the beings, a woman, took a glove with tack-like spikes and pricked him ... and his next memory was of falling into the pasture.

Doctors later noted tiny dots or points on Yanca's left eyelid. They saw no evidence of a hoax. Even after hypnosis and sodium pentothal application, Yanca still could not account for about 2 hours, a period of apparent total amnesia.

August 13, 1975; Alamogordo, N.M.

Air Force Staff Sergeant Charles L. Moody was watching for meteors in the outskirts when a disc-shaped UFO approached. He heard a high-pitched sound and saw shadowy humanoid figures through a window of the UFO. He felt numb ... then saw the UFO depart. When he arrived home, he realized that he could not account for 1-1/2 hours of time. Next day he had some skin inflammation and a small puncture wound on his back.

Over the next two months memory of the "lost" time gradually returned (no hypnosis), and he recalled being on board a craft and having telepathic communication with humanoid beings. They were under 5 feet tall and had whitish-gray skin, large heads, large eyes, and mask-like facial features. Moody was on a smooth, slablike table unable to move, and the beings applied an instrument to his back. He was afterwards given a tour of the craft and shown details of its structure. The beings said they would have limited contact with mankind in the near future.

January 21, 1976; Matles-Barbosa, Brazil.

Herminio and Bianca Reis stopped to rest along the highway, and after a while their car, a Volkswagen, was illuminated by an intense bluish light and levitated into a craft. Inside they saw technological instruments and communicated with two tall beings via "headsets" plugged into an apparent computer. Bianca was examined or tested in a box-like device that glowed red like a grill.

Afterwards they were given a green liquor to drink and more beings appeared; one was a tall, dark-haired woman. They said they were performing medical research, and that they had conquered aging and death in their world.

March 18, 1978; Charleston, S.C.

While observing a UFO through binoculars in a marshy area, Bill Herrmann, an auto mechanic, was rendered unconscious by a beam of light from the object. His next conscious memory was of standing in a plowed field at a different location over two hours later. He ran hysterically toward a distant road where he could see cars passing, and a policeman helped him contact his family who came to get him.

Later, under hypnosis, Herrmann described being examined on a low table (an almost standard feature of physical examination cases) by three small beings using a blinking X-ray-like device. The beings had marshmallow-white skin and fetus-like heads. (In the November 5, 1975, abduction case near Heber, Arizona, Travis Walton also described white-skinned, fetus-like beings, features also present in some of Budd Hopkins' cases.)

Herrmann was told that there are three races of beings from space here to observe and conduct experiments. (In fact, three general types of beings have been reported world-wide:

the diminutive humanoids; beings human-like in appearance and stature; and sometimes very large "monstrous" creatures. Robotlike entities also have been reported.)

November 1978; Trier, West Germany.

Pam Owens, the young pregnant wife of a U.S. soldier, said that she and her family arrived home from a visit to friends with nearly two hours of time unaccounted for after a large oval object hovered over their car. Under later hypnosis she described being examined on a table by two small, hairless beings who had large heads and deep-set eyes. One of the beings inserted a needle just above her navel.

Her next memory after the needle was of standing by the car with her infant son in her arms, watching the UFO depart. Tape recordings of her story were studied by psychological stress evaluator, indicating that she was telling the truth.

April 2, 1980; Pudasjarvi Finland.

Aino Ivanoff was driving across a bridge in the early morning when she entered a "strange fog" and her car headlights were deflected upwards (one of a handful of "light-bending" cases). As she braked to a stop she saw a silvery, domed UFO with portholes. She was taken inside and examined on a table by three "men" (not otherwise described in information presently available).

After she was returned to her car, the fog persisted and she had to drive home in it, most of the way. Later she found five small dots on her right shoulder. She was extremely tired for about a week thereafter. The beings gave her an anti-war message, and also observed that they were unable to have children. Most of the story emerged under hypnosis.

These six cases from 1973 through 1980 illustrate the global nature of the reports, including many similarities as well as differences. The abductions commonly — but not always — occur to motorists at late hours and in comparatively isolated locations. The witness very often — but not always — remembers seeing a UFO immediately prior to an amnesic period. More cases than not involve bodily "examinations" of some kind. (See *Table 3* for case comparisons.)

A critical question, also highlighting some of the internal contradictions in abduction reports, is why some of the presumed aliens reportedly use telepathy to communicate, while others require technological aids. Another critical question is why some "aliens" are communicative at all, while others act zombie-like and conceal their purposes behind a mask of silence. Either there are different "personalities" involved or the reports, in some way, reflect the individual psychology of the abductee. Some witnesses may expect communication because that seems logical to them under the circumstances, while others expect the opposite.

Various sexual overtones are apparent in many of the stories, which may or may not be fodder for Freudian interpretations. They include displayed interest in our reproductive processes (Pam Owens, Nov. 1978) and aliens who say they are unable to have children (Aino Ivanoff, Apr. 2, 1980). The Druffel and Rogo reference (see bibliography) also includes cases with strong sexual overtones, and the most explicit of all is the famous October 1957 reported sexual seduction of a Brazilian peasant, Antonio Villas Boas, by an alien woman. Even the 1961 prototype abduction case in the United States includes what appears to have been the then little-known amniotic pregnancy test, whereby a needle was inserted into Betty Hill's navel.

Is some former race from Earth or a very human-like race from elsewhere, its physiology degenerated by constant spaceflight, now coming here to conduct some genetic engineering? Are we genetic stock — virtual laboratory animals — for their research? The described manipulations of human beings would imply a deep foreknowledge of human physiology and psychology. Its purpose, therefore, would not likely be to learn more about humans per se, and many reports suggest the taking of tissue samples.

Conceivably, alien beings could be making themselves more like us in order to pave the way for open contact and communication, or simply to improve their physical stock (the pale, spindly "fetus beings") which may have undergone evolutionary degeneration as their brainpower (large heads) increased — a well-known science fiction theme. Another possibility is that human beings are being "programmed" or "implanted" in some way to pave the way for human acceptance of the aliens.

Although the aliens (if that is what they are) appear to be compassionate as depicted in abduction reports, sometimes reacting to alleviate pain when the captives display it, the feeling is inescapable that it is the sort of compassion that humans practice with laboratory animals. The stories seem to imply that, just as humans study rats or hamsters for medical knowledge applicable to the human race, we are being studied *in vivo* for some knowledge that is important to the aliens. We are treated kindly overall, then let go bearing some scars and (if we break through the seemingly induced amnesia) some psychological trauma.

Another implication of the reports is that the aliens may not understand our psychology as well as they think they do if they are deliberately trying to help us avoid mental anguish resulting from their experiments. Troublesome dreams and memory lapses often are the impetus for the abductees to undergo hypnosis, thereby bringing unpleasant and painful experiences back to conscious memory. Fear, embarrassment, and mental anguish are the lot of many abductees.

Like the humanoid reports in general, abduction reports seldom are thoroughly and expertly investigated because they are so numerous and complex. All too often amateur hypnotists and biased investigators have "contaminated" the cases through the use of inappropriate methods. Once a potentially valid case subject has been led to tell a "good story," it may be impossible thereafter to ferret out the underlying truth (if any) because the truth will remain cloudy in the mind of the subject — a mixture of suggestion, imagination, and possible truth.

Amateurs can do more harm intruding into abduction case investigations than in any other type of report because of the fragility and suggestibility of the human mind/memory when confronted with frightening or upsetting events. These case investigations are best left to professionals, or at least done with professional supervision.

The probability is high that part (at least) of the stories consist of mental patching and filling by the "victims" in a desperate effort to make sense of what has happened to them. Clinical skills and acute judgment are needed to sort out fact from imagination or fantasy, and mental health professionals often are needed to provide therapy for the "victims."

Budd Hopkins (reference B) has raised the important question of just how many more abduction reports remain to be uncovered. He suggests that the known cases are only the "tip of the iceberg." HUMCAT (the Humanoid Catalogue discussed in Chapter 3) lists over 300 actual or probable abduction cases through 1979, and informal estimates place the figure at a thousand or more cases to date. Since the number of cases coming to light is growing at a near geometric rate, these estimates are subject to rapid upward revision.

Hopkins has provided certain guidelines for case elements suggestive of possible abductions. William Chalker in Australia (see Bibliography) has indicated a number of cases there that contain all the elements typically leading to abduction reports. The following sample cases (summaries in Case Book Appendix) are typical of the widespread proto-abduction reports:

August 1, 1971; Queensland, Australia.

A couple driving at night experienced altered surroundings, a time loss, amnesia, and physical markings on their car. "We felt that something strange had happened to us," they said. Attempted hypnotic regression was given up because they began shaking violently each time.

June 16, 1977; Middelburg, S. Africa.

A newspaper delivery van driver was confronted by a UFO in the early morning, his van engulfed in light. The engine failed and the lights went out after the UFO hovered near the van. The driver could not recall what happened at this point. "I felt that something happened," he said, "but cannot think what."

February 5, 1979; Lawitta, Tasmania.

A man driving home in mid-evening noticed that his car radio stopped playing. His car was engulfed in light and his engine and headlights failed. He blacked out, then "woke up" driving along the highway, until police stopped him for driving without headlights. He was unable to say who he was or where he was going, and was hospitalized. Extensive physical effects later were noted on his car.

July 31, 1981; Lieksa, Finland.

Two vacationing men in a boat saw a UFO and associated lights in the early evening and an object approached the boat. One of the men felt paralyzed, but the two were able to talk with each other. After the object vanished, the men realized that they were not sitting in the same positions in the boat as they had been and 7 hours had passed, unaccounted for. They later experienced physiological effects, including a disrupted sense of balance. Attempts to hypnotize them were unsuccessful.

Such reports as these raise the serious — indeed, scary — question of the dimensions of the iceberg. Even formerly skeptical UFOlogists (like the author) have come to realize that, notwithstanding the sometimes nonsensical story content, something of potentially enormous significance is being described in abduction reports ... if "through a glass, darkly."

An important psychological study of nine purported abductees, sponsored by the Fund for UFO Research, was published in 1985. It included "blind" administration of a battery of psychodiagnostic tests. Dr. Elizabeth Slater conducted and scored the tests before being told what the subjects claimed to have experienced.

Afterwards she wrote an Addendum to her report addressing the question of whether the subjects' reported experiences could be accounted for by psychopathology, or mental disorder. *"The answer is a firm no,"* she stated. "While the testing can do nothing to prove the veracity of the UFO abduction reports, one can conclude that the test findings are not inconsistent with the possibility that reported abductions have, in fact occurred. In other words, there is no apparent psychological explanation for their reports."

Budd Hopkins' 1987 book *Intruders,* based on detailed study of abduction reports and new cases since *Missing Time,* suggests an even more startling thesis. He finds a pattern of multiple abductions over time of single individuals, including more than one member of a family, and recurring reports of what seems to be "genetic engineering." If the reports are valid, the evidence suggests that "aliens" (wherever from) have tampered with or taken human fetuses and created alien/ human hybrids!

As bizarre as this may sound, it is difficult to interpret the "evidence" in any other way. But is the evidence valid? Hopkins' work and some attempts at alternative interpretations (psychological) by skeptics both are reported in the December 1987 issue of *Omni* magazine.

A massive new study of abduction reports by Dr. Thomas E. Bullard, based on a computer catalogue he compiled under a grant from the Fund for UFO Research, also was released by the Fund in 1987. A folklorist by training, Dr. Bullard analyzes patterns in the abduction reports. Among other things, he concludes:

> "Abduction witnesses represent a normal cross-section of society ... (they) seem to be free of any psychological abnormalities which might predispose them to fantasize such a story ... if abductions are

literally true, they are the greatest story of all time. If they are subjective, they offer a seldom-equalled opportunity to gain insight into human mental functions, the interaction of belief with experience, and the social transmission of ideas."

If abduction scenarios do represent some form of psychopathology, it is a raging and world-wide manifestation whose dynamics should be studied at once on those grounds alone. And if abductions really are happening, then apparently we are at the mercy of interventionists from elsewhere whose intentions toward us remain shrouded in mystery.

BIBLIOGRAPHY

APRO. "Higdon Experience," in *Encyclopedia of UFOs* (N.Y.: Doubleday, 1980). Oct. 25, 1974, Rawlins, Wyoming, abduction case.

Barry, Bill. *Ultimate Encounter* (N.Y.: Pocket Books, 1978). The Nov. 5, 1975 Travis Walton abduction case near Heber, Arizona.

Bloecher, Ted (et al.). *Final Report on the Psychological Testing of UFO "Abductees"* (Washington D.C.: Fund for UFO Research, 1985).

Blum, Ralph. "UFOs: An Issue Whose Time Has Almost Come," in *1974 MUFON UFO Symposium Proceedings* (Seguin, Tex: MUFON, 1974). Report on investigation of Oct. 11, 1973, Pascagoula, Miss., abduction case.

Bondarchuk, Yurko. *UFO Sightings, Landings and Abductions* (Agincourt, Ontario: Methuen Publications, 1979).

Bullard, Thomas E. "On Stolen Time: A Comparative Study of the UFO Abduction Mystery" (Washington, D.C.: Fund for UFO Research, 1987). Both the full report and a summary version are available from the Fund for UFO Research.

Chalker, William C. "Australian 'Interrupted Journeys'," *MUFON UFO Journal*, No. 150, Aug. 1980. Vehicle encounter cases suggestive of possible abductions.

Clamar, Aphrodite. "Missing Time: A Psychologist Examines the UFO Evidence," in *1981 MUFON UFO Symposium Proceedings* (Seguin, Tex: MUFON, 1981). Results of hypnotic regression and psychological testing applied to abduction claimants.

Dickinson, Terence. "Zeta Reticuli Connection," in *Encyclopedia of UFOs* (N.Y.: Doubleday, 1980). Discussion of star map shown to Betty Hill in Sept. 19, 1961, New Hampshire UFO abduction case.

Druffel, Ann and Rogo, D. Scott. *The Tujunga Canyon Contacts* (N.J.: Prentice-Hall, 1980). Elaborate series of multi-year abduction reports in California by interrelated persons.

Fish, Marjorie E. "Journey Into the Hill Star Map," in *1974 MUFON UFO Symposium Proceedings* (Seguin, Tex: MUFON, 1974). Article by the original analyst of the star map shown to Betty Hill in Sept. 19, 1961, New Hampshire UFO abduction case.

Fowler, Raymond E. *The Andreasson Affair* (N.J.: Prentice-Hall, 1979). Detailed account of Jan. 25, 1967, S. Ashburnham, Mass., abduction case.

_____. "Andreasson Affair," in *Encyclopedia of UFOs* (N.Y.: Doubleday, 1980).

Fuller, John G. *The Interrupted Journey* (N.Y.: Dial Press, 1966). Detailed account of the Sept. 19, 1961, New Hampshire Betty and Barney Hill abduction case.

Gansberg, Judith and Gansberg, Alan. *Direct Encounters* (N.Y.: Walker & Co., 1980). Survey of abduction claimants.

Hartman, Terry A. "Another Abduction by Extraterrestrials?," *MUFON UFO Journal*, No. 141, Nov. 1979. Abduction report by couple near Owyhee River, Oreg., in Summer 1975.

Hopkins, Budd. (A). *Missing Time: A Documented Study of UFO Abductions* (N.Y.: Richard Marek, 1981). Results of intensive personal and psychological investigation into a sample of UFO abduction claimants.

_____. (B) "UFO Abductions: The Invisible Epidemic," in *1981 MUFON UFO Symposium Proceedings* (Seguin, Tex: MUFON, 1981).

_____. (C) *Intruders: The Incredible Visitations at Copley Woods* (N.Y.: Random House, 1987). Continuing investigations of UFO abduction claimants, including evidence of "genetic engineering."

Lorenzen, Jim and Lorenzen, Coral. *Abducted!* (N.Y.: Berkley Medallion Books, 1977.) Survey of abduction reports.

Lorenzen, Coral E. "Walton Abduction," in *Encyclopedia of UFOs* (N.Y.: Doubleday, 1980). Summary of Nov. 5, 1975, Travis Walton abduction case near Heber, Arizona.

Rueger, Russ A. "Villas Boas Abduction," in *Encyclopedia of UFOs* (N.Y.: Doubleday, 1980). Summary of Oct. 1957 alleged abduction and sexual seduction of Antonio Villas Boas by a female alien.

Smith, Gary. "Unspeakable Secret: What Happened on the Night Michael Shea Can Neither Forget Nor Believe?" in *Washington Post Magazine*, Jan. 3, 1988. A Government attorney abductee "comes out of the closet."

Sprinkle, R. Leo (Ed.) *Proceedings of the Rocky Mountain Conference on UFO Investigation* (Laramie, Wyo., 1980). Summaries of about 13 abduction cases in the words of the abductees.

Stringfield, Leonard H. *Situation Red: The UFO Siege* (N.Y.: Doubleday, 1977). Report on Jan. 6, 1976, Stanford, Ky., abduction case, pp. 198-212.

Walton, Travis. *The Walton Experience* (N.Y.: Berkley Medallion Books, 1978). Personal account of the Nov. 5, 1975, abduction case near Heber, Arizona.

Webb, Walter N.; Story, Ronald; Sheaffer, Robert. "Hill Abduction," in *Encyclopedia of UFOs* (N.Y.: Doubleday, 1980). Summary of Sept. 19, 1961, New Hampshire Betty and Barney Hill abduction case.

Weintraub, Pamela. "Secret Sharers," in *Omni* magazine, Dec. 1987. An overview of abduction reports, including Budd Hopkins' work and alternative views.

PART II
DISCOVERY

"Discovery commences with the awareness of anomaly . . . . It then continues with a more or less extended exploration of the area of anomaly. And it closes only when the paradigm theory has been adjusted so that the anomalous has become the expected."

— THOMAS S. KUHN
The Structure of Scientific Revolutions

CHAPTER 6

THE UFO ANOMALY

The data of UFO reports, surveyed in Part I, constitute a major anomaly that has been "explained" or rationalized in various mundane and exotic ways over the years. (See *Table 4*.) Aside from the skeptics who reject the data, attributing UFO reports to perceptual errors, three basic kinds of explanations have been advanced:

- Thin Air Theories (Postulation of a phenomenon akin to something known and endowing it with the necessary properties to explain the data).

- Origin Theories (Postulation of a source for UFOs, e.g., extraterrestrial, other dimensional).

- Intention — or Purpose — Theories (Postulation of the motives or purposes of the supposed intelligences behind UFOs).

TABLE 4
UFO Theories

ORIGIN THEORIES	
LOCUS	RELEVANT DATA/TESTS
Extraterrestrial	Performance beyond earth technology; humanoids; contact/communication; instrumentation of atmosphere; space exploration.

cont'd

ORIGIN THEORIES	
LOCUS	RELEVANT DATA/TESTS
Other Dimensions/ Parallel Universe	abrupt appearances or "materializations" and disappearances; apparitional appearance; motion through matter.
Time	anomalies associated with time perception.
Human Mind (Collective unconscious)	behavior/activity reflective of human thought and behavior.
Cosmic Mind	baffling phenomena; lack of clear communication.
INTENTION THEORIES	
PURPOSE	RELEVANT DATA/TESTS
Help (Guardian angels)	Angelic, helping behavior
Harm (Demons)	Demonic behavior
Manipulate (Deceptionists, concealing purpose or game plan for ulterior motive)	contradictory and confusing behavior
Control (Warlike, defensive, we pose threat)	military/space connections; encounters with military aircraft; surveillance of military facilities.
Conquer (Takeover)	?
Contact (Preparation for contact or settlement)	?
Fool (Cosmic jokers)	capricious behavior, silliness
Study (Scientific exploring party analogue)	sample gathering; interest in human physiology, technology, etc.

What these theories purport to explain is the testimony describing very close range encounters and abrupt confrontations, plus the variety of physical and physiological effects on vehicles and human beings. These are the core data, and to them we must add the "magical technology" (the observed performance of UFOs), the associated humanoid entities, and the perceptions of many witnesses that they have been abducted and experimented upon or examined by humanoid entities. The latter must either be explained as psychological aberrations, or be considered as an extension of the other data.

Finally, there is the alleged evidence, yet to be adequately documented, of retrieved craft and humanoid bodies. If true, these reports obviously would establish beyond doubt an alien origin for UFOs.

It does not take much comparison of theory vs. data to realize that most theories totally violate the elementary rules of scientific explanation. This is all the more pernicious when such theories emanate from "defenders of science" who sneer at popular attempts to explain UFOs.

Science operates on what is known as the Hypothetico-Deductive Method. Empirical data (observed, measured) are analyzed in terms of existing scientific theories and if they do not fit, either existing theory must be modified or a new theory developed. Any new theory or hypothesis implies or predicts certain things that can be deduced from it, and these allow it to be tested against new data. The process is a continuing one with constant refinements. There is no such thing in complex areas of science as a final or ultimate physical theory, which would imply that we knew all there was to know about the universe.

The word "theory," although often used interchangeably with "hypothesis," technically applies to the underlying principles of science that have withstood the test of time and have been verified repeatedly by observation or experiment, part of a systematic body of knowledge with interlocking predictability and utility.

"Hypothesis," meaning a first rough guess or approximation, is the word more accurately applied to attempts so far to explain UFOs. The *Britannica World Language Dictionary* (1960) defines "hypothesis" as: "A set of assumptions provisionally accepted as a basis of reasoning, experiment, or investigation ... till there has been opportunity to bring all related facts into comparison ... a comprehensive guess." One synonym is "speculation."

Anomalies pose a special problem for science because, by definition, they are observations or facts that are exceptions to the rule and do not fit any accepted theory. A natural tendency exists to discard anomalies as probably mistaken observations, especially if they *seem* to contradict (they may not actually do so) well-established theories and if their implications are sweeping and potentially revolutionary. But this reflexive reaction is not scientific. UFOs, if real, do have potentially revolutionary implications, and it is my conviction that this is the real reason why scientists have failed to come to grips with the problem. Yet, when anomalies showing the same features or characteristics recur year after year as UFO reports do, it is time for science to pay attention. The history of science shows that anomalies sometimes point the way to important new discoveries.

Let us assume that over a period of many months red snow has fallen over the United States, according to local witnesses in 25 States, but has melted before anyone had the presence of mind to freeze some for laboratory tests. Snow is not supposed to be red, so these are anomalous observations.

If scientists followed the same logic they often apply to UFOs, they would reject the reports and assume (without investigation) the witnesses were looking through rose-tinted sunglasses or seeing sunset colors reflecting off the snow. When the scope of the phenomenon was pointed out to them, they would attribute the reports to mass hysteria, or hoaxers and headline seekers. If pointed out to them that trained observers were among the witnesses, they would invoke some assumed local, specialized condition as explanation and mutter about popular fads.

More scientific scientists would interview witnesses, check the pattern of observations, check wind patterns, and seek out good witnesses and physical evidence. Then, if satisfied that the reports were valid, they would attempt to form some hypothesis and proceed to test it — rather than leap to conclusions or prejudge the question as has happened so consistently with UFO reports.

114

The important point in this illustration is that reports of red snow and rain have been made by reliable observers off and on for centuries, and this fact has no credible scientific explanation. The writings of Charles Fort are among the first to compile bodies of data on various recurring anomalies, including red snow and rain, unexplained falls of large chunks of ice . . . and UFOs.

Unfortunately, the UFO subject suffers from an excess of speculation by would-be theorists whose woolly views alienate sensible people, particularly scientists. However, the subject also suffers from the simplistic data-deniers who invoke the full range of perceptual errors, "mass ignorance," and even unique, specialized conditions where necessary, in their zeal to do away with the troublesome anomaly.

THIN AIR THEORIES

Having accepted as valid that witnesses were seeing unexplained luminous phenomena that performed erratically, Philip Klass, avionics editor for *Aviation Week and Space Technology*, in 1966 advanced the theory that a plasma phenomenon akin to ball lightning could explain most of the major UFO cases. He even suggested a mechanism of how balls of light could appear around aircraft and seem to follow them, and how corona discharges around electric power lines could explain a then-popular correlation of UFOs with power lines. In the presence of witnesses, Klass told the author that if plasma wasn't the answer, then UFOs most likely were extraterrestrial.

After his plasma theory was discredited, Klass quietly discarded it, but he has not become a noticeable advocate of the extraterrestrial hypothesis (ETH). Instead, when his theory was found wanting, Klass backtracked on his previous confidence in witness reports and has increasingly invoked perceptual errors and hoaxes as explanations.

Ball lightning itself remains a controversial phenomenon — an anomaly for which no adequate scientific explanation has been advanced. Klass postulated a supposed second cousin of ball lightning to explain UFOs, conveniently ignoring reports of structured, craft-like objects . . . not to mention physical and physiological effects and such non-plasma-like things as humanoids.

Similarly, Donald Robey (Reference A) in 1959 advanced the theory that many UFO reports (including discs with domes) could be explained by ice meteorites ("cometoids") entering the earth's atmosphere from space. In the popular version read by most Americans in *Saturday Review,* Robey seemed to endow the hypothetical ice meteorites with all the characteristics necessary to explain the commonly reported disc shape (oblation in the atmosphere), spinning, wobbling, colors, hissing sound, and rapid disappearance. When queried about the theory in 1981, Robey denied that the *Saturday Review* article accurately represented his views.

Ice falls are another recurring anomaly that has not been widely accepted, much less adequately explained. The known large chunks of ice that have been observed falling or found on the ground contained none of these presumed features and their observed behavior bore no resemblance whatsoever to reported UFOs.

Other Thin Air Theories advanced occasionally are swarms of glowing insects undulating in the sky, and "space animals." These notions are so simplistic that they do not warrant further discussion.

Thin Air Theories share the dubious distinction of selecting out some portion of the UFO data, then extrapolating on some known natural phenomenon in order to create a variant form that, presto chango, has the necessary characteristics to be one and the same with the UFOs . . . or at least the UFO features selected out by the theory proponent. Robey's theory is by far the most ambitious in terms of the data it attempts to explain, and is therefore more scientific in a technical sense.

At bottom, Thin Air Theories represent attempts to dispose of UFOs as "some natural phenomenon that we don't yet know about." In effect, they seek to write off UFOs as something relatively trivial while conveniently ignoring significant portions of the data. None of them can explain (or even attempts to explain) E-M effects, light beams, burns, paralysis, humanoid sightings . . . or abductions.

No doubt the ultimate absurdity in Thin Air Theories was advanced by a scientist in the final report of the University of Colorado UFO study (the "Condon Report"), who said of an airline pilot UFO sighting involving a "mother ship" and attendant smaller objects: "This unusual sighting should therefore be assigned to the category of some almost certainly natural phenomenon, which is so rare that it apparently has never been reported before or since." (Bantam edition, p. 140.) If we are allowed to invoke an assumed one-time phenomenon whenever we choose, then obviously we can "explain" not only all UFO reports, but also every other scientific mystery!

Furthermore, this scientist was mistaken about the rarity of the observation. A larger UFO with smaller ones maneuvering to and fro and around it is a well-recognized case type (Vallee, Type II-B; Hall, "satellite object" cases).

ORIGIN THEORIES

Pre-eminent among the origin theories, once we accept that UFOs are real, is the ETH. Including its variants, the ETH encompasses all but a handful of the theories. If "ETH" is taken to mean non-earthly in origin — in the broadest sense — then the only competitors are Natural Phenomenon and Other Realms. And even "Other Realms" could be viewed as "not of this earth" as commonly understood. Time travellers or beings from another dimension or parallel universe may be considered as emanating from "Other Realms" of space-time as we now, vaguely, understand that concept.

If Other Dimensions or a Parallel Universe exist at all, it could be argued that they co-exist with us and are, in that sense, a facet of this earth and its environment that we simply don't recognize as such. Since we know nothing about such supposed realms to begin with, the distinction is purely semantical. We have no way of knowing how many Other Dimensioners or Parallel Universers can dance through our space-time on the head of a UFO.

Strictly speaking, the Collective Unconscious Projection theory presumably would qualify as a natural phenomenon. The Cosmic Mind theory, on the other hand, is all-encompassing; it postulates that we are part of a larger whole that is working its will on us.

A noteworthy feature of the Origin Theories is that they tend not to be as specifically predictive as Intention Theories. In principle, the ETH could be tested by elaborate instrumentation to detect craft (or whatever) entering the atmosphere from outside, or leaving the atmosphere, and our space exploration conceivably could find evidence of, or make contact with, ET intelligence. But what would constitute a test of time travellers, other dimensioners, parallel universers, or a cosmic mind?

INTENTION THEORIES

Intention Theories accept that some sort of outside intelligence is "visiting" us, and focus on its supposed purpose. The following purposes have been attributed to UFO intelligences by one proponent or another. Their intention is to: help, harm, manipulate, control, conquer, contact, fool, or study. These meta-theories at least have the advantage of being highly predictive in most instances. If UFOs are here to help (guardians of mankind), then we should expect something like angelic behavior. If they are here to harm (demons), then we should expect demonic behavior.

By selecting bits of evidence here and there, it is possible to support — or refute — either of these theories. For example, why would angels zap someone with radiation? Contrariwise, why would demons "heal" ailing humans, as has been reported in a number of cases? Fundamental religionists, of course, can claim that it is the ultimate showdown between forces of good and evil.

If UFOs are the product of intelligences who are interacting with us in the described ways, they must have some reason for their actions. So it is a natural human reaction to try to analyze alien psychology. Probably it is a doomed effort unless "they" choose to communicate something to us. Intention Theories prematurely attempt to supply ultimate answers to the profound questions raised by UFOs, but they tend to share with Thin Air Theories the weakness of not applying to all or most of the core data. They also have the same *ad hoc* air of being forced conclusions.

The idea that the intelligence behind UFOs is intentionally deceiving us or manipulating our beliefs for some hidden purpose has been suggested in some forms by Jacques Vallee in *Messengers of Deception* (also see his position statement in *Encyclopedia of UFOs*), and explicated by sociologist Ron Westrum in a debate with the author in *MUFON UFO Journal*.

Citing books by Vallee and John Keel dealing with the "problem of deception," Westrum in his initial article (No. 81, August 1974) advocated adopting a "strategic" rather than a "scientific" perspective in studying UFOs, saying that it "may be very useful for understanding UFO occupant behavior." He then suggested several types of deceptive practices that the UFO occupants might be employing, including what today, in the jargon of intelligence agencies, would be called "disinformation."

He qualified the comments by suggesting that he was ". . . trying to make the reader consider what a rational opponent might do, not to argue that in fact any one of these methods has been used." Since humans practice such deceptions routinely, he suggested, we ought to consider that aliens would be capable of similar mischief if it suited their purposes.

My response was that making such an assumption would rule out the possibility of scientific research because, if true, we are surely over-matched and any attempt to develop a "counter-strategy," as Westrum had proposed, would be futile. We could no longer trust our senses or anything that we detected, and we would have no way of validating anything.

In the ensuing debate I argued that ". . . we have no way of knowing what strategy to adopt without first knowing where we stand vis-a-vis the ETIs [extraterrestrial intelligences]." Only if they were closely similar to us would "strategic" reasoning have any chance of success, and there could be a huge gap in our intelligence levels as implied by their sheer mastery of natural forces.

Westrum countered that we had no basis for assuming ETIs were omniscient and omnipotent, and preferred to assume that they were not. "I would like to make the reasonable assumption," he said, "that they are both intellectually fallible and physically vulnerable . . . I think the statement that we are being kept in the dark and confused by the ETIs in various ways as to their identities, capabilities, and numbers is readily justifiable in terms of sightings of which we are all aware."

Agreeing that his view was ". . . an interesting idea to keep in mind," I noted that ". . . the same baffling phenomena [he] finds it necessary to account for in this way can, in my view, be accommodated more simply and directly by considering them to be cultural/technological displays for which we have no adequate analogies in our 20th Century . . . society; therefore they baffle us."

The debate was very instructive, and by its conclusion I realized that our very different assumptions had led, quite logically, to different outlooks on how to interpret the observed "behavior," and even on how to investigate UFO reports. He was assuming a relatively narrow gap of intelligence/technology and I was assuming a much larger gap which, in itself, could account for the data that he attributed to deliberate deceptive practices. I could not deny that he might be right, but it all came down to the assumptions one chose to make.

Actually both of us were interpreting the accumulated data and constructing an hypothesis about it. Each hypothesis flowed from a particular reading of the data. This pointed to a serious and important methodological problem of UFO research: Which among the large body of reported UFO data are we compelled to accept as a valid part of the problem to be explained? UFOlogists tend to have wide disagreement on this point, which fundamentally affects all discussion.

How carefully have certain types of reports been investigated and validated? Some controversial areas of data — accepted as valid by some and not by others — are reported manifestations of "psychic phenomena" in association with UFO sightings, associations of Bigfoot sightings with UFOs, and associations of cattle mutilations with UFOs. If these associations are valid and among the data to be explained, then they have profound implications for our understanding of the meaning of UFOs for humanity.

Until a stronger consensus is reached on what constitutes the legitimate data of the UFO mystery, all theorizing is suspect insofar as it *assumes* the validity of many bizarre phenomena that have been reported without being able to put forth and document a catalogue of thoroughly investigated and validated examples.

The two dominant types of report today in terms of widespread interest and controversy are prime examples of the data problem: abduction reports and UFO crash/retrieval reports. That either has actually happened is extremely difficult to validate. The reports are intriguing, but rightfully controversial. Either type of report, if true, would tell us something of immense importance and strongly influence the direction of our theorizing.

If people really are being abducted, then the "spacemen" would appear to be very advanced in intelligence/technology and to have a very strong interest in human physiology. If UFOs have crashed and bodies have been retrieved, then the "spacemen" would seem to be closer to Ron Westrum's "fallible" and "vulnerable" model. Also, the U.S. Government (and probably other governments as well) would know a great deal about the nature of UFOs and their occupants that has been withheld from the public for about 40 years.

If both types of report are true, then there is a missing piece of the puzzle that would explain the seeming discrepancy between the "fallibility" of UFOs that have crashed, on the one hand, and the almost magical technology and powers displayed by the UFO occupants, on the other hand. If both types of report are true, there is another startling implication: Both sides, in a sort of extraterrestrial Cold War, have taken "prisoners" and studied their biological make-up.

Could it be that there are "prisoners-of-war" remaining captive on both sides? And if so, what mad game is the Government playing by not confiding in its citizens for whom the outcome might be life or death, freedom or captivity? Clearly these reports, because of their staggering implications, need to be meticulously investigated.

Similarly, if the "spacemen" are mutilating animals (biological studies parallel to their probings of humans?) and/or utilizing Bigfoot creatures in some manner, then certain implications could be drawn from these facts and our theories would have to be modified accordingly. My personal view is that neither of these alleged associations has been documented sufficiently to compel their acceptance as part of the UFO data. "Mystery helicopters," also on the fringes of accepted UFO-related data, fit the same pattern and have been claimed as part of the cattle mutilation mystery.

As things now stand, one man's data is another man's anathema, severely complicating all efforts at trying to interpret the meaning and significance of UFOs. We are not clear about the true dimensions of the UFO anomaly. My conclusion in the Westrum-Hall debate remains my conclusion today:

> "In my view, we don't have any way of knowing the answer at present, and can only guess from among a number of possibilities. Until we gather and analyze a lot more data ... we ought to back off from over-commitment to one possible explanation; instead, we should objectively gather and study data on those baffling phenomena we all agree are there and discern as much as we can about them, continually testing and exploring various hypotheses in the process. In that spirit, exploring the implications for humanity of various possible explanations is a worthwhile enterprise."

BIBLIOGRAPHY

Aldrich, Hal R. "Rainbows Keep Falling on My Head," *INFO Journal* No. 24, July-Aug. 1977. Reports of colored snow and rain.

Campbell, Stuart. "The Credibility of UFO Hypotheses," *MUFON UFO Journal*, No. 156, Feb. 1981.

Fort, Charles. *Complete Books of Charles Fort* (N.Y.: Dover, 1974). Compilations of ice fall reports, UFO reports, and other anomalies.

Gillmor, Daniel S. (Ed.). *Scientific Study of Unidentified Flying Objects* (N.Y.: Bantam Books, 1969). The University of Colorado UFO Project report, directed by Dr. E.U. Condon.

Greenwell, J. Richard. "Theories, UFO," in *Encyclopedia of UFOs* (N.Y.: Doubleday, 1980).

Hall, Richard H. *The UFO Evidence* (Washington, D.C.: NICAP, 1964). Satellite object cases, pp. 15-17.

——————. "Recapping and Commenting" column, *Skylook* (now *MUFON UFO Journal*), No. 83, Oct. 1974. Concerning the UFO deception theory.

——————. "Recapping and Commenting" column, *Skylook*, No. 86, Jan. 1975. Concerning the UFO deception theory.

——————. "How Do We Cope With Spacemen?" *Skylook*, No. 93, Aug. 1975.

Hynek, J. Allen and Vallee, Jacques. "Brainstorming," Ch. 9 in *Edge of Reality* (Chicago: Henry Regnery, 1975).

James, Trevor. *They Live In the Sky* (Los Angeles: New Age Pub. Co., 1958). Space animals theory.

Klass, Philip J. "Plasma Theory May Explain Many UFOs," *Aviation Week and Space Technology*, Aug. 22, 1966.

——————. "Many UFOs Are Identified as Plasmas," *Aviation Week and Space Technology*, Oct. 3, 1966.

Kuhn, Thomas S. *Structure of Scientific Revolutions* (Univ. of Chicago Press, 1962).

Robey, Donald H. (A) "A Theory on Flying Saucers," *Saturday Review*, Sept. 5, 1959. (In personal correspondence with the author, Robey stated that he never intended his "ice cometoid" theory, popularly reported here, to apply to all UFOs and that the science editor rewrote his article. In fact, he takes seriously some form of the extraterrestrial hypothesis.)

_____. (B) "An Hypothesis on Slow Moving Green Fireballs," *Journal of the British Interplanetary Society*, vol. 17, 1959-60, 398-411. Addressed to "certain bizarre fireballs," including the green fireballs over New Mexico in 1948 and 1949 (see Chapter 11). A more technical exposition of the "ice cometoid" theory that makes clear its limited application to UFO reports.

Sagan, Carl. "UFOs: The Extraterrestrial and Other Hypotheses," in *UFOs: A Scientific Debate* (Cornell Univ Press, 1972) pp. 265-275.

Vallee, Jacques and Vallee, Janine. *Challenge to Science: The UFO Enigma* (Chicago: Henry Regnery, 1966). Type II-B UFO reports, p. 176.

Vallee, Jacques. "The Psycho-Physical Nature of UFO Reality: A Speculative Framework," in *Thesis-Antithesis*, A.D. Emerson, Ed. (Proceedings of Joint Symposium by American Institute of Aeronautics and Astronautics and Los Angeles Chapter of World Futures Society, AIAA Los Angeles Section, 1975).

Westrum, Ron. "Question of Deception by UFOs a Possibility," *Skylook*, No. 81, Aug. 1974.

_____. Letter to Editor, *Skylook*, No. 84, Nov. 1974. Concerning UFO deception theory.

_____. "Matching Wits With Extra-terrestrials," *Skylook*, No. 91, June 1975. Concerning UFO deception theory.

CHAPTER 7

OTHER REALMS

Are the UFO beings from some other space-time realm than those familiar to science? Could they be travellers through time, or from other dimensions or a parallel universe? Popular authors have exploited these themes, especially since the ETH has bogged down for lack of proof, but they remain essentially science fiction notions inaccessible to scientific verification. To what degree this reaching-out for alternative explanations represents only impatience to have final answers remains to be seen. The notions have found advocates among serious UFOlogists who find the data difficult to accommodate to "mere" nuts and bolts spacecraft.

Two types of evidence often advanced are abrupt appearances and disappearances of UFOs (sometimes labelled "materialization" and "dematerialization") and ghostly, apparition-like demeanor of some entities associated with UFOs, including a few who reportedly walk or float through solid matter! If the reports can be accepted as valid observations (as opposed to having purely psychological explanations), then they might suggest the existence of some realm not presently recognized by science.

In 1980 the author assisted Elizabeth Philip and Fred Whiting of *Frontiers of Science* magazine (then *Second Look*) in an investigation of reports by two sisters in Maryland that they had encountered humanoid beings about 5 months apart, both involving "bedroom visitations." Although neither sister saw a UFO nor recalled an abduction experience, the reports otherwise closely resembled many humanoid or abduction reports on record.

The beings floated through the wall of the house and generally seemed more apparition-like than solid. They displayed the typical physiological interest in both sisters, probing the breasts of one (a happily married and seemingly well-adjusted woman in her 30s). They apparently communicated via telepathy. Interestingly, during a long interview including candid life histories, neither of the sisters particularly associated the entities with UFO reports, nor did they seem to be aware that others had made similar reports.

In the Betty Andreasson case investigated exhaustively and documented by Raymond Fowler, the humanoid beings entered through the wall of the house but otherwise seemed to be "typical" solid humanoids.

Early on the morning of October 15, 1973, during the major U.S. UFO wave of that year, another "bedroom visitation" occurred in Omro, Wisconsin. The witness was awakened by a high-pitched sound and the room was illuminated with a bright orange-red glow. Three humanoids with hairless heads and wrinkled grayish-white skin were seen to materialize and move around mechanically. The witness passed out. He awoke briefly to find the entities examining him with an oval object, then passed out again until morning.

On February 3, 1964, in Gum Creek, South Australia, a woman awoke about 2:00 a.m. and through her window saw a figure materialize ". . . like a movie screen descending." The illumination was as bright as day.

About February of 1976, in Hobart, Tasmania, a man and his wife had gone to bed about 11:00 p.m. and the wife was asleep. The man noticed that the closed door appeared to get darker, and three figures came through the closed door (another "bedroom visitation"). One touched the man's leg, which then felt numb, and then they tried to put something over his legs. He resisted and woke his wife, whereupon the figures ". . . stepped over the bed and through the window which seemed to burst open in an orange glow."

It would be easy and perhaps proper at this point to reject such reports as being valid "data," and some of the cases in fact do lend themselves to a psychological interpretation. Generally speaking, many of these reports are so poorly investigated that no one knows for sure how to interpret them. True scientific method does not allow discarding them solely because they do not fit our beliefs. On the other hand, those who use such reports as a springboard to exotic theorizing are on equally shaky grounds.

Overall, enough such "non-materialist" reports have been made to give one pause about assuming they are all nonsense. Unfortunately, they tend to merge with and become indistinguishable from a longstanding body of reports of "apparitions" and "psychic" experiences to which a certain onus attaches. But guilt by association won't do either.

Perhaps the UFO-related cases are simply "more of the same," reports of baffling phenomena previously linked with psychic or religious experiences and now cropping up in the context of UFO reports. Whatever labels we pin on them, people are occasionally reporting encounters with apparition-like beings who behave at times as if non-solid.

Einstein taught us to think in terms of a 4-dimensional universe: length, breadth, and thickness being the familiar three dimensions and time the fourth. Mathematicians talk about multiple dimensions and analyze their mathematical properties. However, it is another question entirely whether these theoretical constructs correspond to physical reality, much less to a realm of existence populated by sentient beings. After all, if *we* talk about another dimension, we are talking about something theoretically detectable or measurable by *us*, something that supposedly exists relative to *our* frame of reference. Just what that might consist of is very unclear, but to think of it as a land, like Oz, that we can visit — or whose denizens can visit us — seems unjustified.

Somewhat more appealing, though an equally fuzzy concept in many respects, is the idea of parallel universes. Essentially this suggests multiple existences of sentient lifeforms who somehow share the same or overlapping Space-Time with us. They differ from us primarily in consisting of matter of a different density, or perhaps variable density. Sometimes, according to this view, the natural environment is right for them to become visible to us and vice versa. Or, through technology, they are able to manipulate the environment in order to interact with us.

Applied to UFOs, this would mean that a technologically advanced society employing UFO-craft is periodically (sometimes very regularly) entering and leaving our perceptual framework, having been "here" (in our Space-Time sphere) all along but invisible to us. They now and then achieve the same or a similar density and then do all the things that UFOs are reported to do, such as confront vehicles and display intense curiosity about individual human beings.

When they are in the state natural to their ordinary existence, presumably they share the same space with us; their craft moving through the atoms of our physical reality with no significant collision. During the transition from their realm to ours, there may be an intermediate state during which they have started to become visible to us but they can still pass through our density of matter. Alternatively, if their density can be controlled thermostat-like, perhaps they turn themselves "off" and "on" as they walk through our walls. And if they become dense enough to be seen but still less dense than us, might they not float in our atmosphere on occasion? Also, when they levitate vehicles or humans they may be applying their superior knowledge of matter. Less mass equals less gravitational attraction.

It is fun to imagine a parallel universe populated by the UFO beings who one day discovered us. Perhaps their society had a history of ghost and apparition reports (pooh-poohed by their scientists), or our atomic tests sent detectable particles into their realm. Anyway, at some point in their evolution they developed the science and technology that allowed them to manipulate matter, and lo and behold they discovered the existence of a parallel universe. Certainly if they were scientific in spirit, this would excite them to the fever pitch of exploration and study that has been observed in UFO reports, or can be read into them.

If we want to give the name "dimension" to the realm of these hypothetical beings, fine. If we want to label them "ethereal beings," fine. But we have now defined some terms at least generally so that if such a realm exists, we can talk about it somewhat more meaningfully. The essence of the concept is that sentient life forms consisting of masses of different densities exist in parallel and, either naturally or by technological manipulation, sometimes are changed to a roughly corresponding level so that they become visible and tangible to each other.

TIME TRAVELERS

But what would time travelers look like, if they exist? Would they appear apparition-like? Would the fact of traveling through time affect the "solidity" of the voyagers so that their matter was less dense than ours? Do such questions make any sense at all?

"Time" is a very slippery concept that is difficult to even talk about without falling into a semantical morass where words and their meanings almost seem to get in the way of understanding. On top of that, the inherent paradoxes of time travel would seem to prohibit it (unless there is some resolution presently beyond our imaginations). Forward time travel implies a fixed order of events that undermines our concepts of free will, and therefore morality.

If it is possible, given the right technology, to travel forward in time and see (and perhaps participate in) events in the future, then that implies the existence of a particular future that *will be* regardless of what actions we take or choices we make. This is the concept of "predetermination" which makes us all actors following a script whether or not we are aware of the parts laid out for us. "Good" and "evil" then become purely illusions, because the noblest saint and the most vicious murderer really have no choice in their behavior.

Backward time travel to the past (which *is* a completed canvas) has a different problem: We could not interact with our ancestors for fear of changing the course of history. The classical paradox has a time traveler going into the past and accidentally killing an ancestor in his direct line of descent, thus destroying the lineage that led to him! Besides, if the past has "already happened," then any kind of meaningful interaction with past human beings seems impossible on the face of it. At best, backwards time travelers could expect to see only images of past events; they could not cause physical effects or abduct and experiment on past humans because this would change what had "already happened."

The logical paradoxes of backward time travel are neatly depicted in the 1980 movie "The Final Countdown" (starring Kirk Douglas, Martin Sheen, and James Farrentino). A modern nuclear-powered aircraft carrier with advanced jet aircraft and weapons systems enters a "time warp" and finds itself near Pearl Harbor, Hawaii, as the Japanese fleet is approaching to attack on Dec. 7, 1941. Should they try to intervene? What would happen if they did try? The movie is fascinating, and highly recommended.

We must also confront the question of traveling "forward" or "backward" in (through?) time. Is time a direction? We travel "to" the past or future. Is time a place? Practically speaking, time as we measure it by our clocks (one earth rotation equals 24 hours) is used to place experienced events in a sequence that we normally refer to as "yesterday," 'today," and "tomorrow." Strictly speaking, "now" — what our senses tell us at the immediate moment — is the only "time" we know or experience directly. Yesterday is only memory, and tomorrow is only anticipation or imagination. Past and future "time" exist only in the mind.

We seem to experience a line-like flow of events to which we assign time measurements ... the "past" (remembered); "now" (experienced); and the "future" (anticipated). If today is July 4, 1983, and our clocks read 5:45 p.m. and the sun is due to rise at 5:45 a.m. on July 5, the sunrise event is minus 12 hours in the future. If we live to experience the anticipated event, a zero hour comes and it is "now." After that the particular sunrise event "recedes" into the past. At 5:45 p.m. July 5, it is plus 12 hours in the past. Eventually it "recedes" into days, months, years . . . millennia.

If the July 5 sunrise was particularly noteworthy for some reason, it might remain in our memory for years. Yet, somehow it does not make sense to think that the particular sunrise event could ever be physically visited and actually experienced again, except perhaps as an image. Nor does it seem to make sense to think that if we discovered a time machine tomorrow, we could somehow travel "to" the future and observe the sunrise on July 5, 2083, by which "time" the earth would have completed some 36,500 more revolutions.

If time is taken to be a human-imposed measure of the relationship among experienced events, we seem to conceptualize a timeline extending from the present to the past, and "moving" forward into the anticipated future. This is sort of like observing the contrail of a jet aircraft at high altitude, trailing behind the present ("now") location of the jet but, as minutes go by, inching across the sky to a new present location. The present ("now") is the cutting edge of reality, yet we anticipate that the contrail will continue across the sky.

What we really seem to be suggesting when we speculate that UFOs may be carrying time travelers is that they are somehow able to re-experience past events by "going" to the scene of their occurrence (implicitly a place) and that we are part of their past experience. Or if they come from our past, that we are their future and they can somehow experience events that are yet to come with reference to their present.

Another semantical confusion is this: Whether the time travelers are our ancestors or our descendents, when they "get here" and experience us, it seems as if we would . . . by the definitions used so far . . . automatically become part of their present, experienced in their immediate "now." And yet, they supposedly have traveled . . . elsewhere from their present.

If our ancestors (the forward time travelers) subsequently returned to their former time frame, would their experiencing of us become a past memory for them? A "memory of their future?" The time-travel event would seem to cause a blending of future and past for the travelers, and when the same experiences came to pass in the natural order of events and "now" arrived, past, present, and future all would be "now!"

It is also interesting to note that, from our "now" perspective, both the present and the future have only a finite existence (before they become part of our past), whereas the past extends infinitely "backwards" as long as there are individual or cultural memories to recall it.

All this having been said, it is entirely possible that our vague concepts of time are all wrong and that it has something to do with other than measuring a unidirectional flow of anticipated, experienced, and recalled events. Different implications would follow if our understanding of the universe and total existence/experience are faulty, as they well might be. If all experience is a Mobius curve looping back on itself, then in some sense time might be a location on that curve that can — given the right technology — be visited, and the concept of time travel might have some meaning.

"Past" and "future" may be human errors of perception, and it may be that all existence simply *is*. "Time" would then be (to us) our immediate slice of experience, our immediate perceptions wherever we happened to be on the curve. "Reality" would be a fixed canvas rolling past us, and if we could roll the canvas at will or travel to the right spot for observation, maybe we *could* see and experience that July 5, 1983, sunrise again. Maybe there is a fixed background of events against which we are allowed some latitude of choice in how we react each time we pass that point on the curve. Perhaps there are alternate "pasts" and "futures" so that we have "parallel realities" . . . an infinite number of canvases.

All this suggests that the popular notions of time travel are extremely simplistic, overlooking the serious scientific, logical, and paradoxical problems raised. The time travel theory, even if true, is not likely to shed any light on UFO reports. If true, we are faced with more mysteries than we began with, and there is no obvious way that real time travelers could be recognized as such.

If time travelers really are here, they clearly do not follow the Rule of Non-Intervention (having caused many changes in individual human lives), so if they are from our future (i.e., events yet to come) they risk influencing events that led to them. And if they are from our past (i.e., our ancestors), then clearly we have lost the technology of our forefathers.

BIBLIOGRAPHY

Basterfield, Keith. "A Possible Psychological Explanation for Certain Close Encounters With the UFO Phenomena," Sept. 1978, UFO Research, South Australia (unpublished). Summaries of Oct. 15, 1973, Omro, Wisconsin; Feb. 3, 1964, Gum Creek, S. Australia,; and Feb. 1976, Hobart, Tasmania, cases.

Fowler, Raymond E. *Andreasson Affair* (Englewood Cliffs, N.J.: Prentice-Hall, 1979).

Frazier, J.T. *Of Time, Passion, and Knowledge* (N.Y.: George Braziller, 1975). Discussions on the nature of time.

Greenwell, J. Richard. "Time Travel Theory," in *Encyclopedia of UFOs* (N.Y.: Doubleday, 1980).

Swords, Michael D. "Are There Parallel Universes ?," *International UFO Reporter*, v. 12, no. 6, Nov.-Dec., 1987. Survey of scientific theory and speculation relating to the possible existence of a parallel universe or universes.

CHAPTER 8

SUPERMIND

Another category of explanations advanced for UFO sightings centers around the concept that UFOs are created or materialized by a Collective Unconscious or mass psyche — a Supermind of one sort or another. The theories differ in the particulars of the mechanism involved and the scope of the Supermind.

Based on the Jungian idea of a collective unconscious, Jerome Clark and Loren Coleman postulated that UFOs are something akin to a global scale poltergeist; psychic energy manifestations projected by collective humanity, or sometimes by individuals. (Clark has since concluded that explanations of this sort are inadequate.) They suggested that ancient archetypal forms that humans have needed to believe in have been absorbed into the UFO phenomenon, and the supposed projections are not a particularly healthy thing. In fact, the repressed unconscious could burst forth and upset human society.

Michael Persinger and Gyslaine Lafreniere, in their ambitious computerized study of Fortean phenomena, suggest the existence of a "Geopsyche" — an entity combining biological systems and their geomagnetic environment — that creates UFOs and other phenomena. At some critical point, they theorize, biological units form a matrix with the capacity to be energized, and ". . . this matrix acquires the potential to display behaviors and patterns of its own."

In both of these theories there is nothing extraterrestrial about UFOs; in fact, they would be distinctly terrestrial and/ or human in origin. In both cases they would — strictly speaking — be natural phenomena, but involving mind and matter in ways not thought of before. Their common feature is the view that a collective mind or psyche (biologically centered) can materialize, or form, or manipulate matter for its own presumably dim and less than conscious "purposes." The range of phenomena displayed probably would have no rational purpose as far as the individual human mind could perceive, and the "intention" of the Supermind would not be to communicate anything to individual humans. It would be sort of a brute monster, possibly dangerous because it is not rational; more of a Super-Id.

Such a theory might have some merit in accounting for the seeming capriciousness of many UFO phenomena, as well as the alleged tie-in of psychic phenomena with UFOs and the amorphousness of some of the phenomena. It seems strained, however, when applied to solid craft and humanoid cases like Socorro, N.M., and other aspects of the UFO data. The Geo-psyche idea might have more merit applied to other sorts of Fortean phenomena centered around oddities of physical nature.

A different sort of Supermind on a much larger scale has been suggested by Terry Hansen, similar to a view expressed by Aime Michel, in which the UFOs are a by-product of an exceedingly complex intelligence organized on a gigantic scale. Michel has suggested the possible evolution in the vastness of the universe of a "cosmic psychic milieu." He cites the need for a new paradigm in which the phenomenon of consciousness is viewed as intertwined with physics before we can begin to understand the very different, possibly omnipresent, order of intelligence involved in the UFO phenomena.

Writing in the *MUFON UFO Journal*, Hansen cited new findings of brain research that suggest intelligence may be nonphysical. He proposes that we should ". . . consider more sophisticated ways in which advanced intelligence may manifest itself. " Taking the J. E. Lovelock concept of earth as a sort of "colonial organism" whose subparts cooperate unwittingly to achieve some form of stability over time, Hansen postulates that the human race itself might be a colonial organism which is a subpart of some gigantic organism "out there" that is the intelligence behind UFOs. In this view, there is such a huge gap in intelligence levels between humans and the Cosmic Mind that communicating with it, much less understanding it, probably would be out of the question.

Just as the cells of the human body perform functions for their larger organism without having more than a vague perception of it (so far as we know), the human race may be dimly experiencing an awareness of a much larger organism of which it is a part. "Just as I would not think of discussing physics or music with my liver cells," Hansen observes, "the higher levels of organization in the universe cannot have an English-language discussion with us. Communication (if you can call it that) between vastly different levels of organization is much more subtle and sophisticated than this, but it does occur."

But at some intermediate level of organization between the Cosmic Mind and us, Hansen suggests, there could exist a nonphysical form of intelligence capable of communicating with us via subjective conscious experience, mind to mind. The recipient of this communication might not be able to recommunicate the "message" to another person except by using limited analogies or symbols. Or, the information may not even be available in the recipient's conscious mind, either because it is suppressed due to shock or the communication was intended only for the subconscious mind to begin with.

Hansen does not say so explicitly, but he could be describing here the experience of abductees who seem to have experienced something shocking or startling, but who often appear to lack the words to describe it. Indeed, the sometimes nonsensical "messages" or communications that they try to convey to others could be an example of a totally subjective experience that defies objective description. The "message" may represent only the feeble attempt of the individual to describe the indescribable.

The Cosmic Mind theory applied to UFO reports has interesting implications. What might it be trying to tell us via UFO displays? Or if not trying to communicate, how is it trying to influence us? Are we, perhaps something analogous to its liver cells, acting up in some way that poses a threat to it? Do UFOs represent its "surgical instruments" performing some sort of an operation on us? Or are UFOs and their explicit or implicit symbolism intended as some sort of "liver medicine" so that we will function more "normally" as the larger organism needs us to do?

The striking symbolism of abduction reports is physiological — medical examinations and biological probes. The messages given to abductees, when intelligible, typically focus on life-or-death themes. Do these represent an overt attempt by a Supermind to alter human behavior? Or are fears related to human survival, lurking just below the surface of our minds, triggered into expression by frightening UFO encounters ... encounters with the unknown? In other words, are we being manipulated by the psychology of a Supermind, or by our own psychology?

All that can be said is that, if the Supermind scenario is true, we are totally dependent on its ability to communicate or manipulate. Rational understanding of what it wants or intends for us would seem to be impossible, and we can only passively await the outcome. The huge gap between our science — our mechanisms for understanding nature — and its scope of intelligence would leave us as purely pawns in the game. Unless we chose to worship it, there would be no point even in trying to study its manifestations. However, if we attribute to it religious significance, then we can await Divine revelation or guidance. At this point the Cosmic Mind becomes an object of worship, or God.

The basic idea of God as a Supermind of which we are part is espoused in the ancient philosophy of Pantheism, which holds that God is the totality of existence, or Nature. Rather than a transcendent Being, God is immanent — everywhere. The modern version of Theosophy as represented by Helena P. Blavatsky in the United States is a religion with roots in Pantheism, that talks of a mind pool in which we participate. Theosophy incorporates reincarnation and transmigration of souls, with karma as the guiding principle.

Inevitably, if we look to a Supermind as "explanation" of UFOs, we are forced into philosophical and religious speculation rather than scientific inquiry. The key questions become our relationship to the Supermind, and what latitude we have for independent choice, right and wrong behavior . . . and all the traditional problems of morality and religion. Is our behavior predetermined? Are we parts of the Supermind that blindly obey its will? Does the Supermind guide or influence our behavior? The answers would appear to lie beyond the province of science.

ANGELS AND DEMONS

Dr. Barry H. Downing, a Presbyterian clergyman, has said that the explanation of UFOs lies within the realm of faith. Citing Biblical examples of UFO-like phenomena, he argues that UFOs are part of a "heavenly transportation system" carrying angels of God who interact with man, and there will never be absolute scientific proof — only acceptance by faith — until God's plan determines otherwise.

Speaking at the 1981 MUFON UFO Symposium at the Massachusetts Institute of Technology, he quoted various Biblical references (Revised Standard Version) to illustrate that angels, who come from a heaven that is vaguely described as ". . . outside of the earth somewhere," appear as very human-like. Abraham met "three men" whose angelic nature was later revealed (Genesis 18:1-5). The Bible also says (Hebrews 13:2), "Do not neglect to show hospitality to strangers, for thereby some have entertained angels unawares."

UFO-like objects reported in the Bible include Elijah's "chariot of fire," and the "pillar of cloud and of fire" during the Exodus (Exodus 12:21-22). In the Exodus, Downing noted, angels of God led Moses and performed such "miracles" as the parting of the Red Sea. Throughout, Moses was guided by the sometimes moving, sometimes hovering "pillar of cloud by day, and pillar of fire by night." UFOs often appear cloud-like in daylight and luminous at night.

Elijah was taken up into heaven in a "chariot of fire," and Jesus was met by Moses and Elijah at the mountain of the Transfiguration ". . . with a 'bright cloud' apparently having provided them with the means of transportation to the mountain." (Matthew 17:5.) The Biblical examples, Downing concludes, indicate ". . . some kind of heavenly transportation which carries the angels between earth and heaven. . . ."

Downing's religious views, which he acknowledges are controversial even among religious leaders in identifying UFOs with literal angels, also merge with those of "other realms" thinkers. His position statement in the *Encyclopedia of UFOs* indicates a belief that UFOs come from a parallel universe "in the midst of us," citing a statement by Jesus (Luke 17:21). The modern UFO mystery, in his view, is merely an extension of events depicted in the Bible and other historical reports showing that angels ". . . are still with us, doing their shepherd work — by night and day."

Thus we have a range of Superminds to choose from, a spectrum from rudimentary consciousness (the Geopsyche) through the subhuman Super-Id, and evolutionary Cosmic Mind, to angels and God. On the low end of the spectrum the theories fit only selected data, and on the high end, explanation ceases and faith takes over. In the middle . . . who is to say? None of the theories seems capable of shedding any light on the nature and implications of UFOs in a scientifically meaningful way.

BIBLIOGRAPHY

Clark, Jerome, and Coleman, Loren. *The Unidentified* (N.Y.: Warner, 1975). Psychic projections theory.

Downing, Barry H. *Bible and Flying Saucers* (N.Y : Lippincott, 1968). Elaboration of angels theory.

_____. "Angels, Biblical"; "Biblical UFO Sightings"; "Demonic Theory of UFOs"; "Religion and UFOs"; in *Encyclopedia of UFOs* (N.Y.: Doubleday, 1980).

_____. "Faith, Theory, and UFOs," *1981 MUFON UFO Symposium Proceedings* (Seguin, Tex: MUFON, 1981).

Fort, Charles. *Complete Books of Charles Fort* (N.Y.: Dover, 1974). Pioneer chronicler of unexplained phenomena, including 19th and early 20th century UFO reports, which have come to be known as "Fortean phenomena."

Hansen, Terry W. "The Mind-Body Problem and Its Importance to UFO Research," *MUFON UFO Journal*, No. 163, Sept. 1981. Cosmic Mind theory.

Michel, Aime. Position statement in *Encyclopedia of UFOs* (N.Y.: Doubleday, 1980). "Psychic cosmic milieu" or Cosmic Mind theory.

"Pantheism." Entry in *Encyclopedia Britannica*, vol. 17-233 (1969).

Persinger, Michael A. and Lafreniere, Gyslaine F. *Space-Time Transients and Unusual Events* (Chicago: Nelson-Hall, 1977). Computer analysis of Fortean phenomena, including UFOs.

Pinotti, Roberto. "Control-System Theory" (Vallee), in *Encyclopedia of UFOs* (N.Y.: Doubleday, 1980).

"Theosophy." Entry in *Encyclopedia Britannica*, vol. 21-1000 (1969).

CHAPTER 9

NUTS & BOLTS

The most popular theory, and that also held by a majority of UFO researchers including many scientists, is that UFOs represent "nuts and bolts" hardware controlled by intelligent beings visiting earth from some civilization in space. What technology — and what mental powers — such beings have attained can only be inferred from reported observations and the evidence of instruments and photographs.

Why such a civilization would want to visit earth, or why its technology and behavior seem incomprehensible to us, are questions for which there are no answers at present. Although skeptics often cite the baffling behavior of UFOs in refutation of the idea that they could be extraterrestrial, this line of argument presumes a great deal about what extraterrestrials *must* be like and how they *ought* to behave.

The late Dr. James E. McDonald, an atmospheric physicist who was highly regarded internationally and served on scientific panels for the National Academy of Sciences and National Science Foundation, studied UFO reports in great detail. At a 1968 Congressional symposium (and in many other forums) Dr. McDonald said, "I am one of those who lean strongly towards the extraterrestrial hypothesis (ETH)." And, ". . . if the UFOs are not of extramundane origin, then I suspect that they will prove to be something very much more bizarre, something of perhaps even greater scientific interest than extraterrestrial devices." He backed up his arguments with ample discussions of specific cases.

At the 1969 meeting of the American Association for the Advancement of Science, Dr. Robert L. Hall — a sociologist

— addressed the question of why physical scientists commonly attributed UFOs to psychological causes. "I, speaking as a behavioral scientist, say that there must be a real physical phenomenon [whereas physical scientists say it is all psychological]. So we pass the buck back and forth without forming any adequate explanation, either physical or behavioral." Dr. Hall also cited specific cases that led to his judgment.

Scientists representing the skeptical position at both forums, notably Dr. Carl Sagan, avoided discussion of specific cases and argued largely from theory. Though Dr. Sagan did concede at the Congressional symposium that ". . . there is nothing in the physics that prohibits interstellar spaceflight" and that visits were possible, he did not find the evidence very convincing.

Any attempt to make a case that UFOs are real and possibly spaceships requires discussion and analysis of particular cases. So does any attempt to write off all UFO reports as "psychological," or errors of human perception. Yet, many scientists and laymen alike are impatient with case reports . . . even bored by them. This is almost certainly a sign of "made up minds" that don't wish to be bothered by facts. The layman who already believes UFOs are extraterrestrial spaceships wants to leap ahead to the presently unanswerable questions of purposes or motives, and the skeptical scientist already "knows" that all reports, regardless of details or witness credibility, have — must have — conventional explanations.

The case for nuts and bolts extraterrestrials is based on 40 years of observations of domed disc-shaped objects or other geometrical forms capable of tremendous speeds (sometimes confirmed by radar) and extraordinary maneuvers, such as sharp turns and abrupt starts and stops. A wide array of physical evidence, including imprints on the ground, has established beyond doubt that UFOs are something physically real. A long history of UFOs pacing aircraft or rockets, circling them, and fleeing when pursued by military jets, suggests some form of both intelligence and curiosity. The vehicle confrontation cases (chapters 1 and 2) establish both the immediacy and the extraordinary nature of UFOs. Since an earthly origin for machines performing in this way for so many years can be ruled out, the ETH becomes the simplest and most direct hypothetical explanation.

Part of the reason for Dr. McDonald's conviction was reports from scientists who would talk only to him for fear of ridicule from their skeptical peers. He also spent a great deal of time in tracking down and re-interviewing airline pilots and other competent observers, and was impressed by what he learned by taking the only true scientific approach — direct investigation.

On April 25, 1952, in San Jose, California, two scientists formerly skeptical of UFO reports saw a small metallic-appearing disc rotating and wobbling on its axis. They were tracked down and interviewed by Dr. McDonald in confidence. While watching the small disc, they saw high overhead a large black circular object joined by two similar objects that dropped out of an overcast. The small disc accelerated upwards and one of the larger black objects, perhaps 100 feet in diameter, took off after it on a seemingly converging course; both then vanished in the overcast.

One of the two remaining black objects then took off to the north, while the final object ascended into the overcast. The shaken scientists reluctantly concluded that they had seen something extraterrestrial, using "... some propulsion method not in the physics books." They were worried about the implications, but reported the sighting only to a handful of scientific colleagues.

One of the most spectacular UFO waves of all time occurred in 1952, including numerous sightings by military and civilian pilots with frequent radar confirmations. On July 13, 1952, while en route to Washington, D.C., from Jacksonville, Florida, National Airlines flight number 611 encountered an unidentified round bluish-white light at 3:00 a.m. about 60 miles southwest of the city. The light was hovering to the west, then "came up to 11,000 feet" level with the airliner, a DC-4, and paced the plane off the left wing. The concerned pilot, Capt. Bruen, turned on all the aircraft lights and the object "took off up and away like a star" with an estimated departure speed of 1,000 m.p.h. Visibility was excellent. (Air Force intelligence report from Project Blue Book files, signed by Lt. Col. Frank M. Allen, in U.S. National Archives.)

On the next night in the vicinity of Newport News, Virginia, Pan American Airways Capt. William B. Nash, in one of the famous classic sightings, watched eight glowing red, disc-shaped objects maneuver in a sharp turn beneath his airliner.

All year long military jet interceptors were scrambled to chase and try to identify unexplained targets on radar, often seeing something ahead of them that also showed on their airborne radar. On the nights of July 19/20 and July 26/27, UFOs congregated around the Nation's Capital, tracked on military and civilian radar right where pilots reported seeing unidentifiable lights capable of hovering, sudden accelerations, and sharp turns. The performance, of course, was "impossible" (by human standards), and the sightings were explained away as aberrations of weather — at least publicly. Recently released Central Intelligence Agency documents show that the 1952 sightings caused the CIA to recommend a major scientific study to identify UFOs.

Is it any wonder that pilots who observed the UFOs maneuvering beyond the capabilities of any known aircraft or rockets, radar operators who tracked them, and Air Force Intelligence as well as the CIA, took the ETH seriously? Assigned the responsibility for investigating UFOs, Air Force Intelligence quickly determined that the Soviet Union, still rebuilding from World War II, had not achieved any miraculous technological breakthrough that could account for the sightings. What did that leave?

But UFO waves (sustained periods of sightings) are not that frequent — though sporadic reports continue during the intervals in between — and memories are short. Particularly when it is easier to think — and hope — that some freak natural phenomenon must have caused the sightings. After all, no spaceship landed and no overt contact or communication took place, so maybe freak weather and a dash of Cold War hysteria caused it all. To think that spaceships were here was . . . mind-boggling, and scientists who were consulted firmly debunked the idea.

The cycle of UFO waves and lull periods, serious attention to the possibility of extraterrestrial visitors and short memories when the wave ends, has been repeated time and time again. The first wave occurred in 1947, leading to the Air Force Intelligence estimate that UFOs were spaceships. The next was in 1952. The 1954 wave, primarily in Europe, was the first to include widespread reports of humanoid UFO pilots observed throughout France and Italy. Publications like LIFE magazine treated the European wave with tongue in cheek, and it was easy to write it off as Continental madness. Then in 1957, following the launching of Sputnik, UFOs were once again seen widely in the United States. A prominent feature of the 1957 wave was widespread reports of E-M effects on automobiles.

A long lull thereafter reduced public interest, and it was not until 1964 that a "trigger" case caused new extensive news media coverage of UFO sightings. In Socorro, N.M., police officer Lonnie Zamora saw an elliptical object resting on stilt-like legs in an arroyo on April 24. Standing near it were two small humanoid figures. As he watched, the craft-like object emitted a loud roar and a blast of flames and smoke, and took off, becoming silent once it cleared the ground. Investigators found four distinct rectangular imprints in the sand and scorched foliage beneath the take-off spot. Project Blue Book (the Air Force UFO investigation unit stationed at Wright-Patterson AFB) made an extensive effort to locate any experimental vehicle which might have caused the sighting, but there was none.

Again, craft-like objects, increasingly observed on the ground and with humanoid beings seen nearby or inside; not human vehicles. What could they be, if not extraterrestrial? However, the aliens, if that's what they were, remained essentially shy about making overt contact or communicating with earthlings.

As with any new or newly discovered feature of UFO reports, historical "firsts" are not easy to establish. Later research showed that E-M effects associated with UFO reports preceded 1957, but were relatively infrequent until then. In the 1960s a seemingly new feature of UFO reports first became prominent: the vehicle encounter. To be sure, pilots had had some relatively close-range encounters with UFOs, but now more and more citizens began reporting some very startling automobile-UFO encounters, more in the nature of confrontations. Then, in the 1970s, the reports of humans being abducted on board craft-like UFOs seemingly began in earnest, though again, earlier cases are known.

The UFO wave that began in 1964 built up to a crescendo in 1966 and 1967 (through the lifetime of the University of Colorado Air Force sponsored UFO study, which in fact resulted from political pressures arising out of the 1960s sightings), and then tapered off again in 1968. For several years another lull period prevailed. The next wave and attendant media publicity was not until 1973, including the October 18 helicopter-UFO encounter over Ohio, E-M effects, numerous humanoid sightings, and the highly publicized October 11 abduction case in Mississippi. More of the same, but with no resolution of the fundamental question: If those craft-like objects and humanoids are not earthly creations, then what are they?

Real extraterrestrial visitors to earth could have profound implications for us . . . under certain circumstances. (If there is too much disparity between our levels of intelligence, meaningful contact and communication might be impossible. This and other factors that could pose barriers to contact are discussed in the concluding chapters.) The observed science and technology would suggest that aspects of nature and physics presently beyond our grasp could be opened up to us, if "they" are willing to divulge the information. Our warlike nature, on the other hand, could be one reason for their apparent reluctance to communicate with us openly and to engage in a cultural exchange.

Conceivably an advanced civilization may have found cures for biological diseases and secrets of longevity (as some of the abduction "messages" say). The society may even have found satisfactory solutions to political stability — indeed, this may be a prerequisite to space travel and exploration. Just imagine the potential for solving the most intransigent human problems that could be inherent in opening up contact with advanced beings from elsewhere.

The other side of the coin is that the advanced technology, the tremendous energies apparently controlled by the ETIs, could be used to take us over or destroy us if that is their design, or if our behavior leads them to that conclusion. The fact that no overt intervention has taken place in 40 years is no proof against it happening tomorrow, for we have no idea of their overall purpose or its time scale. UFOs already have demonstrated the ability to make our vehicles and weapons malfunction, even to take over control of them. These actions could easily be interpreted as demonstrations.

In any case, the significance of UFOs may be that our fate is in the hands of beings from elsewhere, for good or ill. If so, their powers and abilities are being made known to us, one might say, but their minds and thoughts remain shrouded in mystery. If UFOs carry advanced beings from another civilization in space, they may well be a Sword of Damocles poised over our heads.

The abductions, if given credence, could be the beginnings of contact — strictly on their terms. "They" demonstrate an ability to intervene psychologically, to tamper with our minds, and perhaps to alter our perceptions. The abduction reports deserve the most intensive possible study, either to establish that they are some form of hysterical contagion or that they are the real thing. For if they are real, they undoubtedly hold the key to the presently unanswerable questions about motives and purposes.

Taken at face value, the abduction cases would imply that we are totally at the mercy of beings who can intervene and control us at will, beings with a far superior mastery of nature who, for reasons known only to themselves, prefer a one-on-one approach to contact with human beings. But even if the abduction reports are only a psychological spin-off of the UFO problem, not physically real events, the hardcore UFO mystery remains.

Nuts and bolts spacecraft rightfully remains the most viable hypothesis among the choices presently available to us. Is it the answer? And if so, why are the extraterrestrials avoiding open contact?

BIBLIOGRAPHY

Committee on Science and Astronautics, U.S. House of Representatives, *Symposium on Unidentified Flying Objects*, July 29, 1968.

Gersten, Peter "What the U.S. Government Knows About Unidentified Flying Objects," *Frontiers of Science*, v. 3, no. 4, May-June 1981. CIA documents showing serious concern about 1952 UFO sightings.

Greenwell, J. Richard. "Extraterrestrial Hypothesis," in *Encyclopedia of UFOs* (N.Y.: Doubleday, 1980).

Hall, Richard H. (ed.). *The UFO Evidence* (Washington, D.C.: NICAP, 1964). History of UFOs to date, including pilot and scientist sightings and summaries of UFO waves.

_____. "Chronology of Important Events in UFO History," in *Encyclopedia of UFOs* (N.Y.: Doubleday, 1980).

Jacobs, David M. *UFO Controversy in America* (Indiana Univ Press, 1975). Social and political history of UFO controversy, including Air Force Project Blue Book.

Keyhoe, Donald E. *Flying Saucers From Outer Space* (N.Y.: Henry Holt, 1953). Incorporating 1952 radar-visual UFO sightings from Air Force intelligence reports.

Ruppelt, Edward J. *Report on Unidentified Flying Objects* (N.Y.: Doubleday, 1956). History of Air Force UFO investigation projects, including 1952 UFO cases.

Sagan, Carl and Page, Thornton (eds.) *UFOs: A Scientific Debate* (Cornell Univ Press, 1972). Proceedings of the 1969 A.A.A.S. symposium on UFOs.

U.S. Air Force. *Unidentified Aerial Objects: Project "Sign,"* Feb. 1949. Air Materiel Command Technical Report No. F-TR-2274-IA.

Wood, Robert M. "Testing the Extraterrestrial Hypothesis," in *Thesis-Antithesis* (A.D. Emerson, ed.) Proceedings of Joint Symposium by sections of American Institute of Aeronautics and Astronautics and Los Angeles chapter of World Futures Society (AIAA Los Angeles Section, 1975).

PART III
EVALUATING
THE UNKNOWN

"When a man desires to know the truth, his first effort will be to imagine what the truth can be . . . imagination unbridled is sure to carry him off the track. Yet . . . there is, after all, nothing but imagination that can ever supply him an inkling of the truth. He can stare stupidly at phenomena; but in the absence of any imagination they will not connect themselves together in any rational way."

C.S. PEIRCE

CHAPTER 10

SKEPTICAL PRESUMPTIONS

The data of reported UFO sightings contain either the makings of the greatest scientific revolution of all time, or of the most pervasive mass delusion in human history. In neither case does the scientific establishment demonstrate leadership in resolving the problem. Few scientists who argue skeptically about UFOs bother to examine the body of hard-core, unexplained UFO reports; the detailed cases from the best and most credible witnesses. Instead, they react in "knee-jerk" fashion against the notion that UFOs might be extraterrestrial visitors, or they single out crackpot UFO adherents and laugh at their ignorance, or both.

Except for the "scientific underground" known to exist in nearly every major scientific establishment in the United States, with a network of scientists quietly doing the best they can to study UFOs in spare time using only private resources, establishment scientists have engaged in theorizing-away UFOs without confronting the data they claim to be explaining. They typically either (a) deny the validity of the reports or (b) argue that, even if the reports are accurate, they couldn't be describing extraterrestrial visitors "because . . . ."

These skeptical scientists show a dismaying tendency to put the cart before the horse in arguing that the data cannot be valid because extraterrestrial visitation is impossible or improbable. "Impossibility," apparently, is defined by the criterion of our current body of scientific knowledge. These scientists

155

are confusing "impossibility" or "improbability" with "inconsistency." UFO data obviously are inconsistent with our body of scientific knowledge in a number of ways.

If UFOs are maneuvering in the reported ways, they violate (or appear to) the laws of inertia, our cosmological theories, our concepts of propulsion ... not to mention scientific sensibilities and terrestrial provincialism. We cannot comfortably fit them into our scheme of things, because any of the hypotheses that accepts the data as valid does violence to some cherished belief. Anyone who thinks that our cosmological theories deserve to be taken as articles of faith has not read Arthur Koestler's *The Sleepwalkers*, a devastating commentary on "fashions" in science and the historical subservience of science to the winds of politics (or — in an earlier era — religion).

None of the skeptical scientists' arguments establishes the impossibility of UFOs, or even that extraterrestrial contact is unlikely to occur simply because we do not see how it could happen. The point was neatly summed up by Dr. James E. McDonald in a 1968 talk to aerospace scientists:

> "To be sure, we don't yet have any red hot ideas for getting out to Tau Ceti; but the pace and tempo of our own technology ought to give pause to those who would insist that there are no Tau Cetians who can do that which we still regard as impossible."

Those hypothetical Tau Cetians, should they choose to visit us, probably would by the very fact of being able to get here send earth scientists scrambling back to the drawing board for some hasty revisions. Earth scientists may find difficulty in imagining that there could be more intelligent beings "out there" who have a superior knowledge of natural laws. However, we have no way of knowing what the technological capabilities of other intelligent beings might be — including the possible ability to reconnoiter the Earth if they choose to do so.

156

The UFO problem cannot be evaluated objectively by start-ing with the assumption that our science is the pinnacle of achievement in the universe. It is not scientific to reject data because they do not fit present theories. How "they" could muster the propulsion technology to get here, or why they would want to visit us in the first place, or why they don't make overt contact, are irrelevant questions when offered as if they constituted a rebuttal to UFO reports. Yet, these are the central arguments of the skeptics.

In 1949, scientists consulted by Project "Sign," the original Air Force study of UFOs, betrayed their biases about extrater-restrial psychology in the final report of the project:

> "Various people have suggested that an advanced race may have been visiting Earth from Mars or Venus at intervals from decades to eons. Reports of objects in the sky seem to have been handed down through the generations. If this were true, a race of such knowledge and power would have established some form of direct contact . . . they would at least try to communicate. It is hard to believe that any technically accomplished race would come here, flaunt its ability in mysterious ways and then simply go away. Furthermore, a race which had enough in-itiative to explore among the planets would hardly be too timid to follow through when the job was accomplished."

Then, speaking of the higher probability of intelligent life ex-isting outside of our solar system:

> "Conceivably, among the myriads of stellar sys-tems in the Galaxy, one or more races have discov-ered methods of travel that would be fantastic by our standards. Yet the larger volume of space, i.e., greater distance that must be included in order to strengthen this possibility, the lower will be the chance that the

race involved would ever find the Earth . . . . A super-race (unless they occur frequently) would not be likely to stumble upon Planet III of Sol, a fifth-magnitude star in the rarified outskirts of the Galaxy.

"A description of the probable operating characteristics of space ships must be based on the assumption that they will be rockets, since this is the only form of propulsion that we know will function in outer space . . . The lack of purpose apparent in the various episodes is also puzzling. Only one motive can be assigned; that the space-men are 'feeling out' our defenses without wanting to be belligerent. If so, they must have been satisfied long ago that we can't catch them. It seems fruitless for them to keep repeating the same experiment . . . .

"Although visits from outer space are believed to be possible, they are believed to be improbable. In particular, the actions attributed to the 'flying objects' reported during 1947 and 1948 seem inconsistent with the requirements for space travel."

This analysis is signed by J. F. Lipp, Missiles Division, Rand Project. Although it was penned nearly 40 years ago, scientist skeptics use essentially the same arguments today. Once they make all of the assumptions that tend to rule out extraterrestrial visitation — the astronomical distances and the non-humanlike science and behavior displayed — the skeptics uniformly attribute the continued reporting of unidentified craft-like objects to the vagaries of human psychology. Thus, physical and engineering scientists step far outside of their fields of expertise to pass judgment on UFOs; "passing the buck" to behavioral scientists. Not only do they presume to know human psychology sufficiently to conclude it is the source of UFOs, but also they presume to know extraterrestrial psychology!

Put in question and answer form, their dialogue runs as follows:

Q. Why must an extraterrestrial race be confined to rocket propulsion?

A. Because that's the only thing we know will work in outer space.

Q. Why is the "mysterious" behavior of UFOs considered to be evidence that they are not extraterrestrial visitors?

A. Because we wouldn't behave that way if we explored other planets.

Q. Why are the actions of UFOs "inconsistent with the requirements for space travel"?

A. Because the technology displayed is not that we would use if we tried to travel to other planets.

These scientists would flunk out of my logic course, unless I were willing to grant their basic premise: "Man is the measure of all things." Then their logic is flawless.

Otherwise highly competent scientists continue to betray an inability to break free of reasoning by human analogy and to look at UFO reports objectively. If they find the ETH offensive, let them study the data and formulate a better hypothesis. The gratuitous assumption that no one has ever reported a truly unexplainable UFO is not even an hypothesis; it is a denial of the need for an hypothesis. Thus, the skeptics never explain the data; they merely deny that a significant body of data exists. When facts get in the way of their assumption, they invoke some new, previously unknown "natural phenomenon" to account for the facts. I suppose, in their way of thinking, that if they were to grant the validity of the UFO data they would find themselves facing an "unnatural phenomenon."

It does not take much imagination to suppose that we could be dealing with a science and technology that has evolved along lines unfamiliar to us. That alone could cause the displays we see to appear mysterious, and not in the mold of what we have been conditioned by science fiction to believe is "proper" extraterrestrial behavior.

One so-far science fiction concept (though earth scientists have studied the question) is anti-gravity. If we assume that extraterrestrials may have acquired a better understanding of gravity and learned to control it for their purposes, this conceivably could begin to place some of the puzzling features of UFO reports into a conceptual scheme. Those features include the broad array of E-M effects, the displacement of large masses (especially vehicles), reported levitations, and maybe even the reported ability of UFOs to make "impossible" turns and maneuvers. Reports of UFOs seeming to "fall upwards" and seeming to be in a precarious balance while hovering also come to mind.

Control of gravity could lead to a cushioning effect for the occupants of a vehicle, allowing them to survive the inertial forces in sharp turns and in rapid acceleration to hyper-velocities described in UFO reports. If a gravity field were somehow brought to bear on the occupants as well as the craft, as a unit, the occupants would not be smashed against the walls of the craft. Additionally, the cloudy glow often reported around UFOs might be a plasma that cushions the craft against the friction and heat generated by passage through the atmosphere.

Skeptical scientists may eagerly pounce on such speculations as so much nonsense and as a blatant effort to "save the phenomenon," but if so, they miss the point. The speculations are not suggested as answers, but simply to make the point that earth scientists may not know all there is to know about so-called "natural laws." Scientifically advanced beings from elsewhere could easily be far ahead of our science, able to do things we cannot do; not through magic, but simply by technological applications of knowledge we are yet to attain.

The primacy of data over theory should compel scientists to find a better explanation of UFO reports if they think they can, rather than to reject the data. If, in fact, we are being visited by extraterrestrial intelligences, then somewhere along the line there are faults or gaps in our scientific knowledge. That possibility ought not to surprise anyone greatly. Pragmatically, we know that our science works here and in space as far as we have explored. But as Dr. J. Allen Hynek has pointed out, only a fool would say that 20th century science on earth is the pinnacle of achievement in the universe, or even that in another 20 centuries from now, terrestrial science will have changed very little.

The possibility that UFOs may amend our understanding of nature is one of the potential revolutions of human thought inherent in the UFO question. If UFOs prove to be something even more exotic than spaceships, then the revolution could be sweeping indeed.

What seems to be at work among the scientist skeptics is a defense of the status quo against incursions by "believers" or science-fictionists, as they see us, assaulting the body scientific with claims based on careless observations and a poor understanding of science. The substantial body of data they are overlooking (which is by no means all anecdotal) may or may not be explainable only by a theory that would require sweeping amendment of scientific concepts. We won't know until science really confronts the data instead of denying it.

As some of us are convinced, our body of scientific knowledge may be excluding important data or wrongly interpreting cosmological questions. Some UFO data, if taken at face value, might suggest that our basic concepts of perception, "reality," and the mind-body question are faulty; that some built-in "filter factor" may somehow be causing us to misperceive or to overlook a portion of the universe around us. The Answer, if it is ever known, may be simplicity itself.

No one — least of all scientists — should prejudge the outcome of applying scientific resources to the UFO problem. Since no concerted effort has been mounted to gather and study UFO data systematically, we cannot tell how far our instruments and concepts can carry us toward understanding UFOs. Any claim that science has, *by scientific study*, explained UFOs as misperceptions of common phenomena or as anything else is totally unfounded. The sad truth is that scientists have avoided confronting a sticky problem by rationalizing it in ways unbecoming to science. Hasty and ill-informed personal judgments and ridicule of the subject are not science.

An astronomer who, without confirming witnesses, reports a chance observation of a bright meteor is believed, even though many astronomers know little about meteors and are not particularly interested in them. Witnesses to unaccounted-for domed discs with portholes are disbelieved because there "can't be" domed discs with portholes unless we make them, which we don't. When two or three people witness a domed disc with portholes, they are suspected of collusion. When the same disc is tracked on radar, there must be something wrong with the set.

Why it is so difficult for scientists to concede that anomalous things are being reported, and to study the events objectively, is a significant question in itself. The vaunted neutrality and objectivity of science has not been evident in response to UFO reports. To the contrary, the "scientific" response has largely consisted of presumption rather than study, and ridicule rather than open-mindedness.

In the words of the American philosopher Charles Sanders Peirce, "The first step toward finding out is to acknowledge you do not satisfactorily know already . . . ." We look forward to the day scientists recognize that UFO anomalies are occurring and lend their vital talents to a thorough study; when, in the words of Thomas Kuhn, ". . . the anomalous has become the expected . . . and the discovery has been completed."

Until science "discovers" UFOs, the problem is likely to sail on in limbo, unresolved. So far scientists have been (in general) part of the problem rather than part of the solution. One of Dr. McDonald's insights was that scientists consulted by military authorities responsible for UFO investigations had consistently given them bad advice, based purely on prejudices, not on sound scientific principles.

Presumption is the exact opposite of what science is supposed to be.

BIBLIOGRAPHY

Condon, Edward U. "Summary of the Study," in *Scientific Study of Unidentified Flying Objects*, Daniel S. Gillmor, ed. (N.Y.: Bantam Books, 1969) pp. 7-50.

_____. "UFOs I Have Loved and Lost," in *Bulletin of the Atomic Scientists*, Dec. 1969.

Hynek, J. Allen. *The UFO Experience: A Scientific Inquiry* (Chicago: Henry Regnery, 1972).

Maccabee, Bruce S. "Still in Default," in *MUFON 1986 UFO Symposium Proceedings* (Seguin, Tex.: MUFON, 1986) pp. 131-160.

McDonald, James E. Testimony before House Committee on Science and Astronautics, *Symposium on Unidentified Flying Objects*, July 29, 1968, pp. 18-85.

_____. "Science in Default: Twenty-Two Years of Inadequate UFO Investigations," in *UFOs: A Scientific Debate* (Cornell Univ Press, 1972) pp. 52-122.

Menzel, Donald H. Submitted statement to House Committee on Science and Astronautics, *Symposium on Unidentified Flying Objects*, July 29, 1968, pp. 199-205.

_____. "UFOs: The Modern Myth," in *UFOs: A Scientific Debate* (Cornell Univ Press, 1972) pp. 123-182.

Murray, Bruce. "The Limits of Science," in *UFOs and the Limits of Science* (N.Y.: William Morrow, 1981) pp. 255-266.

U.S. Air Force. *Unidentified Aerial Objects: Project "Sign,"* Feb. 1949.

CHAPTER 11

THE BIG SECRET

The idea that the U.S. Government (and probably other governments) knows all about UFOs and is hiding the truth from the public is almost an article of faith among "UFOlogists." The question is a complicated one requiring close study of American UFO history from the beginning, and consideration of fragmentary evidence that is subject to various interpretations.

Is the Government concealing important — perhaps vitally significant — information about UFOs? My answer would be an unequivocal "yes!" The indications of secrecy are overwhelmingly strong, including "leaked" information about spectacular military cases withheld from the public and cases forced into the open through Freedom of Information Act (FOIA) lawsuits. How much the Government knows about UFOs is the more important question.

Why is UFO information being kept secret? If anyone knows, he or she is not talking. The possibilities range from self-serving classification by Government agencies to conceal the fact that they don't have a handle on the problem and have misjudged it over the years, all the way to retrieved hardware and alien bodies undergoing secret study at Government installations. If the crash/retrieval stories are true, the reasons for a high-level policy of secrecy would be more obvious.

Anyone familiar with the Government bureaucracy, however, suspects that the SECRET stamp is applied more often to cover up blunders or potentially embarrassing revelations about procedures than it is to protect legitimate secrets. Although the FOIA has ferreted out many examples of this practice, it also has uncovered hidden UFO reports so spectacular that reasonable people can interpret them as evidence of a conspiracy of silence. The question remains: Why?

My views on Government secrecy have fluctuated over the years. For many years I paid little attention to the question while gathering and analyzing UFO reports, knowing that the Government was being less than candid with the public because various officials were leaking information to me. I was then Acting Director of the National Investigations Committee on Aerial Phenomena (NICAP), in Washington, D.C., the preeminent civilian UFO organization of the 1960s. At that stage of UFO history, there was little time for grand theorizing.

On one occasion I received a phone call from the State Department informing me that an Argentine newsman wanted to interview me. When the "newsman" arrived at my office, along with a State Department interpreter, he turned out to be an officer of Argentine Air Force Intelligence who wanted to compare notes, which we did at length. (According to him, Argentina also had humanoid reports and other bizarre cases.) He also wanted to know how NICAP operated because his government was planning to form a scientific-military group to study UFOs.

More than one State Department official provided copies of airgrams and other diplomatic message traffic from embassies in foreign countries reporting UFO sightings that were not in the newspapers. Confidential reports also came from active duty Air Force personnel, NASA scientists and engineers (some of whom operated NICAP investigative units on the side), and many other quarters. It was clear that UFO reports going through Government channels were considered not for public consumption — at least for official attribution.

Although "leaks" are a Washington institution and in this case could have represented nothing more than the personal interest of the leakers in the various agencies, NICAP did have prominent supporters — both military and civilian — in the Executive and Legislative branches of the Government. Their influence no doubt had something to do with the flow of information. I labored under the perhaps naive belief that "the Government" didn't want to reveal its hand, but trusted NICAP to inform the public in a responsible manner. In fact, we publicized the information content of the reports while carefully protecting our sources.

In the mid-1960s Dr. James E. McDonald, a highly regarded atmospheric physicist at the University of Arizona, became interested in UFO reports and began a whirlwind investigation. We subsequently became close friends, spending long hours discussing all aspects of the UFO question. Under his influence, I first began seriously weighing the pros and cons of "cover-up" vs. "foul-up," his shorthand terminology for the ultimate question of how much the Government knew.

Was there a conscious, high-level cover-up of significant UFO evidence such that the Government was well aware of UFOs and only pretending not to be? Or was the official policy more of a foul-up, a failure to recognize or come to grips with the UFO problem because of its bizarre and potentially revolutionary nature? Strong arguments could be advanced on either side of the question.

Jim inclined toward "foul-up" because of all the undeniable signs of shoddy investigation and general ineptitude in Air Force files, while I inclined toward "cover-up" because of the information being funneled to me. Yet, I was aware that "foul-ups" had occurred too, and Jim was concerned about the type of report he also was receiving from highly credible witnesses who approached him after his talks at scientific and military establishments all over the country.

Neither of us was totally convinced one way or the other, but I played the Devil's advocate. The shorthand expression for my view was: "They can't be that stupid." Too many military pilots had been scrambled to chase UFOs tracked by ground radar, seen something visually, and locked onto it with airborne radar. Too many jet interceptor gun camera films and other movies had been obtained of objects defying conventional explanation. Too many airline pilots and other well-qualified observers had reported encounters with manifestly unexplainable things. "They" (top-level Government officials) had to know that something real and exceedingly strange was being detected.

Since the 1960s, a great deal of new information bearing on the question of Government secrecy has been obtained through FOIA lawsuits and other sources. However, it has not been sufficient to establish beyond a reasonable doubt that a true cover-up exists. The possibility remains that the Government knows only a little more than we do; that (except for periodic reviews forced by new sightings) UFOs are not taken seriously, and that no one is maintaining an overview. I seriously doubt it, but recognize that the possibility exists.

Several scenarios are plausible, depending on how consistently the Government has pursued the subject and what "hard" evidence has been obtained. The first major UFO wave in the United States occurred in 1947, stimulating a Top Secret Air Force project to investigate. The fear was that the Soviet Union had made a dramatic technological breakthrough that threatened our national security. An urgent investigation by the Air Technical Intelligence Center quickly ruled that out, but failed to explain the sightings. Since Air Force investigators took the reports seriously, they considered the extraterrestrial hypothesis, advocated it, but could not "prove" it.

SCENARIO 1

Whatever UFOs were, they apparently posed no threat. They didn't attack, and other than exciting the imagination of the populace, they had little or no impact on society. Scientific consultants to the Air Force pooh-poohed the idea that they could be extraterrestrial, so a decision was made to ignore the reports.

Once the Administration was committed to a position — in this case that UFOs were nothing worth bothering about — inertia set in. Some spectacular new evidence would have to be obtained, something more than "routine" UFO reports, some hard facts, before the Air Force would stick its neck out again. Thus, sightings from 1948 through 1951 easily could be rationalized or "explained-away" as due to stray aircraft or aberrant weather, or excitable witnesses. This, says ex-Project Blue Book Chief, Edward J. Ruppelt, is what happened before he took over the project.

In 1951, Ruppelt was inundated with information from highly reputable professional people, angry about Air Force debunking of their reports. This and various other influences led to a revitalization of the project, including a more vigorous effort to conduct field investigations and to cultivate good witnesses. Perhaps by coincidence, perhaps not, the largest wave of UFO reports to date ensued in 1952, and it included spectacular airborne encounters by military jets, radar trackings, and gun camera film footage of UFOs.

Such evidence could not be ignored, so scientists again were consulted and the CIA became involved. Both Ruppelt's book and CIA documents obtained via FOIA requests clearly show that by the end of 1952, both agencies took UFOs very seriously. In fact, the CIA recommended to the National Security Council that a major scientific investigation be undertaken to identify the nature of UFOs. Yet, the very next year UFOs were officially debunked again. Why? Was it a conspiracy?

Early in 1953 the CIA convened a panel of prestigious scientists (The "Robertson Panel") to review the Air Force evidence. In a few days of meetings the busy scientists took a quick look, found no "proof," and recommended debunking the subject, even going so far as to question the motives of civilian UFO groups in language reflecting the McCarthy hysteria of the times. Some of the scientists failed to attend all the meetings. As Dr. McDonald noted, scientists only superficially knowledgeable about UFO reports and clearly approaching the task with an extreme negative bias repeatedly have given the Air Force bad advice.

Sightings tapered off again after 1952, and treatment of subsequent waves (the next in late 1957) was a reprise of the explain-away pattern. Scientists (though they were physical scientists) insisted the basic cause of UFO reports was psychoogical, and each new wave could be rationalized as more "popular madness." Operational Air Force personnel thought otherwise, but who were they to dispute prestigious scientists?

In this scenario, both the Air Force and the CIA periodically have taken UFO reports seriously but have deferred to outside scientific advice. They have not continuously monitored the problem, instead shelving it and concentrating on their main missions of defense and national security. Personnel have come and gone, and no one has maintained an overview of the evidence. Particular cases have been classified and covered up both because they were puzzling and because their public disclosure might prove embarrassing without convincing explanations. The secrecy has been more self-protective than conspiratorial. A perusal of the Blue Book files alone would tend to support this view.

SCENARIO 2

Because of repeated reports by military pilots, airline pilots, radarmen, and other credible witnesses, the Government (at some high level) has systematically compiled all serious evidence about UFOs and maintains an overview through a classified project. The project continues to gather radar data, movie films, physical evidence, and the like. The reports are viewed as puzzling, possibly evidence of extraterrestrial visitation, but they display no overt threat to national security or to society as a whole, and no direct contact or communication — or other absolute proof — has been obtained.

The Government posture is to keep an eye on the situation without alarming the public, and if they are extraterrestrial, to gather all possible technological information that might allow us to duplicate the propulsion system before the Soviet Union does. Policymakers blow hot and cold about how much to tell the public, and those who favor more public disclosure "leak" information from time to time.

SCENARIO 3

The Government knows what UFOs are (extraterrestrial or otherwise) on the basis of "hard" evidence. That evidence could be unambiguous films, radar data, triangulation by multiple optical and electronic sensors, other physical evidence or "hardware." The nature of the "hard" evidence or proof governs policy. If strong evidence — or proof — has been obtained that abductions really are taking place, this would amount to a "secret state of warfare" in which the aliens intervene in human affairs at will. Without effective countermeasures or ability to control the situation, political and military leaders would not be likely to reveal the truth.

Depending on the degree of evidence or proof in hand, the implications of Scenario 2 and 3 would be that Government leaders fear full disclosure would upset the world economy, the fabric of political structures, and religions. Hence they practice near-total secrecy while trying to figure out what to do. Some carefully controlled public education short of officially acknowledging the seriousness of the problem may be part of the master plan.

Assuming Scenario 2 or 3 to be true — a continuing Government awareness of UFOs and their potential significance since the 1940s — you would expect some hints of the truth would emerge through "leaks" or rumors in 40 years. With few exceptions, even major secrets tend to trickle out in a democratic society with a vigorous free press. The "absolute truth" might be garbled, but traces of it should be identifiable in contemporary sources.

A CRITICAL TURNING POINT?

My suspicion is that certain events late in 1948 and in 1949 led to a significant turning-point in Government policy, namely, the beginning of a true cover-up based on startling information obtained during that period. The indicators of this include both documented facts and candidates for the "leaks" and rumors that would hint at a Big Secret in Government possession.

The September 1948 ATIC Estimate of the Situation, classified TOP SECRET, concluded that UFOs were interplanetary spaceships. No matter that this conclusion was not "officially" accepted (for lack of "proof"), it indicates what Air Force intelligence personnel most intimately involved in UFO investigations believed, and they obviously did not believe Air Force public relations statements. During the 1950s and 1960s, Air Force spokesmen in the Pentagon repeatedly denied that the 1948 Estimate ever existed, but both Captain Ruppelt and Major Dewey Fournet (former Pentagon Monitor of Project Blue Book) certified that it did.

The Project Sign (or "Saucer") report analyzing UFO sightings through 1948 was published in February 1949, classified SECRET. Late in April, a 22-page press summary of the report was released concluding that UFOs ". . . are not a joke" and acknowledging that many puzzling cases could not be explained. Unquestionably, it was the most open-minded appraisal of the problem ever issued by the Air Force, and this despite skeptical advice by consulting scientists. About this time the UFO project name was changed to Grudge.

In December 1949, Project Grudge issued a "final" report claiming that all UFO sightings now had been explained and that the project was being disbanded (a mini-cover-up itself, since the project was not disbanded). Why the sudden turn-around without rational explanations for the many puzzling cases then under study and (as we shall see) the many new cases since the Project Sign report? Either those Air Force or Government officials favoring strict secrecy had won the day and now were establishing policy, or something of unusual significance had occurred to cause a drastic shift in public policy toward extreme secrecy. A review of 1948 and 1949 reports casts serious doubt on the credibility of the Project Grudge findings, and suggests possible reasons for the turnabout.

Late in 1948 a series of impressive aerial encounters with UFOs by military pilots were reported through intelligence channels. At the same time, mysterious "green fireballs" (not at all resembling normal meteors) suddenly began cavorting over military installations in New Mexico, defying explanation by astronomers and missile experts. Ruppelt (p. 75) said:

"All during December 1948 and January 1949 the green fireballs continued to invade the New Mexico skies. Everyone, including the intelligence officers at Kirtland AFB, ADC [Air Defense Command] people, Dr. [Lincoln] LaPaz, and some of the most distinguished scientists at Los Alamos had seen at least one." Dr. LaPaz (an expert on meteorites), he noted, was convinced the green fireballs were not natural phenomena.

Among the message traffic handled by Air Force intelligence in the last quarter of 1948 was the following:

October 1: Air National Guard pilot at Fargo, North Dakota, flying an F-51, chased a glowing, flat, round object in a 27-minute "dogfight." Object made sharp turns, head-on passes, before departing "straight into the air." Object also seen by control tower personnel and a private pilot.

October 15: Crew of an F-61 "Black Widow" night fighter in Japan investigated UFO target on radar, saw silhouette of elongated object travelling about 200 m.p.h. Crew made six attempts to intercept; each time object accelerated to estimated 1,200 m.p.h. and outdistanced interceptor before slowing again.

November 18: Air Force reserve pilot in T-6 chased oval object in 10-minute "dogfight" over Andrews AFB, Maryland. Object also visible to personnel on flight line. Object made sudden changes of altitude, and speed (from 75 to 600 m.p.h.). Pilot maneuvered to flash landing lights directly on object, at which time it glowed white and sped away to East at over 600 m.p.h.

November 23: F-80 pilot near Air Force base at Fursten-Feldbruck, Germany, intercepted target detected by ground radar circling rapidly at 27,000 feet, saw bright red object. Object abruptly climbed to 50,000 feet, speed 900 m.p.h. Report verified by second F-80 pilot.

December 5: Air Force C-47 pilot at 18,000 feet near Albuquerque, New Mexico, watched huge green fireball arch *upward*, then level off to horizontal trajectory at 9:27 p.m. At 9:35 p.m., Frontiers Airlines DC-3 pilot saw full-moon-size orange-red object changing to green approach head-on in flat trajectory, dodge to the side, and fall away toward ground.

Though the project officially lacked "proof" of its September Estimate of the Situation, it did not take much "intelligence" for the analysts to consider reports like these strong evidence that UFOs were real somethings displaying extraordinary performance capabilities, not explainable as natural phenomena. The Project Sign report published the following February cautiously reflected their puzzlement.

Similar reports in 1949 adding evidence of apparently controlled, high-performance UFOs included the following:

April 24: Scientists and technicians tracking a balloon near Arrey, New Mexico, saw and tracked with a theodolite a white, disc-shaped object moving so rapidly that surface details could not be clearly observed. The speed was calculated at 18,000 m.p.h. The object changed course and disappeared in a sharp climb.

June 10: During a Navy upper-atmosphere missile test at White Sands, New Mexico, the missile had attained a speed of 2,000 feet per second (over 1,300 m.p.h.) on its upward flight, when it was suddenly joined by two small circular objects which paced it, one on each side. One of the objects then passed through the missile's exhaust, joined the other, and together they accelerated upward leaving the missile behind. Capt. Robert McLaughlin, who reported the incident in a magazine article, said that he soon received accounts from five separate observation posts at different points of the compass; all had witnessed the performance of the two circular UFOs.

As Ruppelt asked in a similar context, "What constitutes proof?" Two incompletely documented reports from 1949, if true, would be a close approximation. On June 5, 1949, Walter Winchell reported the following in his column:

> "The New York World-Telegram has confirmed this reporter's exclusive report of several weeks before — which newspapermen have denied — about the flying saucers . . . said the front page in the World-Telegram: 'Air Force people are convinced the flying disk is real. The clincher came when the Air Force got a picture recently of three disks flying in formation over Stephensville, Newfoundland. They outdistanced our fastest ships.' "

The other report concerns a Fall 1949 radar tracking over a "key atomic base" (location not specified, but very possibly New Mexico where so many UFOs were reported in this period), and requires a word of explanation.

In April of 1952 LIFE magazine published an article by H.B. Darrach and Robert Ginna titled "Flying Saucers: Have We Visitors From Space?" The article strongly suggested an affirmative answer, and since it was based on Air Force case files also hinted that it reflected high-level Air Force views. The article included a series of spectacular cases attributed to Air Force files. Case 14 was the Fall 1949 atomic base radar tracking.

Capt. Ruppelt, whose book describing the inner workings of the Air Force UFO project is mandatory reading for both cover-up and foul-up theorists, was Chief of Project Blue Book at the time Darrach and Ginna were researching their article. Here is what Ruppelt had to say about it (p. 177):

> "In answer to any questions about the article's being Air Force inspired, my weasel-worded answer was that we had furnished LIFE with some raw data on specific sightings. My answer was purposely weasel-worded because I knew that the Air Force had unofficially inspired the LIFE article. The 'maybe they're interplanetary' with the 'maybe' bordering on 'they are' was the personal opinion of several very high-ranking officers in the Pentagon — so high that their personal opinion was almost policy .... I knew that one of them, a general, had passed his opinions on to Bob Ginna."

The Fall 1949 radar case has eluded complete documentation, probably because the precise date and location were withheld, but there is no doubt about its authenticity. As summarized in the LIFE article, the Air Force officer making the report held the highest security rating given. Formerly he was in charge of radar guarding the atomic installation, but now he held a higher post. The radar scope at the base covered 300 miles of sky up to 100,000 feet. The essence of the report was that a legitimate radar contact had tracked five apparently metallic objects at great height moving South and crossing the 300-mile scope in less than 4 minutes (averaging about 4,500 m.p.h.). The case is one of many missing from the archived Blue Book files.

The sudden "discovery" of explanations for all the previously mystifying cases, and these new ones as well, in the brief period between the two Air Force reports strongly suggests that events forced a shift in policy. My "Estimate of the Situation" is that a high-level, conscious policy of concealing the truth from the public (for whatever reasons) began here.

Ruppelt's depiction of ranking Air Force generals in 1952 encouraging LIFE to suggest that UFOs were extraterrestrial spacecraft provides strong confirmation of the view often expressed by Donald E. Keyhoe. Within the highest levels of the intelligence community and the military establishment there exist two camps: Those who feel the public should be told everything that is solidly known about UFOs, and those who feel that information should be withheld (Keyhoe's "Silence Group") either because it might disrupt society or because the evidence is ambiguous and inconclusive.

The history of Government reaction to UFO reports is best understood by realizing that from the earliest years, the possibility that UFOs were extraterrestrial in origin was clearly recognized. The implications were scary, and strongly influenced policy decisions regardless of the individual beliefs of the policymakers. Obviously many felt that the extraterrestrial possibility, at least, ought to be conveyed to the public. Whether or not the inspirers of the LIFE article had "proof" is another question.

The first widely publicized stories alleging that craft and bodies had been retrieved after UFO crashes also surfaced in 1949 and early 1950. In the parlance of the day, they were known as "crashed saucers and little men." The earliest references are not as well documented as some later 1950s reports, but are definite candidates for "leaks" if crash/retrievals really were taking place. Alternatively, if the stories are hoaxes, the hoax first captured national attention at this time.

The 1950 publicity generally points to 1949 (or earlier) events: rumors of "crashed saucers and little men" in TIME magazine for January 9 (New Mexico) and April 3 (Central America and Mexico), and similar mention in NEWSWEEK for April 17. These, Frank Scully's Fall 1949 article in *Variety* and 1950 book enlarging on alleged crash/retrievals in New Mexico, and the FBI memo (see Chapter 4) attributing to an Air Force source a story of "crashed saucers" in New Mexico, clearly establish that both news media and national intelligence agencies were receiving such reports at this significant point in UFO history.

Mexico and the American Southwest figure strongly into nearly all of the earliest crash/retrieval reports and rumors, and into nearly all of the better documented cases. If they were all hoaxes beginning in 1949, by whom and for what purpose? And are the same supposed hoaxers still carrying on the game in cases just emerging during the 1980s? The persistence of these reports over a 35-40 year period, and the escalation from "wild rumor" status to semi-credibility based on gradually emerging first-hand testimony is intriguing.

On May 31, 1955, in a story filed from London, New York *Journal American* correspondent Dorothy Kilgallen reported:

> "British scientists and airmen, after examining the wreckage of one mysterious flying ship, are convinced that these strange aerial objects are not optical illusions (but) originate on another planet. The source of my information is a British official of cabinet rank who prefers to remain unidentified. 'We believe on the basis of our inquiries thus far, that the saucers were staffed by small men — probably under four feet tall.' my informant told me. 'It's frightening but there is no denying the flying saucers come from another planet.' "

The crash/retrieval reports have come a long way since the unverified rumors of 1949 and 1950, but still fall short of totally convincing documentation. I have talked personally with several of the claimants and have seen some documentation in other cases, enough to seriously advance the *possibility* that hardware obtained by 1949 is the Big Secret that lies behind Government policy on UFOs.

Regardless of possible ultimate physical proof in Government possession, all evidence confirms that by the early 1950s a firm policy was in effect to cope with each new publicized wave of sightings one way for public consumption, and another — far more serious — way in private. Publicly, UFO reports were deemed unworthy of special attention. Privately, secret channels for rapid collection of pilot sightings, films, and radar reports were established.

Both Air Force Regulation 200-2 (specifying procedures for TWX reports to Air Technical Intelligence Center and restricting public discussion of unexplained reports) and a manual for USAF intelligence and operations officers on UFO reporting procedures were issued in 1953, *after* the Robertson panel had recommended debunking UFOs. To their credit, military leaders appear not to have accepted the hasty and ill-informed judgments of "weekend" scientific consultants, no matter their impressive scientific credentials.

The shady role of the CIA in UFO investigations has not been greatly illuminated by the documents obtained under FOIA lawsuits, but here and there significant tidbits of information have emerged. The documents include references to files of "finished intelligence reports" on UFO cases and radar case files maintained by the CIA Physics and Electronics branch. Where are these files, which led the CIA at the end of 1952 to recommend a major scientific investigation of UFOs?

A former Project Blue Book Chief has stated that in the 1960s, gun camera films of UFOs obtained during jet interceptor UFO chases were "routinely" referred to the CIA's National Photographic Interpretation Center (NPIC) for analysis. This cannot be documented at present, but I heard him say so to a UFO researcher colleague. None of the photoanalysis data in these cases has been released, nor has the existence of these films ever been acknowledged.

At least three other indications of high-level concern about UFOs and urgent secret investigation of them came to me at NICAP:

1. Five independent sources — mostly former military pilots — stated that they had been part of secret units of jet interceptors

specially equipped to chase and photograph UFOs in the 1950s and 1960s.

2. In the 1960s a social scientist (also a reserve military officer) employed by a prominent consulting firm spent many weeks at NICAP on a classified project, going through our files looking for a specific type of information. He could not talk about the agency that had contracted for the study (no doubt either the Department of Defense or CIA), nor about its exact nature. But it had to do with UFO witnesses' reactions to their sightings, including indications of fear and panic.

3. A scientist acquaintance then employed by another Government agency, while applying for a position at a National Bureau of Standards facility in the mid-1960s, inquired about the work going on in a classified area adjacent to where he would be working. He was told that the area contained not one, but two secret projects to analyze UFO radar cases. One involved analysis of radarscope photographs of UFOs.

Weighing all the evidence — from documented facts to unverifiable private sources of information — leads me to one conclusion: the Government at the highest policy-making level knows far more than it is saying about UFOs, and a real cover-up — a conspiracy of silence — exists. At a minimum, a large body of photographic and radar evidence has been analyzed, and the findings (much less the data) never released.

If it all were found wanting, the results could be declassified and released, putting an end to the UFO "myth" for once and for all. Instead, each new "leak," each new case forced into the open by FOIA lawsuits, each new revelation by people involved in past cases, confirms that baffling events have occurred, they continue to occur, and a high-level secret study has been going on for at least three decades.

The true dimensions of the Big Secret cannot be known without access to all of the hidden information and all the analysis results. Private information increasingly hints that the dimensions may be colossal.

BIBLIOGRAPHY

Bloecher, Ted. *Report on the UFO Wave of 1947* (privately published, 1967). Detailed reporting, including maps and analysis, of first major UFO wave in the United States.

Center for UFO Studies. UFO Information Service Catalog. Offers Project "Saucer" report, CIA-Robertson Panel report, JANAP-146, and numerous other documents related to Government UFO investigations.

Catoe, Lynn E. *UFOs and Related Subjects: An Annotated Bibliography* (Library of Congress, 1969).

Citizens Against UFO Secrecy. Newsletters and information about FOIA lawsuits and other UFO-related Government secrecy issues.

Darrach, H.B. and Ginna, Robert. "Have We Visitors From Space?" LIFE, Apr. 7, 1952. Based on Air Force UFO reports, including Fall 1949 radar tracking case at atomic facility.

Durant, F.C. *Report of Meetings of Scientific Advisory Panel on UFOs* (U.S. Air Force, 1953). The CIA-sponsored Robertson Panel report.

Fawcett, Lawrence and Greenwood, Barry J. *Clear Intent: The Government Coverup of the UFO Experience* (N.J.: Prentice-Hall, 1984)

Fournet, Dewey J., Jr. Letter confirming existence of Air Force 1948 Estimate of the Situation, in *The UFO Evidence* (NICAP, 1964), p. 110.

Fowler, Raymond E. *Casebook of a UFO Investigator* (N.J.: Prentice-Hall, 1981). Contains relevant chapters on Air Force UFO investigations and cover-up evidence.

Fund for UFO Research. Air Force, FBI, CIA, and other Government agency documents on UFOs.

Gersten, Peter. "What the U.S. Government Knows About Unidentified Flying Objects," *Frontiers of Science*, v. III, no. 4, May-June 1981. Analysis of Government documents on UFOs.

Greenwell, J. Richard. "Conspiracy Theories," in *Encyclopedia of UFOs* (N.Y.: Doubleday, 1980).

Hall, Richard H. "Is the CIA Stonewalling?" *Frontiers of Science*, v. III, no. 4, May-June 1981. Analysis of CIA documents on UFOs.

——————. "The Air Force Investigation," in *The UFO Evidence* (NICAP, 1964), Sect. IX. Overview of official UFO investigation, including AF position statements and trends to date.

Hynek, J. Allen. *The Hynek UFO Report*. (N.Y.: Dell Books, 1977). Recounts author's experience as scientific consultant to Air Force UFO project.

Jacobs, David M. *UFO Controversy in America* (Indiana Univ. Press, 1975). Historical analysis of Air Force UFO investigations, NICAP role, Congressional hearings.

Keyhoe, Donald E. *Flying Saucers From Outer Space* (N.Y.: Holt, 1953). Data from AF intelligence reports, focusing on 1952 sighting wave and jet interceptor, radar-visual cases.

_____ . *Flying Saucer Conspiracy* (N.Y.: Holt, 1955). The case for cover-up. Appendix includes JANAP 146(B), AFR 200-2, and other documents.

McLaughlin, Robert. "How Scientists Tracked a Flying Saucer," TRUE, Mar. 1950. Apr. 24, 1949 and June 10, 1949 UFO sightings in New Mexico.

National Investigations Committee on Aerial Phenomena. *U.S. Air Force Projects Grudge and Blue Book Reports 1-12* (1951-1953), 1968. Reprints of original documents.

Ruppelt, Edward J. "What Our Air Force Found Out About Flying Saucers," TRUE, May 1954.

_____ . *Report on Unidentified Flying Objects* (N.Y.: Doubleday, 1956). Essential reference on Air Force UFO investigations by former Project Chief.

Shalett, Sidney. "What You Can Believe About Flying Saucers," *Saturday Evening Post*. Pt. I, Apr. 30, 1949; Pt. II, May 7, 1949. Review of Air Force UFO investigation following release of Project "Saucer" (Sign) report.

CHAPTER 12

ETH AND THE INTELLIGENCE GAP

Given the mixed bag of raw information and investigated case reports that constitute the "body of data" about UFOs, any attempt to say exactly what UFOs are can only be a guesstimate — a rough approximation at best. A careful sifting of documented cases and reports from the most credible witnesses, however, does narrow down the field to a handful of hypotheses that best fit the data so far.

The Deluded Observer Hypothesis was rejected at the outset, the skeptical view that all witnesses have been mistaken in one way or another and that nothing extraordinary is being seen. The human testimony and the radar and physical evidence simply are too strong and consistent to permit such a sweeping denial of data. UFOs are real somethings that display recurring patterns of appearance and performance.

Also, the hard-core cases militate against the idea that anything as simplistic as secret devices built on earth or an "unrecognized natural phenomenon" could be the answer, yet these two really are the only serious competitors to "beings from elsewhere" if people are seeing what they say they are seeing.

Geometrical UFOs were sighted at least as early as 1904 in a formation that dove, then climbed away, observed by crewmembers of the *U.S.S. Supply*, a Navy ship off the U.S. west coast. Unless the Wright Brothers or Santos Dumont suddenly made a miraculous breakthrough in propulsion that has since been lost to aviation history, these could not have been secret devices. Nor could the structured, craft-like objects observed in controlled air lanes and over urban areas for the past 40 years have been secret devices, unless their operators have gone quite mad.

UFO displays have been observed world-wide, on every continent and in every clime. What government would be operating them and for what mysterious purpose? No practical application of any device capable of performing like UFOs do has ever surfaced. If they are U.S. secret devices, for example, they might have been useful in the Iranian hostage rescue mission instead of plodding, dust-choked helicopters.

The performance of UFOs would imply a revolutionary breakthrough in physics, kept totally secret and used only for the seemingly purposeless buzzing of vehicles and harrassment of human beings. The same arguments used by skeptical scientists to say that UFOs could not be extraterrestrial apply in spades to the secret device hypothesis. Their patterns of behavior and seeming purposelessness (by our standards) for 40 years simply do not fit the idea that they are secret earthly devices.

The only "unrecognized natural phenomenon" idea to attract much attention was "atmospheric plasmoids," advanced by nonscientist Philip Klass and later discarded by him. In the first place, the hypothesis required rejecting those portions of UFO reports that it couldn't explain, including domes, portholes, and other structural features observed on craft-like objects. In the second place, the alleged plasmoids did not make sense scientifically.

Dr. James E. McDonald (atmospheric physicist) in a talk at the Canadian Aeronautics and Space Institute in Montreal, March 12, 1968, noted: "(Klass' theory) fails to deal quantitatively with parts of the argument that are, in terms of existing scientific knowledge, amenable to quantitative analysis." McDonald demonstrated the unreasonableness of claims by Klass that plasma-UFOs would be electromagnetically attracted to aircraft and thus appear to pace them. McDonald privately communicated to the author that he could not find a single scientist who took Klass' idea seriously, since it displayed total ignorance of the relevant physics.

Finally, if some other "unrecognized natural phenomenon" (as UFOs no doubt are, strictly speaking) can do all that UFOs are reported to do, it ought to be the subject of a crash scientific program to study a major anomaly that poses various threats to our physical and psychological well being. Scientists who loosely advance the "natural phenomenon" idea clearly are unaware of the scope and nature of the hard-core UFO reports.

If UFOs are "none of the above," what does that leave? Stated concisely, it leaves "beings from elsewhere" . . . because the craft-like UFOs and humanoid beings are an integral part of the body of evidence that requires an explanation. The only remaining question, but one fraught with great implications for Humankind, is the location of "elsewhere."

The data strongly suggest that beings not of the known physical earth are interacting with us extensively, and sometimes intimately. We cannot rule out the theoretical possibility that they come from some presently unknown realm, such as a parallel universe impinging on our reality in some way; that they are space/time travellers (despite our inability to understand how that could be); or that they are puppets or androids manipulated by some Superintelligence that itself might take a totally non-human form.

Veteran UFOlogist Ted Bloecher, who has studied UFO humanoid reports intensively, has suggested (perhaps more than half seriously) that UFOs come "from behind the scenery." His concept neatly describes the possible alternative to straight "nuts and bolts" visitors from another planet. In my present view, the more exotic alternatives to "nuts and bolts" are not necessary in order to fit UFO phenomena into a conceptual scheme that could account for all reliably reported data.

Unless the presumed intelligence behind the phenomena chooses to provide the necessary evidence, the alternatives are essentially untestable and therefore, in the scientific sense, meaningless. The ETH itself is not easily testable, but it is testable in principle because our space probes and increasingly sophisticated sensors in earth satellites could conceivably find evidence of extraterrestrial life entering or leaving our solar system, or the lack of evidence, if systematically applied in search of UFOs.

Assumptions about what extraterrestrials must be like tend to creep, unrecognized, into the reasoning of those who claim the ETH is inadequate. They begin assuming — unjustifiably — what purposes or intentions extraterrestrials must have, how they ought to behave in order to be recognizable to us as extraterrestrials, and what their galactic timetable must be. They tend to make the same assumptions as the skeptical scientists, but they still view the data as valid and so look elsewhere for the answer. Furthermore, they probably accept more of the full spectrum of everything reported as being more or less equally valid, substantiated data. If they are right in this latter assumption, then they may also be right in doubting the validity of the ETH.

Leaving aside the question of which data can be accepted, their arguments against the ETH otherwise are weak. To scientifically advanced extraterrestrials, 40 years may be only a cosmic eyeblink. Their "baffling" (to us) behavior could be simply evidences of an advanced technology operating on principles presently unknown to us, which Arthur C. Clarke has suggested would appear indistinguishable from magic.

When the UFO beings fail to behave according to the standards we have set for them, these UFOlogists become impatient and begin doubting that they could be "nuts and bolts" extraterrestrials. They then start imagining that something more bizarre must be involved. Although it is frustrating not to have the answers, it is fallacious to conclude that no answers are possible unless we invoke more exotic explanations. There are no shortcuts to science.

The leap to exotic theories displays a naive belief that present scientific concepts should be able to supply the answers at once; indeed, that science has tried and failed, when in fact scientists have been reluctant to study UFOs at all. Clearly there is a scientific vacuum that laymen are trying to fill, but they often lack the disciplined reasoning that scientists could apply to the problem.

The American philosopher William James, talking about "exceptional observations" that science tends to ignore, could have been applying the following words to the UFO problem today:

> "When once they [the exceptional observations] are indisputably ascertained and admitted, the academic and critical minds are by far the best fitted ones to interpret and discuss them ... but on the other hand if there is anything which history demonstrates, it is the extreme slowness with which the ordinary academic and critical mind acknowledges facts to exist which present themselves as wild facts, with no stall or pigeon-hole, or as facts which threaten to break up the accepted system. ..."
>
> (In *The Will to Believe.*)

UFO data are "wild facts" that fit no accepted "pigeon-hole," and have the potential of revolutionizing the accepted system of science, and therefore scientists have been extremely slow to accept the exceptional observations. The pinch-hitting laymen, however, may accept too much too readily, and in some cases lack the needed critical skills.

What do we expect to see if and when extraterrestrials come visiting? Our preconceptions on this point are worth exploring. Little thought seems to have been given to how confusing actual confrontation by an alien culture probably would be. An anthropologist on a UFO panel in the 1960s used the analogy of the North American Indians when the first Europeans arrived:

> "Had there been some kind of Indian CIA collecting and analyzing all reports of European contacts,

it is likely the Indians would have been just as confused about European intentions as they actually seem
to have been. They lacked the scientific, technical and
geographical knowledge necessary for interpretation
of the contacts and could never have guessed at the
motivation behind the exploration and colonization
activity .... . The types of vessels, clothing, equipment and behavior of the crews, their places of appearance and the routes they followed would not
have been susceptible to analysis to a large extent.
So it may be with UFOs and their occupants."

According to Washington Irving in his comprehensive bio-
graphy of Columbus, the Caribbean natives, after witnessing
the arrival of the Spanish ships over the horizon, believed that
the Spaniards were gods who had descended from the skies
and treated them with reverence.

Dr. James E. McDonald used a similar analogy while addressing a seminar of the United Aircraft Research Laboratories,
Connecticut, in 1968. Imagine, he suggested, the bafflement
of Solomon Island natives in World War II with — until then
— only shadowy contact with 20th Century industrial-scientific
technology, suddenly witness to a 1942 amphibious invasion.
How could their Stone Age minds encompass the arrival of
enormous ships of all shapes, unleashing fire, smoke, and
explosions, followed by emergence of smaller ships onto
the beach, in turn disgorging a bewildering variety of men
and equipment:

"Imagine his puzzlement to then see dozens of
aircraft move over, drop bombs, strafe, and engage
in intricate air combat with still other aircraft .... .
We may be like the Solomon Island Stoneager relative
to the bewildering variety and number of UFOs that
seem to be credibly reported as operating in our environment. We cannot understand how any society
could produce such devices, accomplish such feats,

display as many craft of such unprecedented performance characteristics, and do things that to us border
on the miraculous."

That the bafflement might work both ways is something we
tend to overlook. UFOlogist Isabel Davis suggested in 1969:

". . . the extraterrestrials, despite their visits and
their observation, may still be as baffled about our
behavior as we continue to be about theirs."

Why do we automatically assume that extraterrestrials would
be all-knowing just because they are technologically advanced
over us? If their technology has evolved on totally different
lines than ours, our "primitive" piston and jet engines and
rockets could be baffling to them (which might account for
their fascination with our vehicles). At any rate, evolutionary
differences easily could account for our bafflement . . . and
the arguments could cut both ways.

If extraterrestrials long ago learned some means of tap-
ping energy other than the food cycle and fossil fuels (perhaps
cosmic rays or gravity control), or have undergone a different
physiological evolution leading to other forms of locomotion
and communication mechanisms, these alone could cause their
appearance and behavior to seem inexplicable to us. We tend
to take our evolutionary and cultural fundamentals for granted,
as the "norm," but there is no reason to suppose that extraterrestrial evolution and technology would be parallel, much less
so similar as to be readily identifiable and understandable.

Some possible characteristics (as opposed to motives) of
extraterrestrials serve to illustrate why their actions might be
difficult to fathom:

• Scientific/technological differences. They may utilize energy sources and technological applications
  unknown to our science.

- Mental/psychological differences. They may have highly evolved brains or even psychic abilities unlike anything in our experiece.
- Cultural/philosophical differences. They may adhere to cultural values and beliefs totally unknown to us.
- Multiple origins. They may be coming from several different civilizations or represent different factions of a polyglot society, thus multiplying the effects of each of the previous factors.

These very likely possibilities, singly or in concert, would pose serious barriers to easy and immediate communication and mutual understanding. To assume they are very much like us in all these respects is, again, to make Man the center of the universe; the standard to which all things must conform.

The critical question bearing on the possibility of meaningful contact could be the relative intelligence level; the degree to which they (presumably) have a superior understanding of how to control and use natural forces. If the difference is large, communication and contact that would be understandable to us might not even be possible. They might not be able to find, by their standards, intelligent life on earth; only odd creatures who seem intent on fouling their own nests with dangerous waste products.

We interact with prairie dogs, who have a very "advanced" form of social organization and elaborate community life, but it is doubtful that we communicate anything to them, exchange ideas or culture with them.

Only recently have we begun to realize that the intelligence of bottle-nose dolphins (porpoises) and a few other "higher" mammals (as defined by us) may be close to our intelligence. We now think that it might be possible for us to communicate meaningfully with porpoises eventually, even to exchange cultural information, but it has not proved to be easy.

Participants in a 1965 symposium panel on "Communications With Extraterrestrial Intelligence," including Dr. John C.

Lilly of porpoise research fame, pointed out that the possibility of communication probably is a direct function of the relative intelligence levels.

Dr. William O. Davis, a former Air Force physicist involved in the UFO program, then employed by Huyck Corporation, said that verbal communication would be the least likely means of first contact because we would lack common cultural referents. The most likely visitors, he felt, would be beings of higher intelligence than ours. If they were at a similar level of intelligence, which he thought unlikely, they would be the most dangerous to us.

Higher level beings, Dr. Davis said, would realize that their contact with us would pose serious psychological problems for us. Therefore, they would try not to frighten us, instead taking steps to accustom us to their presence so that we would be relaxed and become prepared for communication. The burden of such contact, he felt, would be on the more highly intelligent beings who would be more likely to learn our languages and something about our culture before we did theirs.

In the case of the porpoises, we allegedly are the superior intellects with the advanced technology, and we have not yet succeeded in establishing meaningful communication.

The primitive Tasady tribe, discovered in 1971 in the Philippines and studied by anthropologists, apparently had no knowledge until then that highly technological cultures even existed. No doubt they still understand little of those outside cultures. Chance sightings of helicopters or aircraft may well cause Tasaday UFO reports. If we were to pull out and leave them alone, future generations of Tasaday probably would have legends about strange humanoid beings, oddly garbed and using wondrous machines, who contacted their ancestors.

If we are being examined by extraterrestrial anthropologists who are scientifically far advanced over us, we are not likely to understand their comings and goings, the technological means of it, their cultural values and beliefs, or their ultimate intentions. A cultural/technological gap, rather than a more exotic origin, could easily account for the baffling behavior and incomprehensible technology we are seeing.

The most troublesome question concerning the nature and extent of the postulated cultural/technological gap can be expressed in a ratio. Is it Western Culture: Tasaday? Humans: Porpoises? Humans: Prairie Dogs? Or even Humans: Ants? The answer to this question is likely to determine our entire future relationship to any visitors from the universe, whether they come from presently known or unknown realms.

Dr. McDonald's summation in the 1968 Congressional UFO Symposium is worth repeating, since it remains a valid observation today. The ETH, he said, does appear to be the one "most likely to prove correct." He added: "My scientific instincts lead me to hedge that prediction just to the extent of suggesting that if the UFOs are not of extramundane origin (i.e., not extraterrestrial surveillance devices), then I suspect that they will prove to be something very much more bizarre, something of perhaps even greater scientific interest than extraterrestrial devices."

BIBLIOGRAPHY

Davis, Isabel. "Extraterrestrials: Suggested Motives and Origin," *UFOs: A New Look* (Washington, D.C.: NICAP, 1969).

Hall, Richard H. *The UFO Evidence* (Washington, D.C.: NICAP, 1964). 1904 *U.S.S. Supply* sighting of maneuvering UFOs in formation, p. 13.

Irving, Washington. *Life and Voyages of Columbus*, v.I (N.Y.: G. P. Putnam, 1859).

McDonald, James E. "Science, Technology, and UFOs." Talk presented January 26, 1968, at a General Seminar of the United Aircraft Research Laboratories, East Hartford, Conn. Solomon Islanders analogy.

———. "UFOs: An International Scientific Problem." Talk presented March 12, 1968, at the Astronautics Symposium, Canadian Aeronautics and Space Institute, Montreal, Canada. Includes critique of Klass's "plasmoid" UFO theory.

NICAP. "Scientists Discuss Space Communications." *U.F.O. Investigator*, v. III, no. 4, Aug.-Sept., 1965. Summary of panel discussion on "Communications With Extraterrestrial Intelligence" held at 1965 Conference on Military Electronics, Sept. 22-24, Washington, D.C. Proceedings were published by the Institute of Electrical and Electronics Engineers.

_____. "NICAP Panel Studies Occupant Reports." *U.F.O. Investigator*, v. V, no. 1, Sept.-Oct. 1969. Anthropologist's comments on North American Indians' reaction to European contact.

"Tasaday Stone Age Tribe of Mindanao," *1973 Britannica Yearbook of Science and the Future*, Encyclopedia Britannica, Chicago, Ill.

CHAPTER 13

EXTRATERRESTRIAL PSYCHOLOGY

If we suppose that UFOs carry visitors from elsewhere (extraterrestrial intelligences, or ETIs for convenient shorthand), why are they here? Does the accumulated data provide any clues as to their interests or purposes? Seeking answers may be akin to tea-leaf reading, but we now have 40 years of descriptive information. If we analyze the circumstances of UFO sightings it might be possible to discern some patterns that reveal something about ETI psychology.

We know that the long history of visitation has produced little evidence of overt hostility. Some aircraft accidents and bothersome physiological effects could be evidence of accidental harm or of self-defense. Maybe the ETIs are to us as we are to ants, and if we interfere with their picnic they stomp on us. From the obvious high technology displayed it is possible to infer that if their goal were to destroy us or take us over, this could have been done long ago.

Watching UFO events over a period of decades, you get the feeling of a detached or long-term "program" of some sort that at times of UFO sighting waves seems about to reach a culmination, but never does. Sudden spurts of confrontational behavior and direct intercession in human activities, as if some final contact or communication were imminent, give way to long lull periods during which the waves are forgotten until next time. The waves usually are sufficiently spectacular to make international headlines, but do not penetrate our cultural

195

inertia to the point of upsetting the routines of society, or even to the point of stimulating a larger scale scientific study.

People react and internalize the events, maintaining a high awareness of UFOs as shown by Gallup polls, but governments do not. The few times that governments have reacted and initiated investigations, the inquiries have floundered in a sea of confusion about what to believe and how to go about a study. Busy scientists have half-heartedly looked at the subject and, noting its ebbs and flows, assumed it must have something to do with mass psychology.

Almost everyone knows about UFOs, and that they might be extraterrestrial in origin, but this is taken to be a popular belief rather than a serious theory justified by things seen. So society marches on undisturbed by the ghostly apparitions, through petroleum crises, Middle East war, crippled economies, and assorted forms of human violence and riots.

If the ETIs wanted to raise our consciousnesses without upsetting world governments, they couldn't adopt a better plan than the manner in which they have manifested themselves to us so far.

The major displays that constitute UFO waves (see *Table 6*) typically include episodes of blatant interactions with humans and their vehicles. This blatancy factor embedded in UFO waves alternates with periods in which UFO behavior seems more subtle, even furtive. During the lull periods when conventional news media lose interest in the subject, sighting information is difficult to obtain and is only slowly and painfully reconstructed by UFOlogists using their own limited resources. When the information is in, we learn that startling events have continued to occur but, for reasons unknown, they have not attracted the same degree of attention. Human reactions to UFO sightings perhaps are more cyclical than the sightings themselves.

As indicated in *Table 6*, each wave period has corresponded roughly to major historical events. A far more comprehensive study of such historical correlations is needed before too much significance is attached to them. Something about the nature of news reporting of crises and earth-shaking events may incidentally zero in on UFO reports. But a certain rationale for ETI interest in the rapidly exploding development of human aerospace technology also can be read into the apparent coincidences.

By repeated manifestations in specific contexts of human affairs, UFOs have shown apparent interest in —

- Vehicles

- Warfare

- Strategic technology

- Energy

- Human physiology

In addition to the vehicle encounter cases reported in chapters 1 and 2, some of the earliest significant UFO sightings on record involve aircraft and rocket pacings at such test ranges as White Sands Proving Grounds, New Mexico, and later at Cape Canaveral, Florida. The ETIs, it could be argued, have displayed curiosity about all forms of human propulsion, from piston engines to jets and rockets.

Every major war in modern times has included UFO sightings at the scene of combat. The "foo-fighters" of World War II were the first widely reported UFOs of the 20th Century.

William D. Leet, late Arkansas State Director for the Mutual UFO Network, was a bomber pilot during World War II. On a "lone wolf" bombing mission over Klagenfurt, Austria, November 24, 1944, he and his B-17 crew were on their bomb run when the plane suddenly was caught in a blinding light for 2-3 seconds, and Leet felt a sensation of heat. If it had been searchlights, the Germans would not have broken off contact. They completed the bomb run safely, encountering no flak, and turned to scurry back to their home airfield in Amendola, Italy.

All at once a round, amber light appeared off the left wing of the B-17, showing a perfectly circular outline, and paced alongside the plane for about 45 minutes before abruptly vanishing. During debriefing, Leet was informed that no searchlights were known to be at Klagenfurt. The intelligence officer suggested that the amber disc was a new German fighter or remote control device radioing position information to anti-aircraft guns, but Leet replied that the object did not fire on them, nor had they encountered any flak.

"Foo-fighters" also were seen in the Asian Theater. On August 10, 1944, Capt. Alvah M. Reida was piloting a B-29 on a bombing mission over Sumatra. After leaving the target area he and his crew saw an orange spherical object with a halo effect that paced off the starboard wing. Reida took evasive action, but the UFO followed every maneuver for about 8 minutes. "When it left," he said, "it made an abrupt 90 degree turn, up and accelerating rapidly."

Wayne Thomas, Jr., a former group intelligence officer for B-29's stationed on Tinian also has confirmed that "foo-fighter" reports were common in the Asian Theater. They would typically move along with the bombers for several minutes at a time before breaking off.

A number of very similar Korean War UFO sightings appear in the records of the Air Force Project Blue Book, now on microfilm in the National Archives. In Project Grudge Report No. 4 (Grudge was the immediate predecessor of Blue Book) is the following report:

"On the night of 29 January 1952, 30 miles WSW of Wonson, Korea, three members of a B-29 crew . . . observed a light orange colored sphere for a period of five minutes. The object was on a parallel course to the B-29 at 8 o'clock level. The color of the object was further described as being the color of the sun with an occasional bluish tint. The outer edge of the object appeared to be fuzzy and it seemed to have an internal churning movement like flames or fiery gases.

The object closed in on the B-29 to an undetermined
distance, and then faded away in the distance."

The bomber was at 22,500 feet in, CAVU weather (clear and
visibility unlimited) at 2300 hours local time. At 2324 hours,
another B-29 crew observed an identical object near Sunchon.

During his testimony at the 1968 Congressional UFO Symposium, Dr. Robert L. Hall recounted the following experience:

> "When I was on the faculty at the University
> of Minnesota, a student came to me, having heard
> that I had some interest in this question. He in-
> formed me that his father, a colonel, an artillery
> colonel in Korea . . . had flown over a hill in Korea
> in his observer plane, and found (right next to him
> virtually) a characteristic unidentified flying object
> with the usual kind of configuration. It had prompt-
> ly retreated upwards. It had frightened him, but he
> was an experienced and trained observer, so he took
> notes on it . . . . When he returned he was so ridi-
> culed and laughed at for a long period of time that
> he completely gave up trying to have this taken
> seriously. He refused to talk about it."

During October 1973 when UFOs were once again making headlines after a long lull, Gen. George S. Brown, Air Force Chief of
Staff, said at a press conference: "I don't know if this story has
ever been told, but UFOs plagued us in Vietnam during the war."
He cited an incident in early summer of 1968 when a series of
sightings set off "quite a battle (with) an Australian destroyer taking a hit," and another in 1969 that resulted in "some shooting."

A spectacular sighting occurred in June 1966 at Nha
Trang, an active base on the coastline of South Vietnam.
About 9:45 p.m. there was a flash of light and a UFO approached, descended in plain view of numerous soldiers, and
hovered a few hundred feet off the ground, its glow illuminating the entire area. The base generator failed and the base
was blacked out. Idling aircraft engines, bulldozers, trucks,

everything (including some diesel engines) failed for about 4 minutes. The UFO finally "went straight up" and rapidly disappeared from view.

Colonel Robert M. Tirman, an Air Force flight surgeon, was among those who observed a "huge" cylindrical UFO over southeast Asia on March 14, 1969. Tirman was a passenger on a KC-135 whose pilots and crew also saw the object. The cylinder hovered in a vertical orientation about 2 miles from the plane at about 15,000 feet altitude. When they tried to circle for a closer look, the UFO disappeared. Jet interceptors also were scrambled but could not locate the UFO.

STRATEGIC TECHNOLOGY

During large-scale NATO maneuvers ("Operation Mainbrace") in the North Sea in September 1952, UFOs were sighted for over a week by ships and aircraft of the fleet. Color photographs were taken from the deck of the U.S. aircraft carrier *Franklin D. Roosevelt* of an unidentified silvery spherical object moving at high speed. No technical analyses of the photographs or other sightings have ever been released.

Air Force and CIA documents obtained by lawyer Peter Gersten under the Freedom of Information Act reflect the fact that by the early 1950s the U.S. Government was concerned about the pattern of UFOs being sighted at strategic locations. (Gersten, reference A, bibliography)

On May 25, 1950, the Kirtland, New Mexico, district office of the Air Force Office of Special Investigations (OSI) reported a series of UFO sightings by scientists, pilots, security personnel, and others to the OSI Director, expressing concern about ". . . the continued occurrence of unexplained phenomena of this nature in the vicinity of sensitive installations . . . ."

In a memo dated December 2, 1952 (on the heels of the major UFO wave of that year) the CIA Assistant Director of Scientific Intelligence alerted CIA Director Walter B. Smith to the pattern of sightings at strategic locations: "Sightings of unexplained objects at great altitudes and travelling at high speeds in the vicinity of major U.S. defense installations are of such nature that they are not attributable to natural phenomena or known types of aerial vehicles."

During the 1952 wave, including the Washington, D.C., radar-visual sightings, Air Force intelligence had received a steady flow of reports from jet interceptor pilots who had been scrambled to chase unidentified objects detected by radar. Time after time the pilots obtained visual sightings of the UFOs, often locked onto them with airborne radar, but could not catch them. The UFOs sometimes played a cat-and-mouse game, fleeing just out of range of the fighter aircraft, then turning and following the plane as it returned to base.

Several times during the Washington, D.C., sightings interceptors were scrambled from Dover AFB, Delaware, and roared into the skies over Washington. Just as they arrived the UFOs would vanish off the radar scopes. Later research in the morgue of a Maryland eastern shore newspaper turned up references to UFOs showing up there, some 70 miles southeast of Washington, moments after they disappeared in Washington.

An exception was reported in one case when an F-94 pilot from Dover did intercept a group of UFOs when vectored to them by radarmen. A group of civilian and military aviation experts at National Airport watched on radar as the UFOs surrounded the F-94. The terrified pilot was heard on the intercom meekly asking permission to break off contact and return to base. His personal testimony, which has never been released, would make a fascinating addition to the record. What did he see and experience?

The eerie truth is that the UFOs have reacted differently to armed military interceptors than they have to civilian aircraft. In 1952 they literally followed airliners as they approached Washington Natonal Airport, sometimes hovering in plain sight of them. But they usually stayed out of the way of military jets, behaving almost as if testing their capabilities, or taunting them.

The CIA case files for 1952, once maintained by the Physics and Electronics Division, have never been released to the public. Do they contain reports of effects on the intercepting aircraft or other odd occurrences? In the widely publicized September 19, 1976, Iranian jet case, American-built F-4's were scrambled to chase UFOs which displayed an "inordinate amount of maneuverability." They also displayed an ability to defend themselves; when one F-4 pilot attempted to fire at a UFO, his weapons-control panel abruptly became "inoperable." Another pilot experienced total instrument failure as he closed in on a UFO. A Defense Intelligence Agency evaluation labelled this "an outstanding report."

These reports border on proof that the ETIs know what our weapons are, perhaps even know when we are getting ready to use them. Another indication of weapons awareness is the SAC base reports also belatedly known to the public through FOIA lawsuits. Quoting lawyer Peter Gersten (Reference B, bibliography):

> "DOD, USAF, and CIA documents reveal that during October, November, and December of 1975, reliable military personnel repeatedly sighted unconventional aerial objects in the vicinity of nuclear weapons storage areas, aircraft alert areas, and nuclear missile control facilities at Loring AFB, Maine; Wurtsmith AFB, Michigan; Malmstrom AFB, Montana; Minot AFB, North Dakota; and Canadian Air Forces Station, Ontario. Many of the sightings were confirmed by radar. At Loring AFB, the interloper 'demonstrated a clear intent on the weapons storage areas.' . . . . An Air Force document says that 'Security Option III' was implemented and that security measures were coordinated with 15 Air Force bases from Guam to Newfoundland."

Many other examples could be cited from UFO history to demonstrate an apparent pattern of the ETIs "watching" our technological development, especially our propulsion (delivery) capabilities, our actions in warfare, our nuclear technology ... and our reaching out into space. Wherever they come from, it may be that we are beginning to pose a threat to them because (a) we can now send space vehicles to the outer planets and beyond, (b) we are warlike, and (c) we have nuclear weapons.

TABLE 5
World-Wide Record of Successful Space Launches

[From Congressional Research Service report "Space Activities of the United States, Soviet Union, and Other Launching Countries: 1957-1986." Oct. 1987]

YEAR	USSR	US	CHINA	JAPAN	ESA	INDIA	FRANCE*	AUST.*	UK*	TOTAL
1957	2									2
1958	1	5								6
1959	3	10								13
1960	3	16								19
1961	6	29								35
1962	20	52								72
1963	17	38								55
1964	30	57								87
1965	48	63					1			112
1966	44	73					1			118
1967	66	58					2	1		127
1968	74	45								119
1969	70	40								110
1970	81	29	1	1			2			114
1971	83	32	1	2			1		1	120
1972	74	31		1						106
1973	86	23								109
1974	81	24		1						106
1975	89	28	3	2			3			125
1976	99	26	2	1						128
1977	98	24		2						124
1978	88	32	1	3						124
1979	87	16		2	1					106
1980	89	13		2		1				105
1981	98	18	1	3	2	1				123
1982	101	18	1	1						121
1983	98	22	1	3	2	1				127

con't

YEAR	USSR	US	CHINA	JAPAN	ESA	INDIA	FRANCE*	AUST.*	UK*	TOTAL
1984	97	22	3	3	4					129
1985	97	17	1	2	3					120
1986	91	6	2	2	2					103
Total	1,921	867	17	31	14	3	10	1	1	2,865

*Note that France, Australia and the United Kingdom no longer launch their own satellites. France and the UK are members of the European Space Agency (ESA) which built the Ariane launch vehicle whose first launch was in 1979.

Italy conducted eight launches from 1967 to 1975 using U.S. Scout rockets from the San Marco platform off the coast of Kenya. Since the launch vehicles were American, NASA includes them in U.S. launch statistics and they are treated the same way here.   Prepared by CRS.

As early as 1958 a Yale University social scientist, Dr. Harold D. Lasswell, in discussing space travel, suggested:

> "The implications of the unidentified flying objects (UFOs) may be that we are already viewed with suspicion by more advanced civilizations and that our attempts to gain a foothold elsewhere may be rebuffed as a threat to other systems of public order."

ENERGY

That ETIs would be interested in our sources and applications of energy follows logically from their interest in our strategic technology, but it is difficult to establish any clear correlation. My private studies convince me that an interest has been displayed in atomic energy facilities and petroleum-related activities. Map plottings show a significant concentration of sightings in New Mexico, counter to population trends. New Mexico is extraordinarily high in both strategic facilities and mineral production.

Another State with a significant number of close-range UFO sightings in comparison to its population (see *Table* 7) is Missouri. A separate study by Ted Phillips of 2,108 CE II physical trace cases shows that Missouri ranks third in number of such reports while ranking 13th in population. Missouri contains major aerospace activities, a leading weapons production facility, and is a significant producer of strategic metals and minerals. For the most part, as Table 7 illustrates, sighting frequency tends to reflect population.

Vehicle encounter cases, taken as a whole, could be interpreted as showing an interest in our uses of energy, what makes our vehicles tick. So can the numerous cases of aircraft and rocket pacings.

A possible progression of interest with time is intriguing, but remains only an intuition. During the 1940s and 1950s UFOs were particularly observed around aircraft and rockets. During the 1960s automobile encounter cases came to the fore. Also during the 1960s, when our space program reached the stage of lunar rockets and deep space probes, major waves of UFO sightings occurred after a lull of 7 years. Then, in the 1970s, the "petroleum connection" began to emerge.

It was almost as if the ETIs gradually figured out the motive power of our vehicles, monitoring the sites of advanced propulsion technology (White Sands, Cape Canaveral), checking our energy resources, and tracing our peculiar dependence on fossil fuels to the U.S. oil fields of the West and Southwest (e.g., Levelland and Damon, Texas sightings), and to the Arab nations of the Middle East. Whether a similar pattern has evolved in other countries is unknown.

At any rate, the 1973 UFO wave coincided with the OPEC embargo and the beginning of the U.S. petroleum supply crisis, and the 1978 Eastern Hemisphere wave (largely unreported in the U.S.) was focused in the oil-rich Arab nations. Was this only coincidence?

A series of UFO sightings occurred in Kuwait starting on November 9, 1978. As reported by P. G. Jacob, a marine biologist employed by the Kuwait Institute for Scientific

Research, "All the sightings occurred in the oil fields of Kuwait Oil Company, the major oil producing concern in Kuwait." The final sighting was November 21 over the Al Sabriyah oil field near the Iraqui border, and the UFO was photographed as it flew over a 20-foot water tower and hovered in the area for 30 minutes.

At one point Kuwait Oil Company technicians observed the landing and take-off of a soundless domed UFO which had a flashing red body light. Telecommunications were interrupted during the sighting, and an electrically operated oil pumping station near the landing site ceased to function. Similar E-M effects were noted during the other sightings.

From November 1978 through January 1979, UFOs were seen and photographed from several Arab nations over a wide area near the Persian Gulf coast opposite Iran. During the same time frame there were widespread sightings in Australia and New Zealand, including the famous New Zealand movie films taken from an aircraft in December. The movies received international news media attention, but the Arab oil field sightings and landing did not, at least not in the United States.

Early in 1979 a UFO landing also was reported at a major Argentine oil field. On May 1, engineers of the YPF government oil fields at Vizcacheras, in a remote area accessible only to company employees, were awakened at 4:00 a.m. from the noise made by goats in a corral. When they went outside to investigate, they saw a UFO hovering silently about 70 meters from the encampment and 20 meters above the ground. They waved a lantern and the UFO seemed to respond by blinking a light, then slowly landed nearby. More light signals were exchanged, then the UFO took off and disappeared toward the Andes mountains at 4:35 a.m.

The group went to inspect the landing spot and found a large circle in which the sand had been petrified or hardened into chunks. Soil samples were taken to a Professor Corradi for analysis. Corradi, identified as Director of the Institute for Extrahuman Studies, said the samples were being analyzed by the Office of Mining. He noted that after the sighting, the goats (about 1,500) refused to return to their corral.

Corradi also noted a strategic connection that other South American investigators have commented upon in the past:

> "I have been noticing for some time that the permanent presence of the UFOs over the uranium mines of La Pintada and Cuesta de los Terneros in San Rafael and now in Vizcacheras, is not a coincidence."

Earlier, on March 10, 1977, crew members of two oil tankers anchored a mile apart in the offshore Arjuna oil field of Indonesia at 7:40 p.m. saw a large dark object with a red body light, and emitting yellowish-white beams of light. The UFO approached from the west beneath a 1,000 foot cloud cover, circled the oil field twice, and flew away to the east.

The "petroleum connection" may or may not be significant. The possibility exists that the ETIs have been conducting a broad survey of human technology that, among other things, has touched on petroleum as well as other energy-related factors. The survey might be of such broad scope, so comprehensive, that no particular pattern would emerge from our large-scale data analysis and UFO sightings would correlate with almost everything under the sun. But if the skeptical assumption is made, no science is done and we are left only with speculation. The effort to seek out such patterns in the data seems well worthwhile.

Meanwhile, the attempt to analyze extraterrestrial psychology remains a speculative art that necessarily involves critical assumptions at various points. The scenario presented here amounts to an educated guess and a survey of reasonable possibilities. We are not likely to have any final answers until the full resources of science are applied to the problem . . . or the ETIs reveal their purposes.

TABLE 6
UFO Displays and World History

1939-1946: World War II; German rocket and jet technology advances; Bikini atoll atomic tests; Hiroshima and Nagasaki A-bombs, 1945-46.

1944-46: UFOs ("foo-fighters") observed by Allied and Axis pilots.

1947: V-2 and other rocket/missile tests; Nevada A-bomb tests; flight of X-1, first supersonic aircraft.

1947: First major wave of UFO sightings in U.S. initially focused in Northwest.

June 25, 1950-July 26, 1953: Korean War; first American H-bomb detonated Nov. 1, 1952.

1952: Major UFO wave June-December, including radar-visual, pilot sightings, jet interceptor chase cases; September NATO sightings during North Sea maneuvers.

1954: Bikini atoll H-bomb test March 1 injures Japanese fishermen with radioactive fallout; height of Cold War struggle over fate of Germany; maturation of ICBMs due to improved inertial guidance systems; Algerian War begins, Nov. 1.

1954: Major UFO sighting wave September-October, primarily in Europe, including numerous humanoid sightings for first time.

1957: British H-bomb test May 15 at Christmas Island; first Soviet ICBM successfully launched Aug. 26; Sputnik I, first earth satellite launch, Oct. 4; Sputnik II (carrying dog) launched Nov. 3

1957: Major UFO wave October-December, primarily focused in southwest and midwest United States.

October 1958-September 1961: Moratorium by major powers on further nuclear testing; Sept.-Oct. 1959 Soviet lunar flights, including Lunik II impact on Moon, Sept. 13; Soviet Venus probe launched Feb. 12, 1961; Soviet nuclear testing resumed Aug. 29, 1961.

Apr. 12, 1961-June 16, 1963: First manned Earth-orbital flights, 12 in 26 months; British and American nuclear testing resumed Feb. 7, 1962; Ranger IV impacts on Moon Apr. 26, 1962; Mariner 2 Venus probe launched Aug. 27, 1962; American-Cuban crisis Sept.-Nov. 1962.

Fall 1963: Nuclear test ban treaty signed Aug. 5; President John F. Kennedy assassinated Nov. 22.

1959-1963: Significant lull period in reported UFO sightings.

1964-67: Lunar landings and deep space probes; multiple-manned Earth-orbital flights, 13 between Oct. 1964 and Apr. 1967; Middle East war; height of U.S. involvement in Vietnam War.

1964: Ranger VII impacts on Moon July 31; Communist Chinese explode nuclear bomb for first time Oct. 16; Mariner 4 Mars probe launched Nov. 28.

1965: Ranger VIII launched Feb. 17 for lunar impact; Ranger IX launched Mar. 21 for lunar impact; Soviet Venus probe launched Nov. 12.

1966: Soviet Union first successful lunar "soft landing" Feb. 3; Soviet probe impacts on Venus Mar. 1; Soviet Luna 10 Placed in lunar orbit March 31; Chinese H-bomb detonated May 9; Surveyor 1 launched May 30, lunar landing; Soviet Luna 1 3 Moon landing Dec. 24.

1967: Surveyor 3 Moon landing Apr. 19; third Israeli-Arab war begins June 5; Soviet Venera 4 launched, "soft landing" on Venus; Mariner 5 passes near Venus Oct. 19.

1964-67: Renewal of UFO sightings after 7-year lull; largest volume sighting wave in UFO history 1966-67; Congressional hearings and Colorado UFO Project formed, 1966.

August 24, 1968: First French H-bomb test.

July 20, 1969: U.S. lands men on Moon.

1973: OPEC oil embargo, petroleum crisis and political turmoil in U.S., Agnew resignation; Israeli-Arab war Oct. 6-21.

1973: Major UFO wave October-November after 4-5 year lull, featuring numerous humanoid sightings and Hickson-Parker abduction.

1978: Continuing Middle East crises, petroleum shortage, OPEC price rises.

1978: Sighting wave October-December in Middle East and Australasia (little publicized in U.S.), including Arab Nation sightings and oil field landing.

(Sources: NASA Space Activities Summaries, 1960s; "Chronology of Major European Events," Univ. of S. Carolina, Feb. 8, 1978; *Encyclopedia Britannica*, 1969, atomic energy and space exploration entries)

TABLE 7
Top 10 States reporting
UFO close encounters vs. population
(Based on 379 CE II and CE III cases through 1967)

SIGHTING RANK/STATE
(Population Rank, 1970 Census)

1. California (1)
2. Ohio (6)
3. New York (2)
4. Pennsylvania (3)
5. Texas (4)

6. Illinois (5)
7. New Mexico (37)
8. Indiana (11)
9. Missouri (13)*
10. Florida (9)

*In a study by Ted Phillips (see Bibliography) analyzing 2,108 CE-II physical trace cases through 1981, Missouri ranked 3rd in case frequency vs. 13th in population.

BIBLIOGRAPHY

"Argentine Oil Field Landing" (excerpts from *Radiolanda 2000* magazine, May 25, 1979, Buenos Aires). *MUFON UFO Journal*, No. 139, Sept. 1979.

Brown, Gen. George S. Quoted by UPI (Chicago) about Vietnam War UFO sightings. Washington *Star-News*, Oct. 17, 1973.

Fawcett, Lawrence and Greenwood, Barry J. *Clear Intent: The Government Coverup of the UFO Experience* (N.J.: Prentice-Hall, 1984). SAC base UFO sightings.

Gersten, Peter. (A) "What the Government Would Know About UFOs If They Read Their Own Documents," *1981 MUFON UFO Symposium Proceedings* (Seguin, Tex.: MUFON, 1981). Includes Sept. 19, 1976 Iranian jet case.

_____. (B) "What the U.S. Government Knows About Unidentified Flying Objects," *Frontiers of Science*, v. III, no. 4, May-June 1981.

Hall, Richard H. *The UFO Evidence* (Washington, D.C.: NICAP, 1964). Reida "foo-fighter" report (p. 23); Thomas "foo-fighters" letter (p. 26); 1952 Washington, D.C. sightings (p. 159); 1952 NATO sightings (p. 162).

_____. "UFOs in Arab Nations, "MUFON UFO Journal, No. 133, Jan.-Feb., 1979. See also Arab Times, Nov. 23, 25, 1978; Dec. 5, 10, 1978; Jan. 20, 21, 24, 1979; Kuwait Times, Nov. 16, 18, 1978.

Hall, Robert L. Statement to House Science and Astronautics Committee, Symposium on Unidentified Flying Objects, July 29, 1968, pp. 103-104.

International UFO Reporter, v. 3, no. 2, Feb. 1978 (Center for UFO Studies, Evanston, Ill.) Indonesian oil field case, reported to CUFOS by an Indonesian Air Force officer.

Lasswell, Harold D. "Men In Space," Annals of the New York Academy of Sciences, v. 72, art. 4, Apr. 10, 1958.

Leet, William D. "The Flying Fortress and the Foo-Fighter," MUFON UFO Journal, No. 133, Jan.-Feb., 1979.

Maccabee, Bruce S. "Photometric Properties of an Unidentified Bright Object Seen Off the Coast of New Zealand," Applied Optics, v. 18, no. 15, Aug. 1, 1979; comments (v. 18, no. 23) and author's reply (v. 19, no. 11). Dec. 31, 1978 movie film of UFO taken from aircraft.

Phillips, Ted R. "Close Encounters of the Second Kind: Physical Traces," 1981 MUFON UFO Symposium Proceedings (Seguin, Tex.: MUFON, 1981).

Sinclair, Ward and Harris, Art. "What Were Those Mysterious Craft?" Washington Post, Jan. 19, 1979. SAC base UFO intrusions, 1975, and Iranian jet case, 1976.

Tirman, Col. Robert. Report of southeast Asia UFO sighting taken from Jacksonville Daily News, Arkansas, Mar. 27, 1969. Details confirmed in interview by Dr. James E. McDonald.

CHAPTER 14

IS THE MEDIUM
THE MESSAGE?

One of the salient features of the ongoing UFO mystery is the wave phenomenon: the sporadic outbursts of sightings with lull periods in between. Are waves "real"? Do UFOs actually put on spurts of activity and then "go away" for years at a time, or is something else involved?

The experience of living through and participating in study of every modern UFO wave since the first in 1947 convinces me of one thing: a UFO wave probably is 60% reflective of a real upswing in sightings and 40% reflective of periodic reawakenings by news media when one or more spectacular "trigger" cases capture their imagination.

After-the-fact studies have shown in most cases that an increase in sightings had already begun well before the first headlines appeared. The penchant of newsmen for sensation could explain why early-wave sightings tend to remain "local news," until something sufficiently spectacular occurs that is then deemed "national news" and appears in wire service stories and network TV broadcasts. Unfortunately, it takes a steady diet of sensation for something to remain "national news" for very long. After a while one UFO sighting is pretty much like another, so the publicity "flap" component of the wave fades away. The sightings, however, do not.

Air Force intelligence reports had been showing a very unusual sequence of events early in 1952, with cat-and-mouse jet interceptor cases and military installation sightings, well

213

before the July "invasion" of the Nation's Capital. When UFOs intrude in the restricted Washington air spaces, are tracked on radar, and lead jets a merry chase, that is sensational. The result was national headlines and a major Air Force press conference (reputed to be the largest since World War II) to "calm the waters."

The 1957 wave broke on November 23 with Army jeep patrol sightings at White Sands, New Mexico, and multiple sightings in Levelland, Texas, of large, red, elliptical objects landed on roads and reports of electromagnetic failures in vehicles that came upon them. The reporting was sustained for about two weeks because of continuing E-M reports from credible witnesses across the country, but faded away thereafter. The sightings actually had begun increasing about June.

The April 24, 1964, Socorro, New Mexico, landing witnessed by Officer Lonnie Zamora clearly triggered national news media attention . . . a cop of good reputation, imprints and scorch marks found at the site . . . but Air Force and private UFO group records contain a large number of substantial UFO reports throughout the latter half of 1963 and early 1964.

A particularly striking example of the wave/publicity "flap" interface occurred while I was Assistant Director of the National Investigations Committee on Aerial Phenomena (NICAP), then the largest and most effective UFO group. Through our grass roots national "intelligence" network of field investigators and reporters, we had been well aware of a steady build-up of sightings throughout 1965, but it took the Michigan sightings of March 1966 (patrol cars buzzed, landed object glowing in woods) to trigger major news media interest.

The public perception of UFO waves, therefore, is more a function of the nature of news reporting than an accurate reading of what is really happening. The concept of what constitutes "news" definitely is part of the problem. UFO news reporting has been, by a large margin, more reactive (reporting only the spectacular and citing opinions of "authorities") than investigative. Old-fashioned reporters would dig for a story, but modern news reporting has become so mechanized and homogenized that the news media offer little hope of contributing significantly to a resolution of the UFO problem.

Another lesson learned was that during the so-called lull periods (and there *have* been low points of UFO sightings, notably from 1959 into 1963), a steady flow of substantial cases occur that, for reasons which are not clear, do not strike any sparks. The lull period reports contain all of the same features, but occur with lesser frequency. Many, in retrospect, are just as "spectacular" and convincing as the more famous trigger cases.

The fact of having a central clearinghouse for receiving UFO reports makes a big difference in the perception of UFO activity. I distinctly recall feeling slightly schizophrenic during the 1960s because of the disparity between what the NICAP network was funneling to me and what was being reported in major news media.

If it were possible to screen out poor UFO reports generated by news media coverage, or conversely to compute a loading factor for lull periods when the press is not paying attention, the graphic peaks of UFO waves probably would be blunted but not removed. UFO sightings do not occur at a uniform pace over the years, creating a straight-line graph; but neither do they totally disappear for long periods of time (as you might believe if your only information source was conventional news media) and then suddenly reappear in hordes. The truth lies somewhere in between. The waves of 1947, 1952, 1954, 1957, 1966-67, and 1973 all were real in the sense of representing a distinct increase in sightings, and sometimes in the character of the sightings.

The airborne close encounters by military jets that characterized the 1952 wave had not happened before, at least with the same frequency or intensity. The first widespread humanoid sightings accompanied the 1954 wave. The 1957 wave included humanoid reports, and E-M effects were first widely reported then. Automobile encounter cases seemed to surge in the 1960s and abduction reports in the 1970s. Whether this represents some progression of activities by the ETIs is unknown, but one or more new features or intensification of features seems to emerge with each wave.

A common aspect of each wave is some obvious overt behavior on the part of UFOs that attracts attention to the reports; the sensation factor that triggers publicity. In 1952 it was the brazen violation of restricted air spaces over Washington, D.C., radar tracking, and the aerial encounters. In 1954, it was humanoid beings boldly showing themselves to or accosting citizens; "flashing," as it were. Rare mass landings on the streets of a Texas oil town, Levelland, and sightings at or near New Mexico military installations stimulated press coverage of the 1957 wave, as did the "technological" feature of E-M effects.

Concentrated sightings, car-buzzings, and landings in Hillsdale and Dexter, Michigan, in 1966 first captured the attention of LIFE magazine, newswire services, and network TV news. A UFO landed in woods at Dexter, and sat there pulsating as sheriffs and curious citizens surrounded it. A major case of the 1973 wave that attracted national interest was the October 11 "abduction" of Charles Hickson and Calvin Parker from their riverside fishing site in Pascagoula, Mississippi, onto a hovering UFO where they were examined by an X-ray-like device. Another was the October 18 confrontation of the Army Reserve helicopter by a structured UFO over Ohio; the UFO hovered near the helicopter, shone a green beam of light into the cabin, and affected the controls of the helicopter.

Do the ETIs have such a sophisticated understanding of human psychology that they know how to capture attention when they want to? Or what do such blatant displays mean? One suggestion is that it might be some form of consciousness-raising, perhaps in preparation for overt contact. If the ETIs are non-humanoid in appearance and would be frightening by our standards, then maybe they are staging humanoid appearances while displaying essentially benign behavior, gradually getting us used to the idea that they are

here . . . and that intelligence comes in other forms than purely human physiognomy.

Overall, it is difficult to escape the impression that the
ETIs are trying to "tell us something" when they perform
such demonstrations as confronting our vehicles, inducing
E-M effects, lifting vehicles off the ground, landing en masse
at Levelland, buzzing over the U.S. Capital, and playing games
with military jets. Maybe the medium is the message, and
the answers lie in interpreting the nonverbal communication
inherent in the displays. In his report on a microcosmic UFO
wave in the Uintah Basin of Utah, biological scientist Frank
Salisbury observes:

> "I, and some of the witnesses as well, couldn't
> help but be impressed with the idea that the UFOs
> *wanted* to be seen. Otherwise, why should they dive
> on Joe Ann Harris, follow Thyrena Daniels and many
> other cars, dance around in full view of dozens of
> witnesses for fairly long intervals of time, etc? Why
> indeed should they execute the intricate and involved
> maneuvers? Why do their lights flash or change col-
> or? It is as though they were *putting on a display.*"
> (Original author's emphasis.)

The Utah sightings were primarily concentrated in 1966 and
1967, coinciding with the major UFO wave then in progress
all over the country. This particular wave featured a large
number of "Here-I-Am" cases, with UFOs flaunting themselves
before witnesses as if to call attention to themselves. When
a UFO rose up out of the woods on April 17, 1966, in Ravenna, Ohio, and illuminated the ground around two stunned deputy sheriffs, it set off a chain of events that reached the halls
of Congress.

Deputies Dale Spaur and Barney Neff, on orders from the
dispatcher, began following the UFO as it moved over the
highway, and soon were involved in a cat-and-mouse game
and a high-speed chase across the Ohio border and into Penn-

sylvania, joined by other police witnesses. When the Air Force insisted that the officers had been fooled by the planet Venus and a satellite (neither of which illuminates roadways!), their Congressman and a former Congressman from the district protested vehemently and pressured the Air Force into a re-investigation. The case also added fuel to the fire of internal Air Force reform of its UFO investigation program, leading to the University of Colorado UFO Project established that Fall.

Spaur and Neff were confronted at close range by a structured UFO beaming a brilliant light onto the ground which then led them on a cat-and-mouse chase. Such confrontations typically disrupt the normal affairs of the witnesses and abruptly call their attention to manifestly unconventional and highly maneuverable objects totally alien to their experience.

The cat-and-mouse behavior calls the witnesses attention to the fact that they are dealing with some hidden intelligence, something or someone that reacts to their actions, flees (almost playfully at times) when pursued, reverses course to re-engage the outdistanced pursuers, and more often than not finally departs the scene with a spectacular burst of speed (demonstrating enormous power). Often the departure is vertically upwards, and the UFO dwindles in apparent size to a pinpoint of light or merges into the star field background at night.

The behavior is sometimes reminiscent of porpoises playing around a boat, but at other times the apparitions are menacing. Sometimes the UFO "rattles the cage" of the trapped, frightened human animal or holds him at bay for a while, then tires of the game (or completes the "mission") and departs as abruptly as it appeared.

The salient feature of the confrontations is that one or more humans are, in effect, isolated and manipulated while virtual captives of the forces behind UFOs. A strong element of directedness appears in case after case: the UFO approaches a particular witness or vehicle, interferes with or stops it, interacts sometimes briefly and sometimes for a considerable period of time, and then departs, usually leaving behind a thoroughly shaken witness. On some occasions the UFO abruptly comes directly toward the witnesses and hovers in plain view, but quickly breaks off the encounter and departs after no — or minimal — interaction. Otherwise, the same directedness is evident in the manner of approach.

In the early morning of December 20, 1958, Officers LeRoy A. Arboreen and B. Talada of the Dunellen, N.J., police department were on night patrol, cruising in a slightly elevated area commanding a good view of the surroundings. A glowing red object suddenly approached them from the west, attaining a large apparent size in a matter of seconds. It stopped abruptly and hovered in plain view showing a distinct elliptical shape pulsating with a red glow. Their official report on the incident concluded:

> "The object hovered for a few seconds, then made a left turn and again hovered for a few seconds, then went straight up like a shot. We watched it until it completely faded beyond the stars."

Perhaps their lone patrol car at close to 1:00 a.m. attracted the attention of the UFO, but at any rate its performance seemed to be directed at them. It was not something that just happened to fly past within their field of view.

Late in the evening of September 3, 1965, near Damon, Texas, Deputy Sheriffs Billy E. McCoy and Robert W. Goode had been observing an unexplained purplish light out over the prairie and trying to drive closer to it on some back roads. As they neared a pasture area and Goode slowed the car, a UFO suddenly rushed at them, stopping abruptly about 150 feet away and 100 feet off the ground. It appeared to be about 200 feet long and 40-50 feet thick, tapering toward the ends, flat on the bottom and slightly domed on top. A pulsating purple light flashed on one end and a blue light on the other end.

The purple light illuminated the interior of the car and the surrounding area; "... every blade of grass in the pasture stood out clearly," they said. The frightened officers fled.

Looking back, they saw the UFO shoot upwards at high speed and disappear.

Again, for whatever reason, the UFO seemed to be directed at the particular witnesses or their vehicle. However, here we have the same problem of interpretation if we think in terms of the ETH; by 1958 and surely by 1965, what reason would there be for ETIs — after countless vehicle encounters — to be curious about another vehicle? Most likely it has nothing to do with "curiosity," but instead with a display or demonstration of . . . something.

If the ultimate purpose is open contact and communication, whether to establish cultural interchange or to take over, then it is possible to imagine an elaborate scheme of preparation. The scheme would include general background study of what makes human beings and human societies tick. The results of individual human studies are fed back to help determine what steps to take (appropriate displays) to raise human consciousness, individually or collectively, to pave the way for ultimate contact. The overall appearances and displays, meanwhile, are kept to a level of unobtrusiveness that prevents panic and disruption of human society.

The various methods used to achieve the desired end might include, on one extreme, preparing or programming individuals who are appropriate for this purpose or susceptible to its techniques (abductions and confrontations), and on the other extreme, increasing awareness of social groups in mutually reinforcing ways (waves, mass displays). Depending on their understanding of individual and social psychology, the ETIs could also be experimenting with various techniques to see which best suit their purposes.

National polls indicate that something over 100 million Americans think UFOs are real, and this generally means a belief in extraterrestrial visitation. In certain other countries (including Canada, England, France, and Japan) the awareness level also is very high, conservatively suggesting tens of millions of others around the world who tend to think we are being visited. Yet the governments of the world, judging by what they say and the way they react to UFO sightings and waves, do not think UFOs are real and they often profess to be annoyed by the "popular madness."

By 1978 a Gallup Poll showed that a clear majority of Americans (57%) accepted UFOs as real; comparable figures are not available for other countries. The results indicate that believers increase in direct proportion to level of education. Of respondents with a college education, 66% accepted UFOs as real. The acceptance level overall also has increased from 46% in 1966 to 57% in 1978, a growth rate of approximately 1% of the total population per year.*

Considering the lack of official recognition of UFOs in these years and the lack of positive publicity about them in major news media, the reasons for the steadily growing belief in UFOs are unclear. The basic reason may well be that the ETIs are succeeding in their consciousness-raising master plan. But at what point would the hypothetical master plan be completed? When 75% of the people accept them? 90%?

An interesting study would be to determine through surveys what it took to persuade present "believers" that UFOs are real and what it would take to persuade "disbelievers" and the uncommitted. To what extent have personal sightings, sightings by trusted friends or certain types of witnesses, or readings been the determining factor? What have been the sources — and types — of information for people whose beliefs changed to positive from skeptical or uncommitted?

Since we have little evidence of direct communication from the ETIs, we must look to possible nonverbal communication or demonstration of key ideas that they may wish to convey to us. Some of the repetitive behavior (e.g., car-buzzings,

---

*Since this was written, a new Gallup poll was released on Mar. 12, 1987, with the headline "Only One-Third of Public Deny Existence of UFOs, Extraterrestrial Life." "Belief" in the existence of UFOs declined to 49%, but that belief remains ". . . substantially higher among persons who attended college . . .," and 9% of Americans (a fairly constant figure since 1973) report having sighted a UFO. As a nation, we remain divided about 50-50 on what to believe about UFOs.

sample gathering) could be designed to put across some message. So could the cumulated features of UFO sightings over the years, the recurring patterns and associations that can be found by analyzing the data. Presumably the ETI poll takers have some measure of how the master plan is progressing, though it is possible that we give them too much credit for their ability to figure us out.

As noted previously, the similarity or dissimilarity between the intelligence levels and technological sophistication of the ETIs and humans likely would be a critical factor in the possibility of meaningful communication and contact. If the intelligence/technology gap is great and our evolutions have been vastly different in terms of energy applications and environmental accommodations, chances are that we may baffle them by the very strangeness of our science and culture. It is no foregone conclusion that highly advanced ETIs would have an easy time figuring us out.

On the assumption that the ETIs have figured us out or are in the process of doing so, they could have made mistakes along the way ("Oops, that needle in the navel was not supposed to hurt"; "that plane got too close and we didn't mean to damage it"); and some cases involving burns or radiation could have been accidents.

Regardless, it at least makes sense to consider possible nonverbal communications that may be purposely included in UFO displays. Some of the possible messages are:

1. We can encounter or confront you at will and our technological superiority should be obvious to you. Let there be no doubt who is in control of the situation.

2. We are technological, not supernatural (structural features, physical traces . . .).

3. We are studying your physiology and human energy sources such as food and agriculture (Hill case, Wilcox case, soil and plant sample gathering . . .).

4. Some harm can come to you as side effects of our energy sources; be careful (physiological effect and injury cases).

5. We are studying your energy sources and applications, including military (E-M effects, blackouts, military installation sightings . . .).

6. Your understanding of natural laws is faulty and incomplete. Look what we can do, and think about it. (Levitation, mass displacement cases, E-M effects . . .).

7. We take many forms other than plainly humanoid to which you will have to become accustomed if you want to understand us (humanoid encounters, abductions . . .).

8. We want you to become aware of us gradually, but we don't want to destroy your society or create panic.

9. We are observing the political and military affairs of Earth to determine whether you will react with hostility toward us and whether peaceful contact is possible, or even desirable (sightings in combat areas, military interceptor encounters . . .).

The tremendous power displayed by UFOs implies that the ETIs have mastered energy applications in some way beyond our present understanding. Their behavior patterns also suggest that they probably are very different from us psychologically, even if they are roughly humanoid in form. This would mean that the UFO displays and encounters are a mutual learning experience, and mutual understanding will take time.

The persistence of the ETIs (unless they operate on a very different time scale) implies a strong interest in us and some ultimate purpose to the encounters. Whatever that purpose may be, it almost certainly will have a profound effect on Humankind for good or for ill. Considering the awesome power and "magical" abilities they have demonstrated, let us hope it is for good.

Exactly why 40 years of impressive human testimony and related instrumental and physical evidence has essentially escaped the attention of science constitutes a human mystery of major proportions. Human psychology may provide the explanation. Or maybe the explanation lies in ETI psychology.

We have two possibilities of obtaining meaningful answers about UFOs: One, if science wakes up to the problem and governments support thorough investigation; two, if the ETIs want to and are able to communicate them directly to us. Neither of these possibilities seems probable any time soon, so we are left to ponder a mystery that may determine the fate of Humankind.

We can at least examine what UFOs *might* mean and be a little better prepared for whatever the ETIs have in store for us. Then we will not be totally shocked or surprised when the presently shadowy reality of UFOs comes into daylight. The ultimate meaning of UFOs may be that human life is on the verge of beginning a new phase, a new maturity, perhaps a new relationship to the universe.

BIBLIOGRAPHY

Donderi, Don C. "The Effect of Conscious and Unconscious Attitudes About UFO Evidence on Scientific Acceptance of the Extraterrestrial Hypothesis," *Journal of UFO Studies*, v. 1, no. 1 (Evanston Ill: Center for UFO Studies, circa. 1979).

Friedman, Stanton T. "Do Americans Believe in UFOs?" *Second Look* (now *Frontiers of Science*), v. II, no. 3, Mar.-Apr. 1980. Discussion of Gallup polls and others.

Hall, Richard H. "1967: The Overlooked UFO Wave and The Colorado Project" in *1978 MUFON UFO Symposium Proceedings* (Seguin, Tex.: MUFON, 1978).

Salisbury, Frank B. *The Utah UFO Display* (Old Greenwich, Conn.: Devin-Adair, 1974).

APPENDIX A: CASE BOOK
A CROSS-SECTION
OF THE UFO MYSTERY

INDEX
(The case summaries are arranged chronologically)

ABDUCTION REPORTS
(see also "Humanoids")

ANIMAL REACTIONS

CAT-AND-MOUSE PURSUIT
(see also Keyhoe and Ruppelt references, Chapter 9 for
1951-1953 cases)

1948: Oct. 15, Japan.

1956: Fall-Winter, Castle AFB, Calif.

1960: Aug. 13, Red Bluff, Calif.

1966: Apr. 17, Ravenna, Ohio; June 24, Richmond, Va.

1969: Mar. 4, Atlanta, Mo.

1976: Sept. 19, Tehran, Iran.

1986: May 19, Brazil.

COLORS
(* = light beam or ground illumination; others refer to pre-
dominant color associated with UFO or event)

Red: Nov. 23, 1948, Fursten-Feldbruck, Germany; *Nov. 2, 1957, Levelland, Tex.; Dec. 20, 1958, Dunellen, N.J.; *Aug. 13, 1960, Red Bluff, Calif.; Feb. 11, 1965, Pacific Ocean; Aug. 19, 1965, Cherry Creek, N.Y.; Mar. 20, 1966, Dexter, Mich .; *Oct. 15, 1966, Split Rock Pond, N.J. (red-orange); *Mar. 7, 1967, Keeneyville, Ill.; Jan. 24, 1974, Aische-en-Refail, Belgium; Sept. 30, 1975, Corning, Calif.; Jan. 6, 1976, Stanford, Ky.; July 6, 1978, Mendoza, Argentina (sky); Sept. 17, 1978, Torrita di Siena, Italy (red-orange); Nov. 1978, Trier, W. Germany (flashing light); Nov. 8, 1978, Kuwait (flashing light); Jan. 5, 1979, Auburn, Mass.; Aug. 4, 1979, Toronto, Ont., Canada; Oct. 23, 1980, Morenci, Arizona (body lights); Dec. 29, 1980, Huffman , Tex. (red-orange); May 19, 1986, Brazil (red/red-orange).

Orange: Aug. 4, 1965, Abilene, Kans.; Sept. 16, 1965, Pretoria, S. Africa ("copper"); Feb. 14, 1974, Ely, Nev.; *Feb. 18, 1977, Salto, Uruguay (changed to red).

Yellow: June 29, 1964, Lavonia, Ga. (amber); Mar. 15, 1965, Everglades, Fla.; Sept. 1965, Brabant, Belgium; Mar. 22, 1976, Nemingha, N.S.W., Australia (yellow-green); *Sept. 23, 1978, Buenos Aires Province, Argentina; Dec. 6, 1978, Torriglia, Italy.

Green: Aug. 19, 1965, Cherry Creek, N.Y. (glow in clouds); *Nov. 2, 1967, Ririe, Idaho; Aug. 1, 1971, Calliope R., Queensland, Australia; *Oct. 18, 1973, Mansfield, Ohio,; *Oct. 27, 1974, Aveley, England (green mist); Oct. 21, 1978, Bass Strait, Australia (body light); May 19, 1986, Brazil.

Appendix A

Green-Blue: Nov. 2, 1957, Levelland, Tex.; July 3, 1965, Antarctica; Mar. 18, 1976. Charleston, S.C. ("aquamarine").

Blue: May 31, 1974, Rhodesia; Oct. 27, 1974, Aveley, England; Feb. 19, 1975, Orbak, Denmark; *Aug. 13, 1975, Haderslev, Denmark (blue-white); *Jan. 6, 1976, Stanford, Ky.; *Jan. 21, 1976, Matles-Barbosa, Brazil; *Nov. 29, 1977, Gisborne, N.Z.; *Mar. 29, 1978, Indianapolis, Ind; *Nov. 19, 1980, Longmont, Colo.

Purple: *Sept. 3, 1965, Damon, Tex; Mar. 31, 1966, Vicksburg, Mich. (body light).

Gray: Nov. 18, 1948, Andrews AFB, Md.; Mar. 7, 1967, Keenyville, Ill. (gray mist); *July 30, 1968, Claremont, N.H.; Jan. 7, 1970, Heinola, Finland ("luminous gray fog"); June 28, 1973, Columbia, Mo. ("silvery-white").

Black: Apr. 25, 1952, San Jose, Calif.; Oct. 23, 1980, Morenci, Ariz. (with red body lights); July 31, 1981, Lieksa, Finland.

ELECTROMAGNETIC EFFECTS

1957: Nov. 2-3, Levelland, Tex.

1960: Aug. 13, Red Bluff, Calif.

1964: June 29, Lavonia, Ga.

1965: July 3, Antarctica; Aug. 4, Abilene, Kans.; Aug. 19, Cherry Creek, N.Y.

1966: June, Nha Trang, Vietnam; Oct. 15, Split Rock Pond, N.J.

1967: Mar. 8, Leominster, Mass.

1969: Mar. 4, Atlanta, Mo.

1973: June 28, Columbia, Mo.; Oct. 18, Mansfield, Ohio.

1974: Jan. 24, Aische-en-Refail, Belgium; Feb. 14, Ely, Nev.; May 31, Rhodesia; Oct. 27, Aveley, England.

1975: Feb. 19, Orbak, Denmark; May 3, Mexico City, Mexico; Aug. 13, Alamogordo, N.M.; Aug. 13, Haderslev, Denmark.

1976: Mar. 22, Nemingha, N.S.W., Australia; Sept. 19, Tehran, Iran.

1977: Feb. 18, Salto, Uruguay; May 5, Tabio, Colombia; June 16, Middelburg, S. Africa.

1978: Mar. 29, Indianapolis, Ind.; July 6, Mendoza, Argentina; Sept. 17, Torrita di Siena, Italy; Oct. 21, Bass Strait, Australia; Nov. 9, Kuwait; Dec. 6, Torriglia, Italy.

1979: Jan. 5, Auburn, Mass.; Feb. 5, Lawitta, Tasmania; Feb. 8, Liverpool Creek, Queensland, Australia.

1980: May 14, Simpson Cty, Miss.; Aug. 22, East Texas; Nov. 19, Longmont, Colo.

1981: June 12, Alice, Tex.

1985: March, Santiago, Chile.

1986: Nov. 17, Fort Yukon, Alaska.

HEAT

1957: Nov. 2, Levelland, Tex.

1958: May 5, Pan de Azucar, Uruguay.

1965: Sept. 3, Damon, Tex.

1969: Mar. 4, Atlanta, Mo.

1975: Feb. 19, Orbak, Denmark; Aug. 13, Haderslev, Denmark.

1977: Jan. 21, St. Bernard Parish, La.; Feb. 15, Salto, Uruguay.

1978: Dec. 6 & 27, Torriglia, Italy.

1979: Jan. 5, Auburn, Mass.

1980: Sept. 30, Sale, Vict., S. Australia; Dec. 29, Huffman, Tex.

1986: Nov. 17, Fort Yukon, Alaska.

HUMANOIDS
(see also "Abduction reports")

1964: Sept. 4, Cisco Grove, Calif.

1967: Nov. 2, Ririe, Idaho.

1970: Jan. 7, Heinola, Finland.

1974: Feb. 14, Petite-Ile, France; May 31, Rhodesia.

1978: Sept. 17, Torrita di Siena, Italy.

1980: Apr. 2, Pudasjarvi, Finland; Aug. 22, East Texas; Nov. 19, Longmont, Colo.

LEVITATION

1965: Sept., Brabant, Belgium.

1967: Nov. 2, Ririe, Idaho.

1973: Oct. 17, Midwest U.S.; Oct. 18, Mansfield, Ohio; Oct. 28, Bahia Blanca, Brazil.

1974: Feb. 14, Ely Nev.; May 31, Rhodesia; Oct. 27, Aveley, England.

1975: May 3, Mexico City, Mexico.

1976: Jan. 6, Stanford, Ky.; Jan. 21, Matles-Barbosa, Brazil.

1978: July 6, Mendoza, Argentina; Sept. 17, Torrita di Siena, Italy; Sept. 23, Buenos Aires Province, Argentina; Dec. 6, Torriglia, Italy.

1980: Aug. 22, East Texas; Nov. 19, Longmont, Colo.

1981: June 12, Alice, Tex.

1985: March, Santiago, Chile.

LIGHT BEAMS

1960: Aug. 13, Red Bluff, Calif.

1965: Mar. 15, Everglades, Fla.

1966: Mar. 31, Vicksburg, Mich.; Apr. 17, Ravenna, Ohio.

1967: Mar. 7, Keeneyville, Ill.

1968: July 30, Claremont, N.H.

1969: Mar. 4, Atlanta, Mo.

1970: Jan. 7, Heinola, Finland.

1973: June 28, Columbia, Mo.; Oct. 18, Mansfield, Ohio; Oct. 28, Bahia Blanca, Brazil.

1974: Feb. 14, Petite-Ile, France; May 31, Rhodesia.

1975: Aug. 13, Haderslev, Denmark.

1976: Jan. 6, Stanford, Ky.

1977: Jan. 21, St. Bernard Parish, La.; Feb. 18, Salto, Uruguay; Nov. 29, Gisborne, N.Z.

1978: Mar. 29, Indianapolis, Ind.; Sept. 17, Torrita di Siena, Italy; Dec. 6, Torriglia, Italy.

1980: Oct. 23, Morenci, Ariz; Nov. 19, Longmont, Colo.

1982: Nov. 27, Palatine, Ill.

1985: March, Santiago, Chile.

1986: May 15, Belo Horizonte, Brazil.

LIGHT ENGULFMENT
(of witness/vehicle)

1965: Sept. 3, Damon Tex.

1966: Apr. 17, Ravenna, Ohio; Oct. 15, Split Rock Pond, N.J.

1973: Oct. 18, Mansfield, Ohio.

1974: May 31, Rhodesia; Oct. 27, Aveley, England ("green mist").

1975: Aug. 13, Haderslev, Denmark.

1976: Jan. 6, Stanford, Ky.; Mar. 22, Nemingha, N.S.W., Australia.

1977: Jan. 21, St. Bernard Parish, La.; May 5, Tabio, Colombia; June 16, Middelburg, S. Africa.

1978: Mar. 18, Charleston, S.C.; Mar. 29, Indianapolis, Ind.; Sept. 23, Buenos Aires Province, Argentina.

1979: Feb. 5, Lawitta, Tasmania; Sept. 21, Sztum, Poland.

1980: Apr. 2, Pudasjarvi, Finland ("strange fog").

1985: March, Santiago, Chile.

1986: May 15, Belo Horizonte, Brazil; Nov. 17, Fort Yukon, Alaska.

ODOR

1964: June 29, Lavonia, Ga. ("like embalming fluid").

1965: Aug. 19, Cherry Creek, N.Y. ("pungent").

1979: Jan. 5, Auburn, Mass. ("sweet skunk smell").

1980: Nov. 19, Longmont Colo. ("electrical").

PERCEPTUAL ANOMALIES

1967: Mar. 7, Keeneyville, Ill. (localized "mist"); Mar. 8, Leominster, Mass. (localized "fog").

1971: Aug. 1, Calliope R., Queensland, Australia (altered surroundings).

1974: May 31, Rhodesia (altered surroundings); Oct. 27, Aveley, England ("green mist," abnormal silence).

1976: Jan. 6, Stanford, Ky. (altered surroundings).

1977: Jan. 21, St. Bernard Parish, La. (abnormal silence); May 5, Tabio, Colombia ("fog," or impaired vision).

1978: Mar. 29, Indianapolis, Ind. (abnormal silence, sense of isolation, diminished vision); July 6, Mendoza, Argentina (altered surroundings); Sept. 23, Buenos Aires Province, Argentina ("yellow fog," sense of isolation, impaired vision); Dec. 27, Torriglia, Italy ("blinding mist").

1979: Feb. 5, Lawitta, Tasmania (impaired vision); Sept. 21, Sztum, Poland (enveloping "fog," kaleidoscopic imagery . . .).

1980: Apr. 2, Pudasjarvi, Finland (enveloping "fog," deflected headlight beams); Aug. 22, East Texas ("fog" or "smoke" on floor during abduction).

Appendix A

PHYSICAL TRACES

1964: June 29, Lavonia, Ga.

1965: Mar. 15, Everglades, Fla.; Aug. 19, Cherry Creek, N.Y.,; Sept. 16, Pretoria, S. Africa.

1971: Aug. 1, Calliope R., Queensland, Australia.

1973: June 28, Columbia, Mo.

1974: Feb. 14, Ely, Nev.

1975: Feb. 19, Orbak, Denmark.

1976: Mar. 22, Nemingha, N.S.W., Australia.

1977: Feb. 18, Salto, Uruguay.

1978: Mar. 29, Indianapolis, Ind.; Sept. 17, Torrita di Siena, Italy; Dec. 6, Torriglia, Italy.

1979: Feb. 5, Lawitta, Tasmania; Aug. 4, Toronto, Ont., Canada.

1980: Sept. 30, Sale, Vict., S. Australia.

1986: May 15, Belo Horizonte, Brazil.

PHYSIOLOGICAL EFFECTS

1957: Nov. 10, Madison, Ohio (eye irritation, skin rash . . .).

1964: June 29, Lavonia, Ga. (burning sensation); Sept. 4, Cisco Grove, Calif. (nausea, unconsciousness).

1965: Mar. 15, Everglades, Fla. (eye damage, unconsciousness, numbness, hearing loss); Sept., Brabant, Belgium (prick marks); Sept. 3, Damon, Tex. ("healing").

1966: Oct. 15, Split Rock Pond, N.J. (anorexia, muscle weakness, weight loss . . .).

1967: Mar. 8, Leominster, Mass. (paralysis, sluggish reflexes).

1970: Jan. 7, Heinola, Finland (paralysis, vomiting, headaches, redness and swelling, equilibrium loss).

1973: Oct. 28, Bahia Blanca, Brazil (dot-marks on eyelid).

1974: Jan. 24, Aische-en-Refail, Belgium (abnormal lassitude); Feb. 14, Petite-Ile, France (headaches, impaired vision).

1975: Feb. 19, Orbak, Denmark (aches, nausea); Aug. 13, Alamogordo, N.M. (numbness, puncture wound, inflammation).

1976: Jan. 6, Stanford, Ky. (burning eyes, welts, swelling, weight loss . . .); Jan. 6, Bethel, Minn. (eye irritation, altered menstrual period).

1977: Jan. 21, St. Bernard Parish, La. (hair on end); Feb. 18, Salto, Uruguay (severe: man had skin irritation, dog was "cooked" and died); May 5, Tabio, Colombia (impaired vision).

1978: Sept. 23, Buenos Aires Province, Argentina (impaired vision, or obscuring "fog"); Dec. 6, Torriglia, Italy (headache, pain); Dec. 27, Torriglia, Italy (reddened skin).

1979: Jan. 5, Auburn, Mass. (paralysis, rash); Aug. 4, Toronto, Ont., Canada (prick marks on hand).

1980: Apr. 2, Pudasjarvi, Finland (marks on shoulder); Sept. 30, Sales, Vict., S. Australia (bodily vibrations); Nov. 19, Longmont, Colo. (pneumonia, "healing"); Dec. 29, Huffman, Tex. (radiation sickness: hair loss, vomiting . . .).

1981: July 31, Lieksa, Finland (paralysis, shaking, equilibrium loss).

1985: March, Santiago, Chile.

1986: May 15, Belo Horizonte, Brazil; Aug. 1, Banksons Lake, Mich.

SOUND

1957: Nov. 2, Levelland, Tex. ("like thunder").

1964: June 29, Lavonia, Ga. (hiss).

1965: Mar. 15, Everglades, Fla. (a. jet-like, b. generator-like); Aug. 4, Abilene, Kans. (like "wind through trees"); Aug. 19, Cherry Creek, N.Y. (beep).

1966: Mar. 31, Vicksburg, Mich. (hum or buzz); Apr. 17, Ravenna, Ohio (hum).

1967: Mar. 8, Leominster, Mass. (hum); Nov. 2, Ririe, Idaho (bird-like vocalizations by humanoid).

1968: July 30, Claremont, N.H. (hum).

1970: Jan. 7, Heinola, Finland (buzz).

1973: June 28, Columbia, Mo. ("thrashing"); Oct. 28, Bahia Blanca, Brazil (humming "voices").

1975: Aug. 13, Alamogordo, N.M. (high-pitched); Sept. 30, Corning, Calif. (hum).

1977: June 16 (approx), Nr. Middelburg, S. Africa (buzz).

1978: Sept. 17, Torrita di Siena, Italy (explosive w/flash); Dec. 6, Torriglia, Italy (hiss).

1979: Sept. 21, Sztum, Poland ("high frequency").

1980: Sept. 30, Sales, Vict., S. Australia (a. whistling, b. explosive); Nov. 19, Longmont, Colo. ("swishing"); Dec. 29, Huffman, Tex. (a. "woosh", b. beep).

1986: May 15, Belo Horizonte, Brazil ("voices").

STEERING CONTROL LOSS

1965: Sept., Brabant, Belgium.

1967: Nov. 2, Ririe, Idaho.

1974: Feb. 14, Ely, Nev.; May 31, Rhodesia; July, Bridgewater, Tasmania.

1975: May 3, Mexico City, Mexico.

1977: Jan. 21, St. Bernard Parish, La.; May 5, Tabio, Colombia.

1978: Sept. 23, Buenos Aires Province, Argentina; Dec. 27, Torriglia, Italy.

1979: Jan. 5, Auburn, Mass.

TRANSLOCATION

1971: Aug. 1, Calliope R., Queensland, Australia.

1973: Oct. 28, Bahia Blanca, Brazil.

1974: May 31, Rhodesia.

1976: Jan. 6, Stanford, Ky.

1978: Mar. 18, Charleston, S.C.; July 6, Mendoza, Argentina; Aug. 30, Gobernador Dupuy, Argentina; Sept. 23, Buenos Aires Province, Argentina; Dec. 6, Torriglia, Italy; Dec. 27(?), Arroyito, Cordoba, Argentina.

1980: Aug. 22, East Texas.

VEHICLE ENCOUNTERS
(see also Keyhoe and Ruppelt references, Chapter 9)

1948: Oct. 1, Fargo, N.Dak.; Oct. 15, Japan; Nov. 18, Andrews AFB, Md; Nov. 23, Fursten-Feldbruck, Germany

1951: July 9, Dearing, Ga.; Oct. 21, Battle Creek, Mich.

1956: Castle AFB, Calif.

1957: Nov. 2, Levelland, Tex.

1958: May 5, Pan de Azucar, Uruguay.

1960: Aug. 13, Red Bluff, Calif.

1964: June 29, Lavonia, Ga.

1965: Feb.11, Pacific Ocean; May 28, Bougainville Reef, Australia; Aug. 4, Abilene, Kans.; Sept., Brabant, Belgium; Sept. 3, Damon, Tex; Sept. 16, Pretoria, S. Africa.

1966: Mar. 31, Vicksburg, Mich.; June 24, Richmond, Va.; Oct. 15, Split Rock Pond, N.J.

1967: Mar. 7, Keeneyville, Ill.; Nov. 2, Ririe, Idaho.

1969: Mar. 4, Atlanta, Mo.

1971: Aug. 1, Calliope R., Queensland, Australia.

1973: Oct. 18, Mansfield, Ohio.

1974: Jan. 24, Aische-en-Refail, Belgium; Feb. 14, Ely, Nev.; May 31, Rhodesia; July, Bridgewater, Tasmania; Oct. 27, Aveley, England.

1975: Feb. 19, Orbak, Denmark; May 3, Mexico City, Mexico; Aug. 13, Haderslev, Denmark.

1976: Jan. 6, Bethel, Minn.; Jan. 6, Stanford, Ky.; Jan. 21, Matles-Barbosa, Brazil; Mar. 22, Nemingha, N.S.W., Australia; Sept. 19, Tehran, Iran.

1977: Jan. 21, St. Bernard Parish, La.; May 5, Tabio, Colombia; June 16, Middelburg, S. Africa.

1978: Mar. 28, Indianapolis, Ind.; July 6, Mendoza, Argentina; Sept. 17, Torrita di Siena, Italy; Sept. 23, Buenos Aires Province, Argentina; Oct. 21, Bass Strait, Australia,; Nov., Trier, W. Germany; Dec. 27(?), Arroyito, Cordoba, Argent ina; Dec. 27, Torriglia, Italy.

1979: Jan. 5, Auburn, Mass.; Feb. 5, Lawitta, Tasmania; Feb. 8, Liverpool Creek, Queensland, Australia; July 25, Canoga Park, Calif.

1980: Apr. 2, Pudasjarvi, Finland; May 14, Simpson County, Miss; Aug. 22, East Texas; Nov. 19, Longmont, Colo; Dec. 29, Huffman, Tex.

1981: June 12, Alice, Tex.; July 31, Lieksa, Finland.

1982: Nov. 27, Palatine, Ill.

1985: March, Santiago, Chile.

1986: May 11, Sedona, Ariz; May 19, Brazil; Nov. 17, Fort Yukon, Alaska.

CASE SUMMARIES

OCTOBER 1, 1948; FARGO, NORTH DAKOTA

Features: Aerial encounter, confrontation, "dogfight" maneuvers, evasive action, rapid upward departure.

While preparing to land his Air National Guard F-51 about 9:00 p.m., Lt. George F. Gorman was watching a Piper Cub below him when he saw a light pass him on the right. The control tower said no other aircraft besides the Piper Cub were in the vicinity, so Gorman pulled up to investigate. He closed to within 1,000 yards and saw a somewhat flattened round object (i.e., oblong), small, clear white, and blinking on and off. As he closed on the object its light became steady and it pulled into a sharp left bank. Gorman dove after it but couldn't catch up with it. The UFO then climbed and banked left again, and Gorman turned sharply to try to cut it off.

Suddenly the object made a sharp right turn and came head-on toward the F-51. As a collision seemed imminent, Gorman dove and the object passed about 500 feet over his canopy. As the object circled above him, Gorman once more gave chase. Again the object came straight at him. When a collision again seemed imminent, the UFO shot straight up into the air in a steep climbout and disappeared. The "dogfight" had lasted 27 minutes. Dr. A. E. Cannon and his passenger in the Piper Cub saw both the F-51 and the rapidly moving lighted object. In the airport control tower, Lloyd D. Jensen and H. E. Johnson also saw a round lighted unidentified object passing near the airport at high speed.

Sources: Project Sign report in Project Blue Book files, National Archives, Washington, D.C.; "Gorman 'dogfight' " by Richard Hall in *Encyclopedia of UFOs* (N.Y.: Doubleday, 1980); Fargo, N.D., *Forum*, Oct. 3 & 4, 1948.

OCTOBER 15, 1948; JAPAN

Features: Aerial encounter, radar-visual, cat-and-mouse pursuit.

An F-61 "Black Widow" night fighter crew on patrol over Japan picked up a UFO target on radar moving at about 200 m.p.h. The crew made six attempts to close in on the object, and each time it rapidly accelerated to about 1,200 m.p.h. leaving the interceptor behind. Then it would slow down again until the interceptor began closing in once more. On one pass the crew saw the silhouette of an object shaped like a "rifle bullet" and apparently 20-30 feet long. (Note: A more detailed account, including Air Force witness names and statements, appears in the Hynek reference).

Sources: *Report on Unidentified Flying Objects,* by Edward J. Ruppelt (N.Y.: Doubleday, 1956), p. 68. From Air Force intelligence report; *The Hynek UFO Report,* by J. Allen Hynek (N.Y.: Dell Books, 1977) pp. 134-137.

NOVEMBER 18, 1948; ANDREWS AFB, MARYLAND

Features: Aerial encounter, "dogfight" maneuvers, rapid acceleration, "evasive action."

Summary statement from Project Sign Incident No. 207 in Project Blue Book files: "At approximately 2200 hours Lt. Henry G. Combs (AFRes) sighted an object flying on a 360 degree pattern from West to East over Andrews AF Base. The object had one continuous glowing white light. Combs thought it was an aircraft with the wing navigation lights turned off or burned out. He then made a pass to check. Object then took evasive action. First contact established at 1700 feet over Andrews AF Base. When object started taking evasive action, Combs switched wing and tail navigation lights off.

Maneuvering his ship (a T-6) so that his exhaust flame would not be noticed in an effort to get the object on his left he proceeded to close in but the object quickly flew up and over his aircraft. Then Combs attempted to maneuver the object between his ship and the light of the moon. This was done by making very very tight 360 degree turns with flaps down while making a steady climb. Object was able to turn inside of Combs' aircraft even under this condition. Another amazing feature was the quick variation of airspeed from 80 m.p.h. to 500 or 600 m.p.h. Combs remained in contact with the object for some 10 minutes with the object between the lights of

Washington, D.C., and his aircraft. He could only see an oblong ball with one light and no wings and no exhaust flame. [Elsewhere object is described as a 'glowing white oval.' — Ed.]"

Finally, "Combs pulled back up sharply and came up underneath the object within 300 to 400 feet. He then turned his landing lights on it. It had a very dull gray glow to it and was oblong in shape .... Object then performed a very tight curve and headed for the East coast at about 500 to 600 m.p.h." Other witnesses included Lt. Kenwood W. Jackson, AFRes, who described the object as oval; Lt. Glen L. Stalker, AFRes; and S/Sgt. John J. Kushner on the ground who saw the object make two low passes over the base. Lt. Combs noted the UFO displayed "Evasive controlled tactics and ability to perform tight circles, quick variation of air speed, vertical ascents, evasive movements."

Source: Project Blue Book files, 27-page report, National Archives, Washington, D.C.

NOVEMBER 23, 1948; FURSTEN-FELDBRUCK, GERMANY

Features: Aerial encounter, radar-visual, high-speed ascent.

An F-80 pilot flying in the vicinity of a U.S. Air Force Base saw a rapidly circling red-lighted object at 2200 hours at 27,000 feet. A check with ground radar determined that it was tracking an object at that altitude, now going 900 m.p.h. in the same position as observed by the pilot. The object climbed to 50,000 feet in a matter of minutes and disappeared. Air Force intelligence determined that no balloons or aircraft were in the area that could account for the sighting. The wire report from Germany to Project Sign stated: "Capt. _____ is an experienced pilot now flying F-80's and is considered to be completely reliable. The sighting was verified by Capt. _____, also an F-80 pilot."

Sources: *Report on Unidentified Flying Objects* by Edward J. Ruppelt (N.Y.: Doubleday, 1956), p. 68; *Flying Saucers From*

Outer Space by Donald E. Keyhoe (N.Y.: Holt, 1953), p. 34. From Air Force intelligence report.

APRIL 24, 1949; ARREY, NEW MEXICO

Features: Theodolite tracking, high-speed maneuvering object.

At 10:20 a.m. on a very clear day, Charles B. Moore, Jr., a General Mills Company aerologist and four technicians were preparing to launch a Skyhook balloon and were tracking a small weather balloon, when they suddenly noticed a whitish object rapidly crossing the sky. They turned their theodolite, with 25-power telescope, onto the object and saw that it was a featureless ellipse, its length about 2-1/2 times its width. After about 60 seconds, the object "disappeared in a sharp climb." According to Ruppelt, the UFO at one point passed in front of a range of mountains. From azimuth, elevation, and timing data the object's speed was calculated to be between 18,000 and 25,000 m.p.h.

Sources: *200 Miles Up — The Conquest of the Upper Air,* by J. Gordon Vaeth (N.Y.: Ronald Press, 1956), p. 113; reprint of preceding account in *The UFO Evidence* (NICAP, 1964), p. 2; "How Scientists Tracked a Flying Saucer" by Robert B. McLaughlin, TRUE Magazine, Mar. 1950; *Report on Unidentified Flying Objects* by Edward J. Ruppelt (N.Y.: Doubleday, 1956), p. 101; *The Hynek UFO Report,* by J. Allen Hynek (N.Y.: Dell Books, 1977) pp. 104-105.

JUNE 10, 1949; WHITE SANDS, NEW MEXICO

Features: Pacing of Navy missile, high-speed ascent.

A crew of Navy engineers and technicians under the command of Commander Robert B. McLaughlin were testing an upper atmosphere missile, with observation posts all around the missile test range. When the missile had attained a speed of 2,000 feet per second on its upward flight, it was suddenly joined by two small circular objects that paced it, one on each side. One of the objects then passed through the missile's exhaust, joined the other, and together they accelerated upwards leaving the missile behind. Shortly afterwards, Cmdr. McLaughlin received reports from five observation posts scattered at all points of the compass; all had witnessed the performance of the two circular UFOs.

Source: "How Scientists Tracked A Flying Saucer" by Robert B. McLaughlin, TRUE Magazine, Mar. 1950.

JULY 9, 1951; DEARING, GEORGIA

Features: Aerial encounter with disc-shaped UFO, confrontation.

Air Force Lieutenant George H. Kinmon, Jr., a World War II combat veteran, was flying an F-51 out of Lawson AFB, Georgia, at 1340 hours when a white, disc-shaped UFO ("completely round and spinning in a clockwise direction") confronted his aircraft, at one point making a head-on pass at it. Quotes from Air Force intelligence report: "Object described as flat on top and bottom and appearing from a front view to have rounded edges and slightly beveled ... No vapor trails or exhaust or visible system of propulsion. Described as traveling at tremendous speed ... Pilot had leveled off at 8,500 feet altitude on a course of 247 degrees ... object dived from the sun in front and under the plane and continued to barrel-roll around the plane for a period of ten minutes, when it disappeared under the plane ... object was 300 to 400 feet from plane and appeared to be 10 to 15 feet in diameter ... Pilot states he felt disturbance in the air described as 'bump' when object passed under plane ... Pilot considered by associates to be highly reliable, of mature judgment and a creditable observer. Pilot notified tower, Robins AFB by radio and contacted flt svc [flight service] at Maxwell AFB ... Pilot unable to take photo due to camera malfunction."

Source: Air Force intelligence report, Project Blue Book files, National Archives, Washington, D.C.

OCTOBER 21, 1951; BATTLE CREEK, MICHIGAN

Features: Aerial encounter with silver, highly reflective classic domed-disc UFO, confrontation.

Summary of Air Intelligence Information Report:

"Mr. _____, a civilian pilot of fourteen (14) years flying experience encountered a disk-like, highly polished flying object which closed head on with his Navion aircraft at an extremely high rate of speed, in the vicinity of Battle Creek, Michigan. Altitude of the object was estimated to be 3,000 feet and 1,000 feet below observer's aircraft. Visibility conditions were unlimited above 4,000 feet and a haze restricted visibility to an estimated eight (8) miles below 4,000 feet. Check of available sources both civil and military indicate no known aircraft in the vicinity of the sighting at that time. Mr. _____, Austin Lake, Michigan, Airport Manager, has known observer for three years and considers him a very stable individual. Investigating officer concurs in this estimate of observer."

Other details: The plane was on a heading of approximately 265 degrees, approximately 17 miles due east of Battle Creek, 135 m.p.h. indicated air speed, at 1625Z. UFO was seen straight ahead approaching at "tremendous" speed on an apparent collision course. The pilot's attention was first attracted to it by the sun's reflection on an extremely highly polished surface ("He was particularly impressed with the extremely high polish of the silver colored object and stated that in his estimation, no aluminum surface could ever be polished to such a high brilliance." Compare to Jan. 5, 1965, Brands Flats, Va., humanoid case in Chapter 3). The UFO had a clear-cut dome on top, and when it passed beneath the aircraft it appeared perfectly circular in planform, approximately 30-40 feet in diameter.

Source: Air Force intelligence report, Project Blue Book files, National Archives, Washington, D.C.

APRIL 25, 1952; SAN JOSE, CALIFORNIA

Features: Scientist sighting, disc, oscillatory motion, extraordinary implied propulsion.

Dr. W (biochemist) and Dr. Y (bacteriologist), both employed by a private company, about 11:00 a.m. were driving to their office when Y saw something odd overhead that seemed to be moving against the wind. They entered the company parking lot and got out of the car to look. Directly over a building across the street was a small, metallic-looking disc, tilted at about a 20 degree angle and rotating around a vertical axis, wobbling "like the motion of a disc in a water meter." The distance was estimated to be about 50 ft, and the disc appeared to be 4-5 feet in diameter. The wobble allowed them to judge the thickness as about 1.5 feet as the disc proceeded directly over their heads, continuing to rotate and wobble. No sound or exhaust emission of any sort was detected. It moved in an arc about 40-50 feet overhead very slowly, perhaps 8-10 m.p.h. When it neared some railroad yards, the disc curved around and made a fairly distinct turn, heading back toward them.

At this point Dr. Y suddenly saw something else overhead, which Dr. W also then saw: a black object at high altitude hovering motionless under an overcast (later determined to be about 10,000 ft). It was round, and apparently much larger than the silvery disc, perhaps 100 ft in diameter. As they watched, two identical objects came into position as if they had dropped out of the cloud overcast, and the three objects "jittered around like boats in a stream." About this time the small disc had neared again, still moving slowly. Suddenly it

241

stopped spinning, hung motionless for a moment, then rapidly climbed towards the NNE in the general direction of Mt. Hamilton. At the same time that the small disc began its climb, one of the three black objects left the formation and headed in the same general direction. The black object and the climbing disc seemed to be on a converging course, when suddenly both seemed to disappear into the overcast.

The remaining two black objects maintained their original position for another minute or so, then one of them headed off to the north and out of sight, while the other went directly up into the clouds and disappeared, terminating the incident at about 11:15 a.m. The two scientists immediately went into their offices and dictated accounts of the sighting for a permanent record.

Dr. W felt obliged to make an official report and placed a call to Moffett Field. While waiting on the line for someone to be found to take his account, he had second thoughts about exposing himself to personal ridicule and hung up, so no report was made to the Air Force or other agencies.

Special significance: In addition to the observation by scientifically trained witnesses, and loss of an official report due to the ridicule factor, the scientists' reaction is instructive. They had found it "a most disturbing experience." They had been forced to the conclusion that they had seen some objects of such unusual propulsion characteristics that it was difficult to think of it as anything other than extraterrestrial. As Dr. W said, ". . . it utilized some propulsion method not in the physics books." He had been "worried ever since," mentioning historical evidence that inferior civilizations tend to go under when contacted by more advanced technologies.

Source: Interview with Dr. W by Dr. James E. McDonald; complete account including names and identifications in author's files.

LATE 1956; CASTLE AFB, CALIFORNIA

Features: Aerial encounter, Air Force interceptor "cat-and-mouse" UFO pursuit, partial radar confirmation, evidence of official cover-up.

A.A. and J.R., Air Force interceptor pilots (now United Air Lines pilots), were flying F-86's near Modesto, California, on alert duty due to civilian UFO reports in a nearby town. As they were vectored toward the town, a call came instructing them to return to the base because a UFO was visible from the control tower. Turning on the afterburners, they closed rapidly on a luminous elliptical object that alternately moved above and below a cloud cover at 10,000 to 12,000 feet as if to elude them. The pilots positioned themselves one above and one below the clouds and took turns chasing the UFO as it emerged on their side of the clouds.

During the chase they saw the UFO from various angles, sometimes closing to within an estimated few hundred yards before it accelerated away from them again. In planform, the UFO appeared circular. Ground radar at Madera was tracking the F-86's, but not the UFO. Both pilots got transient returns from their airborne radars, but were puzzled by the curious way in which they lost the echo almost as soon as they picked it up.

Running low on fuel, A. A. started descending to land. When he looked back up and saw that the UFO was now following his wingmate, he elected to go back up despite his fuel situation. Then the UFO shot off and disappeared in the distance terminating the sighting. The pilots were debriefed by several officers flown in from another base who seemed to be seeking "confirmation not information," as if they knew just what they wanted to find out. The pilots were told not to discuss the sighting with each other, nor to make any kind of statement about it. Local citizens, who had seen the UFO and heard the roaring jets, were told that the pilots had been chasing ducks or geese.

Special significance: Numerous cases are known to the author in which military witnesses were debriefed by officers who displayed detailed knowledge of UFOs and sometimes carried notebooks of UFO photographs and drawings for identification purposes.

Source: Interview report by Dr. James E. McDonald including names and affiliations of witnesses.

NOVEMBER 2/3, 1957; LEVELLAND, TEXAS

Features: Multiple landings on roadways, E-M effects, heat, sound, wind, illumination of ground.

From shortly before 11:00 p.m. to about 1:30 a.m., citizens in and around the city repeatedly saw reddish or bluish-green oval or elliptical objects sitting on roadways, then taking off. Vehicles in the vicinity of the UFOs experienced electromagnetic failures, typically the headlights and engine. In one probably significant report at 12:45 a.m., Ronald Martin saw the glowing red UFO land ahead of his truck, then turn to bluish-green. The truck's electrical system failed. When the UFO took off, it turned reddish again. Among the witnesses during the evening was Sheriff Weir Clem, who was searching the roads as a result of earlier reports and saw a reddish oval cross the road, illuminating the pavement.

At 12:15 a.m. Frank Williams saw a bluish-green UFO on the road close to where an independent witness had reported a sighting about 15 minutes earlier. Both his engine and headlights failed. The light from the UFO was pulsating steadily on and off; each time it came on, Williams' lights went out. Finally it rose swiftly making a noise like thunder, after which the car functioned normally. The first sighting that evening, at 10:50 p.m., involved a glowing UFO that rose out of a field and swooped over a farm truck causing the engine and lights to fail. The terrified driver jumped out and hit the deck as the UFO passed overhead with a sound like thunder and a rush of wind which rocked the truck. He also felt heat from the object.

Within the next few hours an Army jeep patrol at White Sands, N.M., reported an egg-shaped UFO that descended to a point about 50 yards above the bunker used during the first atomic bomb explosion, and a major wave of UFO sightings continued for 2-3 weeks.

Sources: *The UFO Evidence* (NICAP, 1964), p. 168; "Levelland (Texas) Sightings" in *Encyclopedia of UFOs* (N.Y.: Doubleday, 1980) p. 210; *UFOs and the Limits of Science*, by Ronald D. Story (N.Y.: Morrow, 1981) pp. 155-159; *The UFO Experience*, by Dr. J. Allen Hynek (Chicago: Henry Regnery, 1972) pp. 123-128.

NOVEMBER 10, 1957; MADISON, OHIO

Features: Brilliant illumination, physiological effects, animal reactions.

Mrs. Leita Kuhn had been going back and forth between her house and backyard dog kennels checking on an overheating stove on a snowy, windy night. About 1:20 a.m. everything was in order, so she shut the kennel door. The snow had stopped and it was dark, with no moon or stars visible. As she stepped away from the kennel she saw a huge glowing object in back, about 60 feet above the ground. It was about 40 feet wide and 10 feet thick with a dome on top, and glowing with a phosphorescent light. The top was brilliant and it hurt her eyes to look at it. Puffs of apparent exhaust appeared around the bottom increasingly, until she became unnerved by the spectacle and ran in the house. When she looked out the window, the object apparently had disappeared. The time was 1:55 a.m.

She stayed up all night caring for an apparently frightened dog that subsequently died of cancer. A few days later she sought medical treatment for eye irritation and skin rash, and was advised to report it to Civil Defense because of suspected radiation effects. She developed an abnormal craving for honey, other sweets, and water. For nearly two years she experienced a variety of physical ailments, some painful and emotionally disturbing.

245

Sources: *The UFO Evidence* (NICAP, 1964), p. 98; *Strange Effects From UFOs* (NICAP, 1969), p. 11.

MAY 5, 1958; PAN DE AZUCAR, URUGUAY

Features: Aerial encounter, heat, confrontation.

Carlos Alejo Rodriguez, an experienced pilot, was flying his Piper Cub in the vicinity of Capitan Curbelo Naval Air Base at 3:40 p.m. when a brilliant top-like object (symmetrical above and below) suddenly approached his plane head-on. The UFO, about 15-20 meters in diameter, stopped about 2,000 meters away and ". . . rocked twice, in a balancing motion." Rodriguez felt strong heat, so he removed his jacket and opened the aircraft windows. The UFO took off abruptly toward the sea ". . . at a fantastic speed," leaving a thin vapor trail.

Sources: *The UFO Evidence* (NICAP, 1964) p. 120; *Strange Effects From UFOs* (NICAP, 1969) p. 16.

DECEMBER 20, 1958; DUNELLEN, NEW JERSEY

Features: Police witnesses, vehicle encounter, hover, rapid upward acceleration.

Patrolmen LeRoy A. Arboreen and B. Talada were patrolling at 12:55 a.m. in an elevated area with an unobstructed view to the North, South, and West. Suddenly a glowing red object came directly toward them at phenomenal speed from the West, increasing rapidly in apparent size, then abruptly came to a complete stop. It was an ellipse proportioned like a football, solid bright red and giving off a pulsating glow. After hovering for a few seconds, the UFO ". . . made a left turn and again hovered for a few seconds, then went straight up like a shot. We watched it until it completely faded beyond the stars."

Source: *The UFO Evidence* (NICAP, 1964) p. 5.

Appendix A

AUGUST 13, 1960; RED BLUFF, CALIFORNIA

Features: Police witnesses, vehicle encounter, light beam, E-M effects, extraordinary maneuvers, cat-and-mouse pursuit.

California Highway Patrol Officers Charles A. Carson and Stanley Scott were patrolling at 11:50 p.m. when they saw what they took to be an airliner about to crash directly in front of them. Instead, when it descended to about 100 or 200 feet altitude, the object "suddenly reversed completely, at high speed, and gained approximately 500 feet ... (and) stopped ... It was surrounded by a glow making the round or oblong object visible. At each end ... there were definite red lights. As we watched the object moved again and performed feats that were actually unbelievable."

The local radar base confirmed a UFO at this time (but denied it next day). "We made several attempts to ... get closer to it, but the object seemed to be aware of us and we were more successful remaining motionless and allow it to approach us, which it did on several occasions." Each time it did so, they experienced strong radio interference as the UFO emitted a red beam of light that swept the area and illuminated the ground. "The object was capable of moving in any direction. Up and down, back and forth ... it moved at high (extremely) speeds and several times we watched it change directions or reverse itself while moving at unbelievable speeds."

The UFO moved easterly away from them and they attempted to follow. A second similar object joined it, and both hovered for some time, occasionally emitting the red light beams, finally disappearing over the eastern horizon. Other officers at the Tehama County Sheriffs' office also saw the UFO and witnessed its incredible maneuvers.

Sources: *The UFO Evidence* (NICAP, 1964) p. 61; "UFOs: Greatest Scientific Problem of Our Times?" by James E. McDonald, presentation to American Society of Newspaper Editors, Washington, D.C., Apr. 22, 1967; *The Hynek UFO Report*, by J. Allen Hynek (N.Y.; Dell Books, 1977) pp. 92-94.

JUNE 29, 1964; Nr. LAVONIA, GEORGIA

Features: Vehicle encounter, confrontation, sound, E-M effects, odor, physiological effects, physical traces on car.

Businessman Beauford E. Parham was driving home in the late evening, and was near Lavonia in northeast Georgia, when he spotted a very bright light in the sky coming directly toward his car. The next instant it was directly in front of his headlights — a top-shaped object, spinning and emitting a hissing sound "like a million snakes." It was amber colored, about 6 feet tall and 8 feet wide, with a mast-like protrusion on top and small portholes around the bottom through which "flames" were visible. The UFO disappeared, then quickly reappeared and stayed directly in front of the car, just in front of the lights (estimated 5 feet), for at least a mile while the car was travelling 65 m.p.h.

The top of the UFO was tilted toward Parham, who said he followed it in a "near trance-like state." Next the UFO went up over the car leaving a strong odor like embalming fluid and a gaseous vapor. Then the UFO appeared for the third time, again heading directly toward the car; the motor began to miss and Parham stopped. The UFO spun "like crazy" and then took off, disappearing in a "split second."

Parham began to feel a burning sensation on his arms, so he drove to an air base and reported the incident to FAA officials. They reportedly detected some radioactivity on the car (no formal report made). Parham's arms continued to burn even after he washed them. An oily substance on the car persisted after many washings, the car hood was warped with bubbled up paint, and the radiator and hoses deteriorated after the incident.

Source: *Strange Effects from UFOs,* (NICAP, 1969) pp. 5-7.

SEPTEMBER 4, 1964; CISCO GROVE, CALIFORNIA

Features: Humanoids and "robots" harassed bow and arrow hunter, physiological effects.

Donald Schrum, 28, and his friends were bow and arrow hunting in an isolated area of Placer County, and Schrum had become separated from his companions. At sunset he decided to sleep in a tree for the night. Later he saw a white light zigzagging at low altitude and, thinking it was a helicopter, jumped out of the tree and lit fires to attract its attention. The light turned toward him and stopped about 50-60 yards away. The object's strange appearance frightened Schrum, so he climbed back up in the tree.

After a while two humanoid beings and a robot-like creature approached the tree. From then on, Schrum was in a state of siege as the beings tried to dislodge him from the tree. At one point a white vapor emanated from the robot's mouth and Schrum blacked out, but woke up again nauseous and began lighting matches and throwing them down to frighten the beings away; they backed away. Finally he shot an arrow at the robot; when it hit there was an arc flash and the robot was knocked backwards. This was repeated two more times, and the humanoids scattered each time. A second robot now appeared and a vapor again rendered Schrum unconscious. When he awoke, he discovered that the two humanoids were climbing up the tree toward him, so he shook the tree and threw things down at them to ward them off. The same actions were repeated all night.

Near dawn more beings approached and "large volumes of smoke" drifted up and he blacked out. He awoke hanging from his belt and the creatures were gone. Later, when reunited with his companions, Schrum found that one of the other hunters, who also had gotten lost and separated from their camp, had seen the UFO.

Source: *Strange Effects From UFOs* (NICAP, 1969) p. 17; *The Hynek UFO Report* (N.Y.: Dell Books, 1977) pp. 210-212.

FEBRUARY 11, 1965; PACIFIC OCEAN

Features: Aerial encounter, radar-visual sighting by Air Force officer and flight crew, aircraft pacing, rapid upward acceleration.

A Flying Tiger freighter aircraft (Flight F-169) en route from Anchorage, Alaska, to Tachikawa Air Base, Japan, encountered three apparently gigantic UFOs. About 4 hours out of Anchorage, a crew member stepped into the cabin and asked Capt. R.W. if he would like to see some UFOs. Capt. W., a rated navigator acting as a military courier, went into the cockpit and observed three targets on the radar indicated at 5 miles off the wing. Three glowing red oval objects were visible out the window in that position.

The UFOs paced the aircraft for about 30 minutes, and when they departed "they climbed straight out at a high angle" tracked at 1200 knots ground speed. The pilot remarked that they often see UFOs on the Alaskan run. Capt. W. reconstructed the apparent size of the UFOs as 2-3 inches in diameter at arms length. At the 5-mile distance, this computes (conservatively) to be objects 1,000 feet in diameter. Even assuming an overestimation of apparent size and reducing the estimate to ¼ inch at arms length, the UFOs would have been close to 200 feet in diameter.

Source: Interview report by Capt. D.M. in author's files.

MARCH 15, 1965; EVERGLADES, FLORIDA

Features: Sound, animal reactions, light beam, reaction to witness, physiological effects, physical traces.

James W. Flynn, 45, was training hunting dogs in the Everglades when at about 1:00 a.m. he saw a cone-shaped UFO hovering about 200 feet over some cypress trees. The UFO moved rapidly and changed positions several times, and Flynn thought it was a helicopter until he looked at it through binoculars. Then, thinking it was "some new device from Cape Kennedy," perhaps in trouble, he tried to approach and offer help. The cone-shaped object appeared to be about 25 feet high and had four tiers of windows emitting a yellowish glow.

Flynn could hear a noise "like a diesel generator," which disturbed one of his dogs who "was howling in his cage and trying to get out."

Within 200 yards of the UFO, Flynn jumped out of his swamp buggy waving his arms. At that point the UFO emitted a jet-like noise and a blast of wind that knocked him off balance. As he continued to approach within a few yards, the UFO emitted a light beam like a welder's torch and Flynn blacked out. "I felt a blow like a sledgehammer between the eyes — and that's all I know," he told the local newspaper. When he awoke the UFO was gone and his vision was severely impaired. About 24 hours had passed. Flynn sought aid from an Indian acquaintance who helped him back to Fort Myers. Flynn required medical treatment, and had a small dark spot on his forehead. He suffered impaired vision in one eye, numbness, and loss of hearing. Extensive physical trace evidence was found at the site, including an area of burnt sawgrass 72 feet in diameter.

Sources: *Strange Effects From UFOs* (NICAP, 1969) p. 12, including opthalmologist's report on Flynn's injuries; Fort Myers, Fla., *News-Press* March 18, 1965, and editorial endorsement of Flynn, March 19, 1965.

MAY 28, 1965; BOUGAINVILLE REEF, AUSTRALIA

Features: Aerial encounter, aircraft pacing, photographs, official secrecy.

An Ansett-A.N.A. DC-6B airliner (call sign "VH-INH") was enroute from Brisbane to Port Moresby, New Guinea. At about 3:25 a.m. the pilot radioed the Townsville Ground Control Tower and informed the operator, Mr. O., that his aircraft was being buzzed by a UFO. He described the object as spherical and slightly oblate — flattened on top and bottom — with what appeared to be exhaust gasses coming from it. The UFO paced the airliner for 10-15 minutes, then shot ahead at a terrific speed. The pilot reported that he had taken photographs of the UFO. Upon return to Brisbane, the pilot was flown to Canberra where the film was confiscated and he was instructed to remain silent about the sighting. The air traffic control tapes at Townsville containing the entire conversation between the pilot and the tower also were confiscated, and O. was threatened with dismissal if he talked about the incident.

Special significance: Sighting and photographs of a geometrical UFO by an experienced observer, and evidence of high level secrecy and confiscation of the confirmatory data in Australia, as often reported in the United States.

Source: Interview report by a police source in Australia (copy in author's files).

JULY 3, 1965; ANTARCTICA

Features: Scientific witnesses, photographs, extraordinary maneuvers, E-M effects, instrumental data.

Argentine, British, and Chilean military and scientific personnel at scientific stations observed a "curious celestial body" for about 20 minutes. At the Chilean station, where 10 color photographs of the object were taken, Air Force Commander Mario Jahn Barrera described it as, "Something that moved at a frightening speed, zigzagging and giving off a blue-green light. . . . it was something solid, which caused interference in the base's electromagnetic equipment. . . . no apparatus constructed by man to date has anything like this, either in shape, speed, maneuverability or other characteristics."

At one point the UFO stopped in midair and "we were amazed to see it hover motionless for several minutes." (Quotes from reference 1, below.) Various news accounts described the UFO as being lens or lentil shaped, or like a "flying saucer." Daniel Perisse, commander of the Argentine station "Orcadas," confirmed that the UFO alternately hovered, accelerated and maneuvered at tremendous speed. While being tracked by theodolite and watched through binoculars, the UFO also registered on magnetograph tapes and caused strong interference with variometers used to measure the earth's magnetic field. Strong radio interference occurred at the Chilean station, temporarily blocking efforts to report the UFO to the other bases.

Special significance: Multiple scientific witnesses and simultaneous instrumental and photographic confirmation. Apparent official secrecy since the photographs, scientific data, and witness reports have never been made public. Personal efforts by the author to obtain analysis reports through embassies in Washington, D.C., were unsuccessful.

Sources: Manitoba *Standard* July 9, 1965 (dateline Santiago, Chile, July 7); Baltimore *Sun* July 7, 1965 (Santiago, Associated Press, July 6); *La Razon*, Buenos Aires, Argentina, July 6, 1965.

AUGUST 4, 1965; Nr. ABILENE, KANSAS

Features: Vehicle encounter, confrontation, landing on highway, E-M effects, sound.

Don Tenopir, a Nebraska truck driver, was driving his grain truck north on Highway 15 about 25-30 miles south of Abilene about 1:30 a.m. when an object swooped over his truck from behind and landed on the roadway ahead of him, forcing him to jam on his brakes. His headlights failed but his engine, a GMC diesel, did not. When the UFO moved ahead his lights came back on, and he could see the UFO hovering about 2 feet off the road surface: a domed disc about 15 feet in diameter, hat-shaped, and orange in color. What looked like square windows were visible around the top.

Tenopir was "scared to death" and never got out of his cab. A car coming in the opposite direction just as the UFO landed had swerved around it and stopped behind Tenopir's truck. The driver got out and approached the truck, saying something as he approached, but before they could compare notes the UFO suddenly began emitting bluish sparks out of the bottom center and took off making a sound like "wind blowing through trees." Both drivers fled the scene. Tenopir

reported the incident to the Abilene police, but was not interrogated by the Air Force or other Government authorities.

Source: Interview report by Dr. James E. McDonald (copy in
author's files).

AUGUST 19, 1965; CHERRY CREEK, NEW YORK

Features: Landing, physical traces, E-M effects, animal reactions, sound, odor.

About 8:10 p.m. Harold Butcher, 16, was milking cows on his
parents' farm with a tractor-powered milking machine, when
static suddenly interfered with his transistor radio, the tractor
motor stopped, and a bull tethered in the barnyard bellowed
and reacted violently, bending a metal stake. Looking out the
window, Butcher saw a large elliptical object apparently landing about a quarter mile away, emitting an audible beep-beep
sound and a red vapor from around its edges. After a few
seconds , the UFO shot straight up into the clouds overhead.
Family members detected a strange odor in the air, and saw
a peculiar greenish glow in the clouds where the UFO had
vanished. At the apparent landing site were a purplish liquid,
disturbed and singed grass, and two track-like depressions in
the ground.

Sources: "UFOs: Greatest Scientific Problem of Our Times?"
by James E. McDonald, presentation to American Society of
Newspaper Editors, Washington, D.C., Apr. 22, 1967; *Strange
Effects From UFOs* (NICAP, 1969), pp. 42-44; *The Hynek UFO
Report*, by J. Allen Hynek (N.Y.: Dell Books, 1977) pp. 170-172.

SEPTEMBER 1965; BRABANT, BELGIUM

Features: Vehicle encounter, steering control loss, levitation,
physiological effects.

Mrs. A.V. was driving home from Brussels on a secondary
road in her MG sports car traveling about 90 kph (56 mph)

just after 7:30 p.m. Her headlights were on. Following behind her at a distance of about 500 meters was her husband in his own car. At a bend in the road she suddenly noticed that the car was no longer responding to the steering wheel, so she started to slow down. Then a "small neon light" appeared near her windshield and the car was lifted a few centimeters off the road. The light was yellow and tube-shaped with even luminosity and sharp contours. It felt as if the car were floating on a cushion of air without her control.

After 3-4 seconds the light disappeared and the car once again made contact with the road, and she regained control of it. Badly frightened, she hurried home. Her nervous tension and fear of ridicule prevented her from telling her husband of the incident when he arrived moments later. He had seen nothing unusual. A few hours later she noticed on her wrists (a long-sleeve dress covered the rest of her skin) line-like markings consisting of a multitude of small points; the mark on her left wrist was reddish, sharp in outline, and itched like a light burn.

After 3 days she told her husband the story. About a week after the incident the marks disappeared. She had not consulted a doctor. Two years later, in 1967, the left wrist marking reappeared for a while, but no other aftereffects were reported. Belgian investigators of the SOBEPS organization interrogated Mrs. A.V. and reconstructed the incident with her, and judged her to be a credible witness.

Source: *MUFON UFO Journal*, No. 126, May 1978 (from *SOBEPS News Bulletin*, Brussels, Belgium, Sept. 1977).

SEPTEMBER 3, 1965; DAMON/ANGLETON, TEXAS

Features: Vehicle encounter, confrontation, brilliant illumination, heat, physiological effects.

Deputy Sheriffs Billy E. McCoy, 38, and Robert W. Goode, 50, were investigating a purplish light over the prairie which they thought might be a gas-well fire between 11:00 and 11:30 p.m. While trying to approach the light on back roads, an object with body lights seemed almost instantaneously to shoot towards them and stop about 150 feet away and 100 feet off the ground. The UFO appeared to be 200 or more feet long and 40 to 50 feet thick in the center. A bright purple light on one end illuminated the ground and the interior of the patrol car. "Every blade of grass in the pasture stood out clearly," they said.

Goode, who was driving, felt heat on his arm which was resting on the open window. (A later report indicates that a cut on Goode's arm healed with astounding rapidity after the incident.) They fled in fear, and the UFO shot away as they left the scene. When their curiosity overcame their fear, they began searching for the object again; but when they again spotted a purple light, they fled for fear of a recurrence of the first experience. Air Force investigators termed the officers ". . . intelligent, mature, level-headed persons capable of sound judgment and reasoning."

Sources: Air Force Project Blue Book files, U.S. National Archives, Washington D.C.; *UFOs: A New Look* (NICAP, 1969), p. 7; "UFOs: Greatest Scientific Problem of Our Times?" by Dr. James E. McDonald, presentation to American Society of Newspaper Editors, Washington, D.C., Apr. 22, 1967.

SEPTEMBER 16, 1965; PRETORIA, SOUTH AFRICA

Features: Vehicle encounter, confrontation, police witnesses, landing, physical traces, official secrecy.

Constables John Lockem and Koos de Klerk were patrolling on the Pretoria-Bronkhorstspruit highway just after midnight when their police van headlights suddenly illuminated a domed, disc-shaped object sitting on the road. The UFO was copper colored and about 30 feet in diameter. In seconds, the object lifted off the road, emitting tongues of flame from two tubes or channels on the underside. "Its lift-off was quicker than anything I have ever seen," Constable Lockem said. Flames from the macadam road surface shot up in the air about 3 feet as the UFO departed, blazing long after it was out of sight.

Later investigation showed that part of the road was caved in as if from a heavy weight, and gravel had been separated from the tar in a severely burned area about 6 feet in diameter. Lt. Col. J.B. Brits, District Commandant of Pretoria North, told the newspaper that the incident was considered "as being of a highly secret nature and an inquiry is being conducted in top circles." Samples of the road surface were taken for analysis by a leading scientific agency, whose report has never been made public.

Source: *UFOs: A New Look* (NICAP, 1969); Associated Press, Johannesburg, S. Africa, Sept. 17, 1965.

MARCH 20, 1966; DEXTER, MICHIGAN

Features: Landing, structured object, multiple witnesses, animal reaction, mist.

About 8:30 p.m., Frank Mannor, 47, a farmer, heard his dogs barking loudly and ran outside to investigate. In a swampy area to the east he saw flashing lights and called his son Ronald, 19. Together they crossed the swampy and hummocky terrain toward the lights trying to get a better look. They saw a domed, elliptical object with a quilted surface hovering about 8 feet off the ground, in a patch of apparent mist. The object then glowed "blood red" and the body lights disappeared. As they tried to get closer in the tricky terrain, they lost sight of the object and did not see it take off.

Mrs. Mannor, meanwhile, had called the police and a crowd gathered around the area. Many, including sheriffs' deputies, saw the flashing lights or a red glow. According to the sheriffs' office, police officers saw the UFO take off, make several sweeps over the area, then fly away joined by three other objects. The incident was one of dozens reported in Michigan in the latter part of March, capturing national news media attention. In a hastily called Air Force press conference, then USAF spokesman J. Allen Hynek suggested the Dexter UFO and others seen in a swampy area near Hillsdale next day may have been marsh (or swamp) gas that had spontaneously ignited.

Sources: "Swamp Gas Episode" by Allen R. Utke, in *Encyclopedia of UFOs* (N.Y.: Doubleday, 1980); LIFE magazine, Apr. 1, 1966.

MARCH 31, 1966; Nr. VICKSBURG, MICHIGAN

Features: Vehicle encounter, brilliant illumination, light beam, wind, sound, possible E-M effect.

Carpenter Jeno Udvardy, 32 (a Hungarian refugee and former aircrew member in the Hungarian Air Force), was driving home from a late work shift shortly after 2:00 a.m. At the crest of a hill on 27th street, he observed a cluster of lights ahead on the straight, level road several hundred yards distant. Thinking it was an ambulance at the scene of an accident, he slowed and approached cautiously. Reaching the scene, he was startled to see that the supposed ambulance was hovering just off the road and his headlight beams were illuminating the road beneath and beyond. Startled, he jammed on his brakes and stopped within 10 feet of the object. It had a rounded undersurface and was bobbing up and down gently.

A brilliantly glaring white light from the left side of the object suddenly fell on him like a searchlight, and smaller red, green, and white body lights blinked randomly. Above (perhaps on a superstructure concealed by the lights) was a blinking purplish light. Suddenly overwhelmed with fear, Udvardy began backing the car away, but was dazzled by the white light and could not see the road behind him. At that moment the car was shaken by gusts of wind, and the object suddenly appeared behind him. He rolled down the window and looked out, shielding his eyes with his arm from the bright glare. A low hum was audible, like a swarm of bees. About this time he noticed that his motor had stalled.

Shortly afterwards the UFO rose vertically and sped off at a steep angle to the east. He acknowledged being more frightened by this encounter than by any past experiences, including being wounded and being shot down in an airplane.

Source: *UFOs: A New Look* (Washington, D.C.: NICAP, 1969) p. 23; Investigation report in author's files.

APRIL 17, 1966; RAVENNA, OHIO, TO CONWAY, PENNSYLVANIA

Features: Police witnesses, confrontation, light beam, brilliant illumination, light engulfment, sound, cat and mouse chase, rapid upward departure.

Deputy Sheriffs Dale Spaur and Wilbur Neff of Portage County were investigating an abandoned car about dawn when a brilliant glowing object rose out of the woods to treetop level and stopped overhead, illuminating them and the surroundings. A humming sound like an overloaded transformer was audible. They fled to the patrol car and notified the station, and were instructed to keep the object in view until a camera car could reach the scene. The UFO began moving away about 300-500 feet above the road emitting an inverted cone of light (narrower at the bottom) to the ground. The light beam rocked back and forth in unison with a slight wobble of the UFO. A dark area and a projection like a large antenna were visible at the upper rear.

The officers chased after it at speeds up to 100 m.p.h. when it pulled away, and each time found it hovering over the road as if waiting for them. At East Palestine, Ohio, near the Pennsylvania border, Officer Wayne Huston heard the frantic radio calls and waited at an intersection they were headed toward to see what was going on. Shortly he saw a glowing object racing along over the highway with the police cruiser in hot pursuit. He wheeled around and joined the chase, guiding Spaur and Neff (whom he had not previously known) through territory that was unfamiliar to them. Running low on gas and with tires worn out by the grueling chase,

Spaur pulled up in a gas station in Conway, Pa., where Officer Frank Panzanella was sitting in his police cruiser.

When briefed by Spaur, Panzanella called his dispatcher and the Pennsylvania police alerted the Air Force, who sent fighter planes to investigate. The UFO had moved on to the east and was visible hovering in the distance. Spaur, Neff, Huston, and Panzanella, from three different police jurisdictions, stood watching and saw the Air Force planes approaching. Spaur: "When they started talking about fighter planes, it was just as if that thing heard every word that was said; it went PSSSSHHEW, *straight* up; and I mean when it went up, friend, it didn't play no games; it went *straight* up."

Sources: *UFOs: A New Look* (NICAP, 1969), p. 8; "UFOs: Greatest Scientific Problem of Our Times?" by Dr. James E. McDonald, 1967; interview transcript and other supplementary material in author's files; *UFOs and the Limits of Science*, by Ronald D. Story (N.Y.: Morrow, 1981) pp. 163-173; *The UFO Experience*, by J. Allen Hynek (Chicago: Henry Regnery, 1972) pp. 99-108.

JUNE 1966; NHA TRANG, VIETNAM

Features: Brilliant illumination, extensive E-M effects at U.S. Army base, hover and rapid upward departure.

At this active base on the coastline of South Vietnam, soldiers were watching an outdoor movie about 9:45 p.m., made possible by recent installation of six new, independently operated 100-kw diesel-powered generators. A Shell oil tanker lay anchored in the bay, two Skyraider prop planes were warming up on a nearby airstrip, and eight bulldozers were at work on nearby hills. Suddenly the sky to the north lit up, thought at first to be a flare, and then a UFO approached (no descriptive details) alternately moving at high and low speeds. It descended toward the gathered soldiers, stopped dead, and hovered at an altitude of about 300-500 feet.

The entire valley and surrounding mountains were illuminated brightly. The generators failed and *everything* blacked out on the base. The engines of the Skyraiders, the bulldozers, the trucks, the power system of the offshore Shell Oil tanker — everything (including some diesel engines) all failed for about 4 minutes. Then the UFO ". . . went straight up and completely out of sight in about 2-3 seconds." After the incident, a plane-load of officials from Washington arrived to investigate.

Sources: *The U.F.O. Investigator*, NICAP, July 1973; *UFOs: Interplanetary Visitors*, by Raymond E. Fowler (N.Y.: Exposition Press, 1974), pp. 101-103.

JUNE 24, 1966; RICHMOND, VIRGINIA

Features: Police witness, vehicle encounter, cat-and-mouse chase, mist, reaction to witness.

Officer William L. Stevens, Jr., was cruising on the Richmond outskirts at 3:30 a.m. when he noticed some odd greenish-yellow lights near the fair grounds. Then he saw that the lights were on the perimeter of a dirigible-shaped object about 100 feet long and 30 feet thick, sharply outlined against the sky. Around the object was a mist or vapor. Stevens turned on his emergency flasher lights and accelerated toward the object (an interesting and totally in character reaction for a police officer!); the UFO reacted immediately, moving swiftly away over the Richmond-Henrico Turnpike.

Stevens continued to speed up in an effort to catch the object, but it maintained the same distance away from him though Stevens altered his speed several times. "The object seemed to be playing with me," Stevens said. He reached speeds of over 100 m.p.h. as the chase continued across Henrico County and into Hanover County. After 10-15 minutes the UFO suddenly accelerated and sped away. A private check on Stevens by a Richmond newsman revealed that he was considered to be of excellent character and had received awards for police work.

Sources: *UFOs: A New Look* (NICAP, 1969) p. 9; "UFOs: Greatest Scientific Problem of Our Times?" by Dr. James E.

McDonald, presentation to American Society of Newspaper Editors, Washington, D.C., Apr. 22, 1967; personal communication to the author.

OCTOBER 15, 1966; SPLIT ROCK POND, NEW JERSEY

Features: Vehicle encounter, confrontation, E-M effects, brilliant illumination, physiological aftereffects.

Jerry H. Simons, 22, a forester, had been camping out and was driving home shortly after 4:30 a.m. He noticed a bright red-orange glow in his rear vision mirror and, thinking a brake light was stuck, stopped the car and leaned out the window to look back. He was shocked to see an illuminated disc-shaped object behind the car, and immediately hurried to get out on the main road.

The UFO followed directly behind and above the car. Then his headlights and engine failed and he saw that the UFO was now above the car. When the UFO retreated, the engine and lights worked again and he tried to flee. The same sequence of events was repeated three times. ". . . three times my car refused to give any electrical response until this object either moved to the rear or to one side of the car," he said.

The UFO illuminated the ground around the car, and the E-M effects occurred when the car was within the illuminated area. Finally the UFO fell back and disappeared. When Simons stopped to report the incident and returned to his car, he found that the engine had apparently started up spontaneously. Several weeks later the engine inexplicably exploded. Shortly after the sighting he experienced a cyclical recurring illness lasting 3 months, including fatigue, anorexia, soreness, muscle weakness, chills, and weight loss. He was hospitalized, but no exact cause for the illness could be determined. After 6 months he had recovered and showed no further aftereffects.

Sources: *UFOs: A New Look* (Washington, D.C.: NICAP, 1969) p.9; *Medical Times*, October 1968.

Appendix A

MARCH 7, 1967; KEENEYVILLE, ILLINOIS

Features: Vehicle encounter, confrontation, light beams, animal reaction, abnormal mist.

Mrs. Lucille Drzonek and her two daughters were driving on U.S. 20 at 12:30 a.m. when they saw a "solid object (about 15 feet in diameter), outlined in bright white lights with two big beams in front." As it descended, the UFO displayed flashing green and red lights and took on a round or disc shape. Their dog, Bugle, reacted with fright, his hair standing straight on his back. As they turned off the highway, the UFO appeared to descend into the woods, lighting the area in a red glare. Then something zoomed out of the woods directly toward the car and projected two white beams of light through the back window. As they arrived home, the UFO was still following and was now about 10 feet above a tree in their yard. Then a strange "gray mist appeared only in our backyard," Joyce Drzonek said. When the mist cleared away, the UFO had disappeared. The dog ". . . was upset for two days."

Source: *Strange Effects From UFOs* (NICAP, 1969) p. 34.

MARCH 8, 1967; LEOMINSTER, MASSACHUSETTS

Features: Abnormal "fog," E-M effects, physiological effects, sound, rapid upward departure.

Mr. & Mrs. William L. Wallace were returning home when, about 1:05 a.m., they noticed a heavy fog patch at St. Leo's cemetery but none elsewhere in the area. As they drove through the fog, Wallace saw a strange light and turned the car around to investigate; he then saw a flattened egg-shaped object hovering 400-500 feet over the cemetery. Wallace stopped the car, got out, and pointed at the UFO, whereupon his arm was pulled abruptly against the roof of the car, the engine stalled, the headlights went out, and the radio ceased playing.

263

Wallace felt something like an electrical shock or numbness and was paralyzed. His immobile state lasted for about 30 seconds, and then the car lights came on again and the radio resumed playing. The UFO, at this point rocking back and forth and emitting a humming or whirring sound, suddenly accelerated upwards and disappeared. Wallace's reflexes remained sluggish for a considerable period of time after the event.

Sources: *UFOs: Interplanetary Visitors*, by Raymond E. Fowler (N.Y.: Exposition Press, 1974), pp. 145-148; *Strange Effects From UFOs* (NICAP, 1969) p. 7.

NOVEMBER 2, 1967; RIRIE, IDAHO

Features: Vehicle encounter, confrontation, humanoids, steering control loss, green illumination, levitation, mass displacement, animal reactions.

Guy Tossie and Will Begay, Indian youths, were driving on Highway 26 about 9:30 p.m. Suddenly there was a blinding flash of light ahead, and a small domed UFO appeared. Through the transparent dome they saw two small beings. As the UFO hovered about 5 feet above the road, the car was slowed and brought to a stop by some external force. The UFO had flashing green and orange lights around its rim and the area was bathed in a vivid green light. The dome opened as if on a hinge and one of the beings emerged and floated down. It was about 3-1/2 feet tall, with a kind of "backpack," its face oval and heavily lined, with small eyes, slit-like mouth, and large ears.

The being approached the driver's side of the car, opened the door and slid behind the wheel, as the terrified pair pushed over to the right. Then the car began to move and was displaced into an adjacent field of stubble wheat as the UFO kept a fixed position a few feet in front. Tossie then bolted out of the door and fled to the nearest farmhouse, as Begay cowered in the front seat in near shock. The being emitted high-pitched unintelligible sounds "like a bird." A second being, who apparently had followed Tossie, then returned to the car and the two beings floated back up to the UFO, which then ascended in a zig-zag path and disappeared.

A number of local farmers reported that their cattle had bolted during the evening for unknown reasons, and a second witness was found who reported a similar encounter that same night.

Source: *UFOs: A New Look* (NICAP, 1969) p. 31.

JULY 30, 1968; CLAREMONT, NEW HAMPSHIRE

Features: Brilliant illumination, light beam, sound, animal reactions.

A land surveyor and his wife saw a dome-shaped object about 20 feet in diameter hovering about 10 feet above the ground a little over 200 feet away at 2:00 a.m. A wide grayish beam of light extended to the ground, causing sharp shadows on the terrain. Their sleeping children moaned and cried out in their sleep, and their German shepherd dog whimpered and whined. Their poodle also was visibly shaking and upset. The couple heard a high-pitched humming sound, like a transformer, as the UFO moved about 25 feet and then stayed in the same position until 4:30 a.m. At one point an arm-like projection from the object descended to the ground. Finally, the humming sound grew "very loud," the light brightened to "high intensity," and the UFO moved away to the west and disappeared. As it moved away, the German shepherd "whined loudly." The couple described the experience as "very terrifying."

Source: *Strange Effects From UFOs* (NICAP, 1969) p. 38.

MARCH 4, 1969; Nr. ATLANTA, MISSOURI

Features: Vehicle encounter, light beam, E-M effects, cat-and-mouse pursuit, heat.

William R. Overstreet, 51, City Marshal and Star Route Mail Carrier in Elmer, Missouri, was driving to work on Highway J at 6:40 a.m., headed east. He noticed a large red object to the right moving on a northerly (crossing) course. When the object reached the road it turned east ahead of him, its size (compared to the road) 100 feet diameter, and about 50 feet altitude. As Overstreet gained on the object he saw a strong beam of white light — tapering at its lower end to about 8 feet diameter (compare to Apr. 17, 1966, Ravenna, Ohio) — beam down onto the road. Debris within the light beam seemed to be magnified in size, and he felt strong heat "like I was sitting out in the sun on a hot summer day ..." (compare to Aug. 13, 1975, Haderslev, Denmark). At this point the UFO began changing colors, its center now a quivering bright blue; around the blue a wide red band; and a narrower yellow band on the outside, apparently rotating clockwise.

The light was so brilliant that Overstreet pulled down his sun visor and shielded his eyes with his hand. He tried to report the sighting on his CB radio, but it was dead. As he neared the conical beam of light, his truck motor and radio quit. Releasing the clutch, he coasted, and as the light beam eased off a few feet he heard static on the radio, so he let the clutch out and the engine restarted. He inched forward toward the light beam again, and when within 6 feet his engine started skipping. When he stepped on the gas, both his engine and radio failed again.

Once again, when the UFO pulled ahead the engine restarted. After that, Overstreet dropped back and cautiously trailed the object for about 4 miles. He noticed that the object, moving at about 40 m.p.h. ahead of him, rose and fell as if following the contours of the ground. At the crossroad of Highway 36, the UFO veered off to the southeast and went out of sight. Elapsed time: 7-8 minutes.

"I had never believed in them too much until I saw this," he said. "Now I know that there is something to these UFOs."

Sources: NICAP investigation report, copy in author's files; Macon, Mo., *Chronicle-Herald*, Mar. 5, 1969; Fulton, Mo., *Sun-Gazette*, Mar. 6, 1969.

JANUARY 7, 1970; Nr. HEINOLA, FINLAND

Features: Sound, "luminous fog," light beam, humanoid, black box with light beam, paralysis, physiological effects.

While skiing close to sunset, Aarno Heinomen, 36, and Esko Viljo, 38, heard a strange buzzing sound which became louder. A very bright light approached and hovered about 15 meters in front of them. An apparently metallic object could be seen surrounded by a "luminous gray fog." It was a domed disc about 3 meters in diameter with three hemispherical protrusions spaced around the lower surface and a tube about 25 cm in diameter in the center. The UFO descended slowly and the "fog" disappeared. About 4 meters from the ground the buzzing sound stopped and a beam of light emerged from the central tube to the ground.

Within the light beam was a small humanoid figure (90 cm) with a white face, and a cone-shaped bright metallic "hat." He had on gray coveralls and green boots. He was holding a small black box from which came a blinding ray of light. The fog then reappeared and red and green sparkles burst out from the luminous circle as the fog became heavy. The light beam re-entered the tube and suddenly the UFO was gone. Heinoman was fainting, and paralyzed on the right side.

It took the two men two hours to reach the nearest village which was 2 km away. Heinoman was suffering headaches, vomiting, and breathing with difficulty. He felt pain all over, was cold, and could not keep his equilibrium. Viljo had a red, swollen face and also lost his equilibrium. His hands and chest were covered with red spots. Other witnesses had also seen a bright light that night.

Source: *Inforespace*, Aug. 1975, No. 22, Brussels, Belgium.

UNINVITED GUESTS

AUGUST 1, 1971; CALLIOPE RIVER, QUEENSLAND, AUSTRALIA

Features: Vehicle encounter, altered surroundings, time loss, amnesia, physical markings on car, translocation (?).

Ben and Helen K. (name on file with UFO Research-NSW), a Finnish couple, were returning home from Gladstone to Rockhampton soon after 11:35 p.m. They were short of gas, but hoped to find a station open. The night was dark and foggy. After passing one closed station they became aware of a green light at treetop level behind them, and shortly afterwards felt that they had been driving straight for an abnormal period of time (the roads are winding), and that they were repeating the same words over and over. Then they saw a circle of lights above and to the left, and the next thing they saw was the Port Alma road sign, about 40 km north of the Calliope River. Immediately after this, they found themselves at a railroad crossing outside Rockhampton, about 20 miles from Mount Morgan.

"We wondered how we had managed to get so far and why we had not seen any villages on the way ... We felt that something strange had happened to us." In Rockhampton, they found an open station and they discovered that it was only 12:15 a.m. Only 40 minutes had elapsed, and at the speed they were driving (35-40 m.p.h.) the trip should have taken close to two hours. They discovered an oily film and four round marks on the hood of the car.

Another motorist then arrived and said he had passed them before the Calliope River and was puzzled about how they could have arrived at Rockhampton before him. The couple reported the experience to the police, who brushed it off as somnambulism. Hypnotic regression was later attempted, but nothing further was elicited. Each time it was attempted, they began to shake violently and the hypnotist gave up the attempt.

Special significance: Features suggestive of a possible abduction.

Source: *MUFON UFO Journal*, No. 150, August 1980.

JUNE 28, 1973; COLUMBIA, MISSOURI

Features: Landing, physical traces, sound, E-M effects, animal reaction, light beams, wind, brilliant illumination.

James Richard, 41, was relaxing in his mobile home at 12:30 p.m. before going to bed. His daughter Vanea, 16, called him from the kitchen, alarmed by a persistent "thrashing sound" audible through the open north window. Looking out, they saw two very bright silvery-white light beams about 5 feet apart and 50 feet away, tapering to about 2 feet diameter at the bottom (compare to Apr. 17, 1966, Ravenna, Ohio, and Mar. 4, 1969, Atlanta, Mo.) The beams faded and a 12-15 foot bright oval object appeared close to the ground. Richard had to avert his eyes due to the brilliance; the area was "lit up as bright as day."

The thrashing sound continued, and the trees swayed as if in a strong wind; one seemed to be pulled toward the ground, and a large limb snapped off at a point 17 feet above the ground. Richard noticed that his dogs were lying quietly outside the house, not barking. Richard got a gun and watched cautiously for a while, then decided to call for help. The UFO then moved away to the north, passing beneath tree limbs, rose slightly and hovered about 200 feet away, its brilliance slightly diminished. Blue and orange bands of lights now appeared, visible on a silvery surface. Then the UFO smoothly and silently moved back to its original position.

Richard called the trailer court switchboard and asked the person on duty to call the police; during the call the house lights dimmed twice. The UFO next moved toward the mobile home, but then away again to a new position where the bands of light could be seen again. Finally the lights diminished and the UFO disappeared. The police arrived at 1:45 a.m., took a superficial look around, and left. Afterwards broken limbs, damaged foliage, and scorched leaves up to a height of 35 feet above the ground were found where the UFO had moved back and forth. Later, more leaves turned brown and wilted. Also, imprints as if from landing gear were found indented as much as two feet in the hard ground. A complex pattern of other imprints was visible along the flight path.

Sources: *Skylook* (now *MUFON UFO Journal*), No. 70, Sept. 1973; *Physical Traces Associated With UFO Sightings*, July 1975, Center for UFO Studies, p. 90.

OCTOBER 17, 1973; MIDWESTERN STATE

Features: Bedroom visitation, abduction with four children, levitation, technological instruments, physiological exam on table, human being working with aliens, occurrence during 1973 UFO wave.

Patty "Price," divorced and sole provider for seven children had just moved into a new house, and the tired family settled down to sleep on the night of October 16/17. The young boy woke up screaming that he had seen a "skeleton," the cat was yowling, and a dog barking furiously. Patty also had vague feelings of having seen a prowler, and took her children to sleep at a friend's house. Next morning Dottie, 7, said the prowler was a "spaceman" and described a craft and creatures on it, and two beings who had come into the house.

Under later hypnosis Patty recalled seeing two figures standing over her, slender, and wearing clothes like uniforms. She resisted their efforts to abduct her, as did the children, but they grasped her by the arms and floated her and four of the children on board a craft and into a large, bright, round room which had computer-like machines, displays, and buttons. Four or five aliens slightly over 4 ft. tall were standing around; they had large slant eyes, masklike faces, long arms, and claw-like hands. With them was a taller, normal human being wearing horn-rimmed glasses.

Patty was placed on a table and something fastened to one leg and arm. She was given an examination, including gynecological, and a needle was inserted into her abdomen and elsewhere. During one such episode she felt that they were "taking her thoughts." Finally she was floated back to the house, where she found the children. The oldest daughter, Betty, recalled seeing her mother nude on the exam table, and seeing the one human being with the aliens. Dottie said she saw other people from the neighborhood also being abducted. Patty said the aliens seemed emotionless, and she felt like a guinea pig that they were using.

Source: *Abducted*, by Coral and Jim Lorenzen, ch. II, "Patty Price's Ordeal" (N.Y.: Berkley Medallion Books, 1977).

OCTOBER 18, 1973; Nr. MANSFIELD, OHIO

Features: Aerial encounter, mass displacement, loss of vehicle control, light beam, E-M effects.

Capt. Lawrence J. Coyne was commanding the Army Reserve Huey helicopter on a return flight to Cleveland from Columbus. Lt. A.D. Jezzi was at the controls when, at about 11:00 p.m., Sgt. Robert J. Yanacsek yelled out that a red light was closing rapidly on them from the east. Thinking it was a military jet, Coyne grabbed the controls and took evasive action, cutting the power and dropping into a dive. The object then loomed overhead in front of the helicopter, stopped and hovered. It was cigar-shaped with a dome on top, a steady red light on the front and a white light on the back. From the underside of the UFO, a green beam of light swung around 90 degrees and shone into the cockpit, which lit up eerily with a green glow.

The helicopter had been descending to 1,700 feet, but now inexplicably the altimeter read 3,500 feet and climbing. Suddenly the crew felt a "bump," and the UFO took off to the west, disappearing in seconds. They had tried to radio Mansfield airport, about 7 miles away, but the radio would not work after initial contact. Both UHF and VHF channels malfunctioned. The unusual communications blackout persisted for about 10 minutes. Although the UFO was so close that it filled the entire windshield of the helicopter, the crew felt no turbulence and heard no noise. The sighting occurred during a major UFO wave.

Sources: *Helicopter-UFO Encounter Over Ohio*, by Jennie Zeidman (Center for UFO Studies, Mar. 1979); Cleveland *Plain Dealer*, Oct. 22, 1973; Cincinnati *Enquirer*, Oct. 22, 1973; *UFOs and the Limits of Science*, by Ronald D. Story (N.Y.: Morrow, 1981) pp. 181-184

OCTOBER 28, 1973; BAHIA BLANCA, BRAZIL

Features: Humanoids, mental blackout, light beam, levitation, abduction, technological instruments, communication, sound, markings on body.

Dionisio Yanca, 25, a truck driver, stopped to change a flat tire at 1:15 a.m. Suddenly he saw a rapidly approaching light that resolved itself into a 4-meter-diameter UFO, which stopped and hovered about 4 m off the ground. Three human-like beings appeared, two short-haired blond men and one long-haired blond woman, wearing silvery clothing. Yanca blacked out. His next conscious memory was of falling — slowly — into a pasture, confused about his identity, where he was, and the time. Later, under hypnosis and sodium pentothal treatment, he told of rising in a beam of light with the beings and entering a craft after they had pricked him with some instrument. The craft had a variety of "dashboard" panels resembling radios and TV screens, one showing a star field.

The beings seemed to communicate among themselves with a humming sound, like a swarm of bees. A voice communicated with Yanca through an apparent radio set, in Spanish, saying that he should not be afraid; that they had been coming here for a long time and would return again. They were studying humans in order to find out whether we could live on their planet. The woman donned a black glove with tack-like spikes in the palm and approached him . . . his next memory was of falling into the pasture, his mind blank. Doctors who treated Yanca when he was found noted tiny dots or points on his left eyelid. After a thorough examination, they concluded that his story was consistent at all points and found no evidence of a hoax. Even after hypnosis and sodium pentothal, Yanca still could not account for about two hours, a period of total amnesia. (Note: This is one of the few abduction reports that depicts contactee-like golden-haired beings.)

Source: *Skylook* (now *MUFON UFO Journal*) No. 76, Mar. 1974 and No. 82, Sept. 1974.

JANUARY 24, 1974; AISCHE-EN-REFAIL, BELGIUM

Features: Vehicle encounter, landed object, E-M effects, physiological effects.

Shortly after 4:00 p.m. on a clear day, Mrs. N.D. was rapidly approaching a hill in her Volkswagen 1300 model when she noticed a red object about 150 meters away on the ground to the left of the road. Suddenly her engine began to lose power and she thought she was running out of gas, or had a carburetor problem. Her car continued to slow, the radio went dead (except that its light remained on), and the car coasted to a stop as the engine failed, with the gearshift still in 4th gear. She was now only about 10 meters away from the object, which was about 1 meter in diameter and ½ meter high, with a red flattened dome on top and two rows of "spots" or ports around the circumference. The surface appeared like unpolished metal, non-reflective.

After 4-5 seconds the UFO began to move, rising about 50 cm, then dropping back to the ground. This action was repeated a second time. The third time it rose slowly and steadily to 3 or 4 meters off the ground and moved above the car, revealing a flat, gray, featureless underside. After a few seconds it moved silently away on a curved trajectory. As it left, the car engine restarted by itself without Mrs. N. D. touching the starter and, still in 4th gear, the car began moving forward as the UFO could be seen disappearing to the east-northeast.

Investigators could find no physical traces on the hard clay ground, and no radioactivity was detected. The car had recently been through a thorough check-up and was in good working order. The witness had nightmares for several days and suffered from "abnormal lassitude." Otherwise she was unaffected. Later that Spring the engine began misfiring, and in July a faulty distributor had to be replaced.

Source: *Skylook* (now *MUFON UFO Journal*), No. 99, Feb. 1976

FEBRUARY 14, 1974; PETITE-ILE (REUNION), FRANCE

Features: Confrontation, "magnetic force," light beam, humanoids, physiological effects.

M. Severin, 21, a commerce clerk, was walking home about 1:30 p.m. on a road adjacent to a cornfield in an uninhabited area. Suddenly he felt a strange force pulling him from the back, as if pulled by a giant magnet, and he felt a tingling in his head. Then he saw an object the size of a car, bright white, shaped like "two half-eggs on a plate." The UFO was hovering 50 cm off the ground, and a luminous ray from it was being directed onto Severin.

Through an opening in the UFO he could see stairs with three steps which reached down to the ground. In that opening was a small being who moved down the stairs and joined another being who appeared to be scraping the ground. Then a third being appeared with a "bag" in his hand and began to move around the one scraping the ground as if trying to help him.

The humanoids were estimated to be 1-1.2 meters tall, dressed in bright white, apparently metallic suits, and had antennalike projections on each side of their heads. After a few moments a fourth being started down the stairs, appeared to see the witness and react to his presence, and all the humanoids re-entered the UFO, the opening closed, and the object took off and disappeared. Severin was badly frightened. He lost his voice, suffered from headaches, and had impaired vision for two days.

Source: *Ouranos*, No. 14, 2nd Quarter 1975 (France).

FEBRUARY 14, 1974; Nr. ELY, NEVADA

Features: Vehicle encounter, confrontation, wind or "force field," E-M effects, levitation, steering control loss, feeling of isolation, severe damage to vehicle.

Two brothers, businessmen, were driving a U-Haul truck from Buhl, Idaho, to Hemet, California, carrying their parent's furniture. About 4:15 a.m. on Highway 93, about 55 miles north of Ely, the driver woke his sleeping brother to tell him that a UFO was following them. A round, orange object about 10 feet above the desert was visible out the left side; three smaller objects (lights) were visible to the right, one flickering on and off. The orange object had moved from a position on the right ahead of the truck, crossed the road, and approached on the left. ". . . at that moment it felt like we had been hit by a blast of wind or force field. [At this point they discovered that the truck was floating off the road.] The lights on the truck flickered on and off and the engine started to miss . . . he [the brother driving] lost control of the truck and couldn't steer it. I told him to stop, and then before we could stop, the transmission selector jumped out of 'drive' into 'neutral,' and we coasted to a stop in the middle of the road."

A huge silver "metal ball with a dome on top and sharp wings" was visible hovering over a hill to the left. Then they noticed a huge lighted object on the road ahead of them that seemed to be approaching. The second brother (non-driver) got out and shone a flashlight at the object, but nothing happened. He then looked under the truck and discovered that the drive shaft was still turning and, frightened and "fearing for my life," got back in the truck and watched the object move closer. "We felt that we were in a vacuum of some kind and isolated from the rest of the world." (Compare to Mar. 29, 1978, Indianapolis, Indiana.) After about 20 minutes the phenomena disappeared and the effects ended.

The truck was totally disabled, so they flagged down a passing driver who took them into a town where they rented another U-Haul truck. The entire rear end of the truck they had been driving had to be replaced — including the tires, the rear axle, the outside housing, and the gears. According to the U-Haul station owner who went to the scene, "The back axle was twisted right off." He said that when they tried to lift up the back of the truck with their tow truck, ". . . the rear wheels just fell right off!"

Sources: *Skylook* (now *MUFON UFO Journal*), No. 78, May 1974; Klinn and Branch UFO column, Santa Ana, Calif., Register, Mar. 27, 1974.

MAY 31, 1974; SALISBURY, RHODESIA, TO DURBAN, S. AFRICA

Features: Vehicle encounter, confrontation, light engulfment, E-M effects, steering control loss, light beam, translocation, altered surroundings, cold, abnormal silence, humanoids, amnesia, levitation.

On the night of May 30/31 Peter X, 24, and his wife Frances, 21, (last name on file at MUFON) experienced a series of strange events along the highway between 2:30 and 7:30 a.m. A very bright revolving light paced their car, a Peugeot 404 sedan, and the headlights dimmed and faded; the engine and radio functioned normally. A brilliant bluish neon-like light engulfed the car, and the interior became so cold that they turned on the heater and wrapped themselves in blankets. Peter discovered that he had no control over the car; "I couldn't stop the car, I had no power over braking. I put my foot on the brake and it went in the normal distance, but had no effect." When he took his foot off the accelerator it had no effect; the car continued moving at high speed.

They passed two abandoned buses about 7-10 km apart, which they thought odd. Now they could see that the UFO was oval, and a beam of light from it extended to the horizon. As they entered Fort Victoria, Rhodesia, the UFO sped off over the horizon and Peter regained control of the car. They stopped for gas (the car took the normal amount) at 4:30. After about an hour, they resumed the trip.

About 10-12 km beyond the city the same or a similar UFO, along with a smaller object, reappeared and the car again was engulfed in light and no longer could be controlled. The car accelerated from about 80 to 120 mph with little engine noise or sensation of speed. They were travelling through a swampy area (unknown to the region, which is dry) that looked ". . . very wet and . . . very lush." The normal sounds, such as crickets and locusts, were strangely absent. "It was as though someone had switched the sound off." No animal or other life was visible.

Just before reaching the South African border, about 7:00 a.m., the strange effects ceased and Peter resumed normal driving. They had travelled 288 km in 1 hour and 45 minutes (averaging about 100 mph), and arrived about an hour earlier than expected. However, the odometer registered only 17 km from Fort Victoria and only 2 liters of gas had been used. Afterwards the electrical system and transmission of the car deteriorated and had to be repaired. Frances began having prophetic dreams, foreseeing small life events that came true.

Under hypnosis December 3, Peter described audible contact and extensive communication with the beings controlling the car, and an apparently humanoid form that was beamed into the back seat. He also recalled seeing inside the UFO, which he described in some detail. He also recalled that the car had been off (above) the road.

(Note: The full story is very complex and needs to be read completely for proper evaluation. The portion emerging under hypnosis contains some vagueness and inconsistency, and is based on an unanalyzed tape recording of the session. An abduction is suggested but not clearly indicated.)

Source: *Skylook* (now *MUFON UFO Journal*), No. 88, Mar. 1975.

JULY 1974; BRIDGEWATER, TASMANIA

Features: Vehicle encounter, steering control loss.

The witness whose name is on record, prefers to remain anonymous. Excerpts from interview tape:

> ". . . it seemed to be oval . . . It had a front top light — a red one, and this larger bottom light . . . . We went along the highway and turned off. It hovered as we turned and seemed to keep pace with us . . . [Describes the UFO speeding up when they did and slowing down when they slowed. As they passed some houses the UFO remained higher, and on a more isolated stretch it again descended below hilltop height and resumed pacing the car.] After it came down again I felt as if I was in its power, as if it was definitely going to take over the controls of the car; it was hard to steer. We did wander right over to the right side of the road where the object was; to pull it back onto the right [correct] side of the road was quite an effort. I can remember that after it disappeared that my arms ached around the shoulders, so I was making quite an effort to keep the car where it should be . . . [It] seemed as if the car wasn't in my power."

The car, a Valiant Safari Station Sedan, suffered no other effects and there were no reported aftereffects.

Source: Transcript of tape-recorded interview by Tasmanian U.F.O. Investigation Centre, *Skylook* (now *MUFON UFO Journal*), No. 101, Apr. 1976.

Appendix A

OCTOBER 27, 1974; AVELEY, ENGLAND

Features: Vehicle encounter, E-M effects, engulfment by "green mist," abnormal silence, cold, time loss, teleportation, abduction, medical exams.

John and Elaine "Avis" (pseudonym), a young married couple with their three children, had been visiting relatives near London. They left at 9:50 p.m. for the normal 20-minute drive home. The two younger children were asleep on the back seat and Kevin, 7, was awake and listening to the radio. A blue, oval light was seen paralleling the car, then passing across the road ahead of them. When they were close to home about 10:10 p.m. they suddenly felt there was "something wrong": an abnormal silence was noted, except for the radio which crackled and began smoking. Just after seeing an eerie green mist covering the road ahead, the headlights went out. They felt the car jerk as they entered the green mist, then there was silence and a strange coldness. What seemed like a second later, the car exited from the mist with another jerk and everything returned to normal.

A few minutes later they reached home, and discovered that it was 1:00 a.m. — leaving nearly 3 hours unaccounted for. Subsequently John had a nervous breakdown and the family underwent various peculiar behavioral changes. John and Elaine had dreams about weird creatures and medical examinations. They thought vaguely that all of this was related to the UFO sighting, so 3 years later underwent regressive hypnosis. Under hypnosis they described the car being teleported up a column of light into a craft where they were medically examined by 4-ft.-tall birdlike entities. Other entities over 6-ft.-tall gave them a tour of the craft, and John was shown a holographic "map" of space that included the beings' home planet. Finally the car was teleported back down onto the road.

Source: "Aveley (England) Abduction" by Jenny Randles, in *Encyclopedia of UFOs* (N.Y.: Doubleday, 1980).

FEBRUARY 19, 1975; ORBAK, DENMARK

Features: Vehicle encounter, confrontation, E-M effects, brilliant illumination, heat, physiological effects, physical traces.

Mrs. X had just driven her daughter to Ryslinge High School and was returning to Orbak when the engine and all other electrical equipment in her Volkswagen failed. She coasted to the curb and stopped, just as a very large circular object descended above the car from behind. A brilliant bluish luminescence was emitted from the object, unlike any light she had ever seen. Shortly afterwards the light and the UFO vanished. For a while the heat in the car became unbearable and she felt a "prickly sensation" on her face. After the UFO disappeared, the car started with no problem. Next day she felt restless and sick with nausea. She told the newspaper that when she went out in the open, her face ached; she had never had this problem before. The red car had a number of blue stripes on the roof which were not there before the incident.

The case was known to Danish investigators within a week, but no information was reported on whether Mrs. X underwent any medical tests or any tests were made on the car paint.

Sources: Jyllands *Posten*, Feb. 25, 1975; *UFO-Aspekt*, Denmark, Apr. 1975 (including photograph of marks on car).

MAY 3, 1975; Nr. MEXICO CITY, MEXICO

Features: Aerial encounter, confrontation, levitation, E-M effects, steering control loss, radar tracking.

Carlos Antonio de los Santos Montiel, 23, was flying a Piper PA-24 from Zihuatenejo to Mexico City at about 15,000 feet. Passing over Lake Tequesquitengo at 1:34 p.m., he felt a strange vibration in the plane. Then he saw to the right, pacing alongside his plane, a 10-12 foot disc-shaped object with a dome or turret on top, and another to the left of the plane. A third disc approached head-on, dropped beneath the plane, and Carlos felt a jolt as if the object had collided with his plane.

Instinctively, he pulled the landing gear lever, but it failed to operate. He felt as if the plane was being pulled or lifted, and his controls refused to respond. Feeling helpless and badly shaken, he maintained radio contact with the Mexico City airport describing what was happening to him. Air control radar, at the same time, was showing unexplained objects near the plane that made sharp turns beyond the capability of aircraft, finally merging into one radar "blip" and speeding away toward Mt. Popocatepetl. After the UFOs left, Carlos was able to lower his landing gear manually and to land safely. Aviation personnel who know him testified to his sobriety and trustworthiness.

Source: *Skylook* (now *MUFON UFO Journal*), No. 93, Aug. 1975.

AUGUST 13, 1975; Nr. HADERSLEV, DENMARK

Features: Vehicle encounter, brilliant illumination, vehicle engulfment by light, E-M effects, heat, photographs, rapid upward departure.

Police Officer Evald Hansen Maarup was driving home to Knud in a police car at 10:50 p.m. As he headed downhill into a hollow to a crossroads, the car suddenly was engulfed by a bright bluish-white light; at the same time, the engine died and the headlights went out. Maarup coasted to the side of the road and stopped. Shielding his eyes from the dazzling light with his arm, he groped for the radio and tried to call the station, but the radio was dead. (Compare these details and following to Mar. 4, 1969, Atlanta, Mo.) The temperature in the car rose, feeling like the sun on a warm summer day. The light, shaped like a cone tapering to a bottom diameter of 4-5 meters, then rose up and into an opening in the bottom of a circular object about 10 meters in diameter.

The UFO was only about 20 meters overhead, and two dome-like protrusions were visible on the underside. Maarup activated a special camera mounted on the patrol car, with automatic film advance, and took three pictures. He stepped out of the car, and seconds later the UFO moved vertically upward and accelerated rapidly out of sight. No sound was heard. The headlights and dashlights then came back on and the car started normally. His radio resumed functioning and he reported the incident to the station.

Developing the film next day, Maarup found that a light source had been captured on it and he delivered the film to the Danish Air Force. No follow-up report is available on the results of photoanalysis.

Sources: *Scandinavian UFO Information Newsletter,* Aug. 1975, Soborg, Denmark; *MUFON UFO Journal,* No. 106, Sept. 1976.

AUGUST 13, 1975; ALAMOGORDO, NEW MEXICO

Features: Confrontation, humanoids, E-M effects, sound, numbness, time loss, abduction, physical exam on table, telepathic communication, physiological effects.

Staff Sgt. Charles L. Moody, U.S. Air Force, after a late work shift drove to the outskirts to watch for meteors. When a disc-shaped UFO descended to low altitude and moved toward him, he tried to flee but his car wouldn't start. He heard a high-pitched sound, saw shadowy humanoid figures in the UFO, felt a numbness ... then saw the UFO depart. His car then started without difficulty and he drove home, discovering a time loss of 1-1/2 hours.

Next day his lower back was inflamed and there was a small puncture wound over his spine; a few days later he had a body rash. Over the next two months, memory of the "lost" time gradually returned. He had been on a craft and in telepathic communication with small humanoid beings, about 4'8" tall. They had whitish-gray skin, large heads, large eyes, small slit-like mouths, and masklike facial features overall.

Their clothing was black and skin-tight, except the "leader" who was dressed in silver-white. Moody was on a smooth, slablike table unable to move; he felt drugged. One of the beings applied a rodlike device to his back. They told him he had resisted fiercely and was slightly injured in a scuffle. Moody was given a tour of the craft and shown details of its structure. Among the messages/communications received was the information that limited contact with man would be made in the near future, but only gradually over a period of time; they are susceptible to nuclear weapons; radar interferes with their navigational devices; there are several different alien races working together.

Sources: "Moody Abduction" by L. J. Lorenzen, in *Encyclopedia of UFOs* (N.Y.: Doubleday, 1980); *Abducted*, Coral and L. J. Lorenzen, ch. IV (N.Y.: Berkley Medallion, 1977).

SEPTEMBER 30, 1975; Nr. CORNING, CALIFORNIA

Features: Sound, brilliant illumination, atmospheric disturbance, animal reaction.

At 3:30 a.m. Hubert Brown, 22, was at work at the Kent Plott Dairy 7 miles south of Corning, off Highway 99W. When he went to the back lot to round up the cows, he saw a domed, disc-shaped object hovering, its light illuminating the whole lot "like daylight." Brown ran back to the milk house to get Tyrone Philips, 38, and the two men stood watching the UFO. The object was emitting a bright red light and making a humming sound. It had raised a huge cloud of dust behind the barn, and the cows fled from the area. After 3-5 minutes the UFO took off and soared out of sight "in the blink of an eye."

Source: *Skylook* (now *MUFON UFO Journal*), No. 95, Oct. 1975.

UNINVITED GUESTS

JANUARY 6, 1976; Nr. BETHEL, MINNESOTA

Features: Vehicle encounter, confrontation, brilliant illumination, physiological effects.

On a cold, frosty night (minus 15 degrees F with windchill factor of minus 50 degrees), Mrs. Janet Stewart, 29, married and the mother of three children left Bethel at 7:20 p.m. headed for Moundview. She planned to pick up her friend, Mary Root, along the way. Rounding a curve, she saw a group of red and green lights crossing the sky and assumed it was an airplane. But it suddenly came toward her, the green lights blinking rapidly. Then she thought it might be a helicopter. As she slowed to round a sharp curve on County Road 15 the flashing object abruptly dropped down above the hood of the car, just above the windshield, and was instantaneously going in the same direction as the car. She crouched over the steering wheel to look up at the object, which maintained the same position for about a mile. Then it moved above the car roof and she could no longer see it.

The back and side windows of the car were coated with frost. Though the brilliant lights obscured the exact shape, she thought she saw something like a ring and a dome shape on the UFO, which was at least as large as her car. She drove on to Mary Root's house, and they returned to the site to look around, but saw nothing unusual. Next day Mrs. Stewart began having menstrual cramps and the following day a full-fledged period, totally out of her normal cycle. Oddly, Ms. Root had the same problem. Mrs. Stewart's eyes began to bother her, and by January 11 they were runny and burning painfully. She considered going to a doctor, but that afternoon the discomfort eased and then cleared up the next day.

Source: *Skylook* (now *MUFON UFO Journal*), No. 101, Apr. 1976.

Appendix A

JANUARY 6, 1976; STANFORD, KENTUCKY

Features: Vehicle encounter, light beam, steering control loss, levitation, translocation, altered surroundings, time loss, abduction, physical exam on table, physiological effects, effects on watch.

Louise Smith, 46, Mona Stafford, 36, and Elaine Thomas, 49, had been at a restaurant having a late dinner. They left at 11:15 p.m. to drive home to Liberty. Near Stanford they saw a reddish, disc-shaped UFO with a white glowing dome and body lights. The UFO descended, circled, and swung in behind the car, illuminating the interior with a blue beam of light. Mrs. Smith, driving, felt the car pull to the left and she no longer had control of it. The car sped up out of control (speedometer reading 85 m.p.h.). All three women felt a burning sensation in their eyes, and Mrs. Smith experienced strong head pain.

Next it felt as if the car were being pulled backwards, bouncing as if on a bumpy road. They saw a strange, wide, brightly illuminated road stretching into the distance, unlike any known road in the area. The phenomena ceased and they noticed a familiar landmark in Hustonville, 8 miles from the encounter point. They proceeded to Mrs. Smith's trailer, where they discovered that about 1-1/2 hours of time could not be accounted for.

All three had burning, tearing eyes and red marks on the backs of their necks. Mrs. Smith's watch hands were noted to be moving at an accelerated speed; Elaine Thomas' watch had stopped; Mona Stafford was not wearing a watch. In following days they had redness and swelling of the skin and Mona Stafford had severe conjunctivitis. Mrs. Smith's pet parakeet behaved oddly after the incident, acting frightened of her, and died within a few weeks.

The women experienced weight loss and personality changes. Under later hypnosis they told of being taken and placed on an exam table under constraints, where 4-foot-tall humanoids examined them. Their impressions of the humanoids remained vague and only fragmentary information, differing somewhat in details, emerged with regard to the abduction scenario.

Elaine Thomas died in September 1979 of an apparent heart attack.

Sources: "Kentucky Abduction," by APRO and R. Leo Sprinkle, in *Encyclopedia of UFOs* (N.Y.: Doubleday, 1980); *Situation Red: The UFO Siege*, by Leonard H. Stringfield (N.Y.: Doubleday, 1977), pp. 198-212; *Abducted*, by Coral and L.J. Lorenzen, ch. VIII, "The Casey County Abduction" (N.Y.: Berkley Medallion, 1977); *International UFO Reporter*, v. 2, no. 3, Mar. 1977 (Center for UFO Studies, Evanston, Ill.); "The Stanford, Kentucky, Abduction," by Leonard H. Stringfield, *MUFON UFO Journal*, No. 110, Jan. 1977.

JANUARY 21, 1976; MATLES-BARBOSA, BRAZIL

Features: Vehicle encounter, brilliant illumination, levitation, humanoids, abduction, technological instruments, communication, physical exam.

Herminio and Bianca Reis, a couple in their 30's, became tired while driving on the Rio de Janeiro-Belo Horizonte highway about 11:30 p.m. and stopped to rest. Herminio fell asleep over the wheel. Later he was awakened when Bianca screamed and an intense bluish light illuminated the area. Suddenly their Volkswagen was "absorbed as if through a chimney" and they found themselves in a brightly lighted circular area. Two dark beings, about 2 meters tall, approached and gestured for them to get out of the car. The beings talked in a language that was unintelligible to the Reis's. They were escorted up a staircase and into a large room full of instruments. There they were given headsets; one of the beings also donned a headset and plugged them into an apparent computer. They then heard a voice say in Portuguese, "My name is Karen, calm down . . . ."

Bianca was later examined (skin, ears, and eyes) and placed in a box-like device that glowed red like a grill. Something like an electric shock caused her to lose consciousness for a while, after which she was placed on something that conformed to the shape of her body. Both were given a green liquor to drink, which they said tasted like a mixture of sugar and iodine. Then more beings appeared, including a tall, dark-haired woman with clear eyes. They said they were performing medical research, that they had conquered the "disease" of old age and there was no death in their world. Bianca was given a technological device and later claimed to be still in communication with Karen via the device.

Source: Argentine newspaper reports, translated by Jane Thomas, Buenos Aires.

MARCH 22, 1976; NEMINGHA, N.S.W., AUSTRALIA

Features: Engulfment by light and haze, E-M effects, white deposit.

A Murrurundi couple returning from a holiday arrived in the small settlement of Nemingha, near Tamworth in the early morning. About 5:45 a.m. they stopped to study a road map, when a small white car approached from the direction of Tamworth. They stepped out, hoping to ask the driver for directions. Suddenly a bright greenish-yellow light descended from above and completely enveloped the small car. The light disappeared, and as the car started to drift to the wrong side of the road, a thick ball of white haze enveloped it. The car then stopped on the wrong side of the road, its lights out.

As the couple watched, a woman stepped from the car and proceeded to wipe a white substance from the windshield with a cloth. The lights came back on, and the woman briefly stood looking at the car. Then she threw the cloth away, whereupon it burst into flames. She climbed back into the car and drove slowly toward the witnesses, turning off on a side road and continuing on her way. As the car passed, the witnesses saw that it was covered with "a thick white substance not unlike white paint," except where the windshield wipers were working. Upset by the experience, the couple wrote a letter to the Tamworth *Northern Daily Leader* newspaper, which was published on April 8.

Source: "A Road Hazard Down Under?," by Bill Chalker, report for UFO Investigation Centre, Lane Cove, N.S.W., Australia.

SEPTEMBER 19, 1976; TEHRAN, IRAN

Features: Aerial encounter, radar-visual, jet interception, E-M effects, physiological effects, extraordinary maneuverability, possible landing, cat-and-mouse pursuit, reaction to witnesses.

At 1:30 a.m. the Iranian Air Force scrambled an American-made F-4 jet interceptor to investigate citizen reports of a UFO. As the F-4 was vectored toward a brilliant light north of Tehran, all communications and instrumentation were suddenly lost. The pilot broke off the mission to return to base, and normal aircraft functions then resumed. A second F-4 took off at 1:40 a.m. and closed on the UFO, making radar contact with an object about the size of a B-707. Flying at a speed greater than Mach 1, the jet obtained a closure rate of 150 nautical m.p.h., but the UFO accelerated (confirmed by radar) and stayed ahead of the pursuing jet. Multi-colored flashing lights were visible on the UFO.

At a position south of Tehran, a smaller brilliant object was seen to emerge from the UFO and came directly toward the F-4. The pilot started to fire an AIM-9 missile at the oncoming object, but at that instant his weapons control panel went off and all communications failed. The pilot took evasive action, and the projectile turned to follow, then sped up and returned to the UFO. The F-4 pilot, his electromagnetic equipment now functioning normally again, once more attempted to intercept the UFO. Another object emerged from the UFO and dove at high speed toward the earth. It then appeared to settle down gently in the hills below. The UFO then sped away. The landed object was illuminating the ground in an area estimated to be 2-3 kilometers in diameter, so the pilot descended to investigate, noting the position, until the light went out. The F-4 crew experienced night vision problems after looking at the brilliant light. They experienced additional E-M interference en route back to base.

Shortly after dawn the F-4 crew in a helicopter inspected the landing area, a dry lake bed, but found no traces but did pick up a beeper signal. A resident in the area had heard a loud noise and seen a bright light during the night in the area of the landing site. A report on the incident circulated through the U.S. intelligence community and a Defense Intelligence Agency "Defense Information Report Evaluation" (IR No. 6846013976), 22 Sept 1976, termed it, "An outstanding report. This case is a classic which meets all the criteria necessary for a valid study of a UFO phenomenon." The analysis termed the UFO performance "awesome," noting that, "An inordinate amount of manueverability was displayed by the UFOs."

Sources: *U.F.O. Investigator*, NICAP, Nov. 1976; Defense Intelligence Agency evaluation report by Maj. Roland B. Evans, USAF, Military Capability Analyst, DIA (Maj. Evans was currently flying as an Electronics Warfare Officer); Tehran *Journal*, Sept. 20, 1976; *UFOs and the Limits of Science*, by Ronald D. Story (N.Y.: Morrow, 1981) pp. 160-162.

JANUARY 21, 1977;
ST. BERNARD PARISH, LOUISIANA

Features: Boat engulfment by light, gravitic (?) effect, abnormal silence, heat, light beam, time loss.

A nutria hunter was plying his trade along a canal about 8:45 p.m. when his boat was engulfed in a brilliant light and all sound ceased and he felt heat from the light. A glowing object then shot away and things returned to normal. The hunter picked up a friend and resumed his work; then a light again approached and hovered above the boat. Again, silence prevailed, and the hunter's hair was standing on end "like wire." Everything felt warm. The engine continued to run, but the boat was standing still as if being held by "strong gravity forces." Later investigation showed that normal impediments could not have held the boat; the channel had recently been dredged.

The UFO was roundish and about 20 feet in diameter, with a textured surface showing a pattern of connecting diamonds or squares. When it departed, the boat suddenly lurched forward throwing both men down, as if the force gripping them had been turned off. They saw the UFO retreat and hover near an oil refinery, where a company guard also saw it, then hover again in a new spot and emit a beam of light downward. After about 30 minutes it disappeared. The hunter reported a time period of 20 minutes that he could not account for during the sighting.

Source: *MUFON UFO Journal*, No. 111, Feb. 1977.

FEBRUARY 18, 1977; SALTO, URUGUAY

Features: E-M effects, animal reactions, brilliant illumination, paralysis, severe physiological effects, physical traces.

Rancher Angel Maria Tonna, 52, his family and farmhands all witnessed UFOs during February and March. About 4:00 a.m. February 18 while herding cows to a barn to be milked, all the generator-powered lights in the barns and other buildings went off. A bright light appeared at the east end of the barn, and Tonna and his watchdog, Topo, ran to investigate fearing a fire. Tonna heard a noise (unspecified) and saw a disc "like two plates facing each other." The cows were running wildly and all the dogs were barking. The UFO began moving, with a rocking motion, breaking off some tree branches, alternately hovering then moving again. As he and Topo, a 3-year-old police dog weighing more than 60 pounds, walked toward the UFO — now glowing bright orange — it turned and began moving toward them. It stopped about 20 feet above the ground next to a water tank, its light illuminating the whole barnyard.

Topo ran toward the UFO to attack it, but suddenly stopped, sat down, and began howling at a point within 15 feet of the object. Tonna saw six beams of lightning-like light, three on each side of the UFO, and felt electric shocks and intense heat. He felt paralyzed. After several minutes the UFO began moving away, its color turning to red, gradually accelerating out of sight. Then the generator resumed functioning but without producing electricity because the wires were burned out. Topo refused to eat and uncharacteristically stayed in the house all day.

Three days later the dog was found dead on the spot where he had sat howling at the UFO. An autopsy by a veterinarian found evidence of extreme internal heating, ruptured blood vessels, and discolored internal organs. The dog had literally been cooked. Tonna experienced severe skin irritation, but refused further medical examination. Broken trees and circular markings on the ground were found around the farm property; one 35-foot circle contained burned grass and three circular impressions arranged like a triangle within the circle.

Source: *MUFON UFO Journal*, No. 125, April 1978.

MAY 5, 1977; TABIO, COLOMBIA

Features: Aerial encounter, confrontation, E-M effects, loss of steering control, impaired vision.

Student pilot Manuel Jose Lopez Ojeda, 22, took off at 9:15 a.m. for a routine solo training flight above the 8500-foot mountains north of Bogota in a 100 h.p. Cessna 150. An hour later, as he was practicing steep turns near the town of Tabio, he noticed that all his instruments either read "zero" or indicated danger. He looked down to his right for a field to make a forced landing and saw a pure white, circular UFO, like an inverted dish about 15-20 meters in diameter and about 3 meters thick, just below him. On the top center was a red-yellow light. The UFO was stationary with respect to his plane, and when it moved it did so with quick zig-zag motions. Ojeda then discovered that his controls had failed. "The whole aircraft seemed to be locked into this machine, or being controlled by somebody else," he said.

Next his vision began to fade; "It was like being in a fog . . . I couldn't distinguish any objects too far, so I asked for guidance . . ." The last thing he saw before his vision failed completely was the UFO departing, and his controls then worked again. But at this point he ". . . couldn't see anything . . . not the dashboard . . . I couldn't see outside my airplane." Two flight instructors from Bogota came to his aid and "talked him down" to a safe landing as his vision slowly returned. He was rushed to a hospital, and recovered quickly under a doctor's care. Interviewers reported that Ojeda's reputation is as a serious and capable pilot, and airport personnel took his report seriously.

Source: *MUFON UFO Journal*, No. 115, June 1977 (from El Tiempo, Bogota, and interview by noted Colombian pilot Rudy Faccini).

JUNE 16 (approx), 1977;
Nr. MIDDELBURG, S. AFRICA

Features: Vehicle encounter, confrontation, vehicle engulfment by light, E-M effects, sound, amnesia.

At 5:15 a.m., Mr. At Gouws was driving a newspaper delivery van on the National Road between Noupoort and Middelburg to meet newspaper editor Arthur Knott-Craig with news from the north for Saturday's paper. At the Wolwekop quarry, he saw a dull glow which he first thought was the moon, but suddenly a glowing object confronted him, enveloping the van in light. The engine failed and the lights went out. The UFO hovered in front, next to and above the van, and Gouws could not recall what happened at this point. "I felt that something happened, but cannot think what," he said. "I really had a terrible fright." What seemed like moments later, the UFO left making a buzzing noise and the van's engine and lights came on of their own accord. Then the engine failed again, but started easily and ran normally thereafter. Mr. Knott-Craig reported that when Gouws reached him, he was shaking like a leaf with fright. Gouws reported the experience to the Middelburg police.

Special significance: Investigation report and detailed information lacking, but circumstances suggestive of possible abduction.

Source: *MUFON UFO Journal*, No. 118, September 1977 (from *Die Vaterland*, June 23, 1977, which dates the event as "last week.")

NOVEMBER 29, 1977; WAIMATA VALLEY, GISBORNE, NEW ZEALAND

Features: Confrontation, light beam, illuminated tree, animal reaction.

Hamish McLean, an investigator for the Aerial Phenomenon Research Group (APRG), received an anonymous phone call from someone in the valley who said a "flying saucer" had landed in a nearby paddock. He drove to the indicated site about 16 miles from the city, arriving at about 10:15 a.m., but saw nothing. Continuing on a little further he rounded a bend and saw a large domed object, flat on the bottom (hemispherical), hovering above a hill to his left. It was about 500 feet away and about 300 feet above the road level. When McLean stopped the car and got out to observe the UFO, it suddenly sped toward where he was standing and stopped about 200 feet away. After about 3 minutes, a bright beam of blue light shot out of a small square aperture on the lower left side of the object and focused on a dead Macrocarpa tree trunk about 50 feet from the UFO and 150-200 feet from McLean.

The tree instantly "lit up like a Christmas tree," fluorescing a different color on each branch (e.g., pink, orange, violet). This lasted for 7 seconds, until the blue beam disappeared. Sheep in the paddock bleated and ran down the hill away from the tree, and milled around in small groups. The UFO then moved about 50 feet to the right where it hovered for 2 minutes before swooping back over the hill and hovering again in its original position. McLean drove off to get another APRG investigator, but by the time they returned to the site the UFO was gone. Later investigation of the tree site turned up nothing unusual.

Sources: Aerial Phenomenon Research Group, Gisborne, N.Z., investigation report; *Xenolog*, Timaru, N.Z., 1st Quarter 1978.

MARCH 18, 1978; CHARLESTON, SOUTH CAROLINA

Features: Light beam, memory loss, abduction, physical exam on table, messages, translocation, artifact.

About 9:25 p.m. while observing a UFO through binoculars in a marshy area, Bill Herrmann, 26, an auto mechanic, was rendered unconscious by an aquamarine light beam from the object. His next conscious memory was of standing in a plowed field at a different location about midnight, surrounded by a light glow. He ran hysterically toward a distant road where he could see cars and was picked up by a policeman who phoned his family. Under later hypnosis he described being examined on a low table by three small humanoid beings who employed a blinking, X-ray-like device. They were about 4-1/2 feet tall with marshmallow-colored skin, fetus-like faces, hairless, and without eye pupils. They told Herrmann there are three races of beings from space visiting here to observe and conduct experiments.

On April 21, 1979, a mysterious metal bar with symbols on it materialized in a globe of blue-green light in Herrmann's bedroom. On May 16 he felt an urge to return to the abduction site and voluntarily went on board a waiting craft. He was told the metal bar was a token of appreciation, and that they would return for him again.

(Note: Some details of these news stories, as is common, may be garbled. The case has been investigated by others and a source of detailed additional information is given.)

Sources: *The Journal*, Summerville, S.C., Jan. 31, 1979; *News & Courier*, Charleston, S.C., Nov. 18, 1979; *UFO Contact from Reticulum*, by Wendelle C. Stevens with William Herrman (privately published, 1981).

MARCH 29, 1978; INDIANAPOLIS, INDIANA

Features: Vehicle encounter, engulfment by light, E-M effects, abnormal silence, sense of isolation, altered perception, physical effects.

Three truckers travelling on I-70 near Indianapolis about 9:30 p.m., while talking back and forth on their CB radios, suddenly were enveloped by a bright blue light from above, blacking out their radios and causing their engines to sputter and lose power. They were not able to see beyond the hoods of the trucks, and all road sounds ceased. After a few seconds the phenomenon disappeared and everything returned to normal. When one of the drivers jokingly suggested on the CB that he wanted to go with the UFO, the phenomenon was repeated for about 15 seconds, the truck engines again sputtering and losing power. While engulfed in the light, the drivers felt a sense of isolation as if there were no one else in the world. Everything was restful and quiet.

Other drivers outside the light also witnessed the phenomenon, including a woman across the highway who said on the CB: "It looked like a big bright blue lampshade over the three trucks." Above the roughly dome-shaped region of light was a long, narrow spout of light stretching vertically upwards. One of the drivers later told a MUFON investigator that his truck clock, which had been working perfectly, began losing about an hour a day after the event and his battery had been drained of power, requiring about 1-1/2 hours to regain a full charge.

Source: *MUFON UFO Journal*, No. 126, May 1978.

JULY 6, 1978; MENDOZA, ARGENTINA

Features: Vehicle encounter, altered surroundings, levitation, E-M effects, cold, translocation.

Francisco Nunez, a man in his 60's and his son of the same name, about 23, both mechanics, were driving toward Lujan south of Mendoza at about 9:00 p.m. Suddenly, as if by magic, a pickup truck ahead of them vanished. Then their car was levitated and they experienced motion at great speed along an unfamiliar, illuminated 5-lane highway surrounded by buildings so tall that they could not see the tops, and the sky was red. (Compare to Jan. 6, 1976, Stanford, Ky.). Up until the strange experience started the sky had been clear and starry. Their car engine stopped and they felt very cold. Their next memory was of being at a new location at a railroad crossing about 9 km away from where the experience began, and their car was facing in the opposite direction. Hypnosis was later attempted but elicited only some color patterns on the tall buildings. No UFO or beings were recalled.

Sources: *Cronica*, Buenos Aires, Aug. 30, 1978, Aug. 31, 1978, Sept. 1, 1978, Sept. 2, 1978, Sept. 3, 1978.

AUGUST 30, 1978;
GOBERNADOR DUPUY, ARGENTINA

Features: Humanoid, paralysis, abduction, communication, body probings, translocation, artifacts.

Miguel Freitas, 23, a wood cutter was in an open area when he saw a UFO approach and a bluish-lighted humanoid emerge. He was paralyzed, then taken on board and submitted to "questioning." The beings communicated with him via a "voice box." They "pricked" his arms with some instrument, and released him about 40 km from the abduction site, after smearing him with a liquid substance (reportedly analyzed as a bactericide). The "voice box" and other artifacts reportedly were turned over to the San Luis police. (No follow-up information is available as of this writing.)

Source: Argentine newspaper reports translated by Jane Thomas, Buenos Aires.

296

Appendix A

SEPTEMBER 17, 1978;
TORRITA DI SIENA, ITALY

Features: Vehicle encounter, confrontation, brilliant illumination, humanoids, E-M effects, levitation, light beams, light flash, sound, physical traces.

About 8:15 p.m. a woman and her son saw a descending red ball illuminating the area, and watched houselights black out. Shortly afterwards a barber got in his car and drove a few meters, when suddenly his engine and lights went out as a bright object descended over the road just ahead of his car. Hovering about a half meter over the road was a 3-meter diameter orange-red domed disc with three light beams extending to the road. A panel opened and two humanoids about 1-2 meters tall, wearing green coveralls and helmets with antennae, "floated" toward the car. They circled the car, apparently more interested in it than in the passengers. Then they re-entered the UFO which took off with a flash of light and explosive sound. Three scorched circles about 50 cm in diameter and 4 meters apart were found on the road surface, apparently corresponding to the three light beams. The encounter was one of numerous CE II and CE III cases occurring during a major UFO wave in Italy, peaking late in the year.

Source: "Italian UFO Wave of 1978," by Richard Hall, *MUFON UFO Journal* No. 153, Nov. 1980 (Information from Massimo Greco, Brescia, Italy).

SEPTEMBER 23, 1978;
BUENOS AIRES PROVINCE, ARGENTINA

Features: Vehicle encounter, brilliant illumination, impaired vision, levitation, translocation, time loss, loss of vehicle control, missing gasoline.

About 3:00 a.m. during a road rally (endurance race), Carlos Acevedo, 38, businessman, and Miguel Angel Moya, 28, mechanic, were completing the final 1,000 km after withdrawing from formal competition due to mechanical problems. Acevedo was driving at about 100 km per hour. A bright yellow light approached from the rear at high speed, illuminated the interior of the car and blinded them. He lost control of the car, and then saw that they were about 2 meters above the ground. The car continued to float, and their vision was restricted by the brilliant light. They lost all sense of time. Finally they felt a bump and noticed that the car was back on the road, a considerable distance away from the point where the encounter began. They saw a yellowish object retreating in the distance. When they analyzed the circumstances, they found that it had taken 2 hours and 20 minutes to travel a distance that should have taken only 1 hour and 15 minutes. They also discovered that their reserve gas tank, recently filled, was now empty. They stopped at the nearest police department, in Pedro Luro, and reported the incident. (Note: Some additional details are included in Chapter 2.)

Sources: *MUFON UFO Journal* No. 140, Oct. 1979; Servicio de Investigaciones Ufologicas UFO Press, v. III, no. 9, Buenos Aires, Argentina; *Cronica*, Buenos Aires, Sept. 24 & 25, 1978.

OCTOBER 21, 1978; BASS STRAIT, AUSTRALIA

Features: Aerial encounter, confrontation, E-M effects, aircraft disappearance.

Frederick Valentich, 20, took off from Melbourne at 6:19 p.m. in a Cessna 182, bound for King Island in the Bass Strait. At 7:06 p.m. he radioed to air traffic control inquiring about an apparent aircraft near him. In subsequent reports he described an elongated object with a green light and shiny "metallic" appearance that confronted his plane and circled above him. "It seems to me that he's playing some sort of game; he's flying over me two, three times at speeds I could not identify," Valentich reported. Just after 7:10 p.m. he said: ". . . it seems like it's stationary; what I'm doing right now is orbiting and the thing is just orbiting on top of me also; its got a green light and sort of metallic; it's all shiny [on] the outside." At 7:12 p.m. he reported that his engine was running roughly.

His last transmission seconds later was, "That strange aircraft is hovering on top of me again ... it is hovering and it's not an aircraft." This was followed by a scraping metallic sound through the open microphone. Valentich and his aircraft vanished, and no trace was ever found despite an extensive search. Australian investigators subsequently located numerous witnesses to UFO sightings in the same vicinity just before and after the aircraft's disappearance, including several who saw a green light over Bass Strait.

Sources: *MUFON UFO Journal*, No. 129, Aug. 1978; *Australian Flying Saucer Review*, Moorabbin, Victoria, June 1981 (including transcript of communications between the witness and air traffic control); *Melbourne Episode: Case Study of a Missing Pilot*, by Richard F. Haines (to be published).

NOVEMBER 1978; TRIER, WEST GERMANY

Features: Vehicle encounter, confrontation, time loss, abduction, examination on table, humanoids, telepathy (?).

Pam Owens, 19, pregnant wife of U.S. soldier Chris Owens, said that they were returning home with their infant son, Brian, from a friend's house on a trip that normally took 30 minutes. Suddenly a large oval object hovered above their car, intermittently flashing a red light. They arrived home at 12:10 a.m., unable to account for about an hour and 40 minutes of time. Under later hypnosis, Pam described getting out of the car as the UFO hovered overhead. She found herself being examined on a table in a room with dim yellow light, by two beings about 2-1/2 m tall. They were hairless, with large heads, large and deepset eyes, and rough-looking greenish skin. One, with fingers twice as long as those of a normal human, took a needle about 8 cm long and inserted it just above her navel.

When she inquired about Brian, whom she had been carrying in her arms, they replied, "We are taking care of him." When she asked that her husband not be hurt, they replied that everything would be all right. Their lips did not move when they spoke (telepathy?). Pam's next memory recall after the needle was of standing by the car with Brian in her arms and watching the UFO depart. C. R. McQuiston, co-inventor of the psychological stress evaluator, studied tape recordings of her story and said: "This is one of the strangest stories I have heard in my life, but it is evident that she is telling the truth."

Source: Argentine newspaper reports translated by Jane Thomas, Buenos Aires.

NOVEMBER 9, 1978; OIL FIELDS OF KUWAIT

Features: Landing, E-M effects.

Kuwait Oil Company technicians observed a domed UFO with a flashing red light that landed at "Gathering Centre No. 24" causing disruption of all telecommunications and an electrical malfunction at an oil pumping station near the landing site. Sightings continued in Arab Nations for 3 months and a number of photographs were obtained. The Kuwait Institute for Scientific Research conducted an investigation of the oil field landing, but apparently found no physical traces.

Source: *MUFON UFO Journal*, No. 133, Jan.-Feb., 1979; letters to MUFON by P.G. Jacob, Kuwait Institute for Scientific Research, Nov. 24, 1978 and Jan. 1, 1979; Kuwait *Times*, Nov. 16 & 18, 1978; *Arab Times*, Nov. 23 & 25, 1978.

DECEMBER 6, 1978; TORRIGLIA, ITALY

Features: E-M effects, sound, blackout, physical traces, time loss, levitation, abduction, physical exam(?), physiological effects, loss of vehicle control, heat.

Fortunato Zanfretta, 26, a night watchman, was patrolling about 11:45 p.m. when he saw lights in a courtyard and approached to investigate. His car lights, engine, and two-way radio failed. Approaching on foot, he clashed with a 3-meter-tall monstrous being and fled. Then he heard a loud hiss, felt a wave of heat, and saw a huge triangular UFO rise up from behind the building and disappear toward the sea. His radio was now working so he called his base station after experiencing a time lapse. His colleagues found him lying in a meadow 80 meters from the building. Landing trace marks were found, and independent witnesses saw a triangular UFO that night.

Zanfretta had a persistent headache for several days. Under hypnosis on December 23 he described several "monstrous beings" who abducted him to a hot, round room where something was placed on his forehead that caused pain. Left alone, he fled yelling for help. Due to his anxiety at this point the hypnosis was terminated, and another session scheduled for December 30.

Back on the job on December 27, at 11:46 p.m., his base station heard him on the radio describing a headache, a blinding mist, and the fact that he had lost control of his car which moved at high speed, then stopped abruptly. He then described a bright oval object. His colleagues began an immediate search, locating him about 1:09 a.m., confused, hot, and apparently "sunburned."

Under follow-up hypnosis on January 7, 1979, he recalled being taken on board a yellow, triangular craft by a green light beam and encountering 10 or more beings who were tall, greenish, with yellow triangular eyes but humanlike hands and legs. Instead of mouths, they had "nets" that emitted light.

On February 6 under sodium pentothal examination at a major Milan Medical Center, Zanfretta told exactly the same story.

Source: "Italian UFO Wave of 1978," by Richard Hall, *MUFON UFO Journal*, No. 153, Nov. 1980. (Data from Massimo Greco, Brescia, Italy).

DECEMBER 27, 1978; TORRIGLIA, ITALY

Features: Vehicle encounter, steering control loss, blinding "mist," physiological effects.

Continuation of Fortunato Zanfretta case. (See Dec. 6, 1978, Torriglia, Italy.)

DECEMBER 27 (approx.), 1978; Nr. ARROYITO, CORDOBA, ARGENTINA

Features: Vehicle encounter, amnesia, translocation.

Orlando Carrizo, 40, Severiano Brunetto, 53, and the latter's son Daniel Omar, 20, all employees of the power company, were travelling to San Francisco in a company truck about 4:30 a.m. They sighted a UFO hovering a short distance from the ground, and as they prepared to cross a bridge near Arroyito ... they suddenly found themselves 15 km away in the district of Transito in the middle of the road. None of them recalled crossing the bridge or continuing along the road. The cigarettes they had been holding as they approached the bridge were still the same size. The news report, without elaborating, states that "One man even exchanged signals with the occupants of the object."

Special significance: Features suggestive of a possible abduction.

Source: Buenos Aires *Herald*, Dec. 29, 1978 (originally reported in *Cordoba*, the local newspaper).

JANUARY 5, 1979; AUBURN, MASSACHUSETTS

Features: Vehicle encounter, confrontation, E-M effects, paralysis, heat, physiological effects, loss of vehicle control, odor.

At about 6:20 p.m., Anmarie Emery left Cambridge, Mass., to drive to her parent's home in Springfield. Near Auburn, she noticed three, red-glowing triangular objects flying over woods to her left. Just past the Route 90/86 interchange she found herself travelling alone. When she rounded a corner, she saw three glowing red UFOs hovering over the road directly in front of the car. Simultaneously, her radio (AM) stopped playing and her CB radio went off, and the car slowed smoothly to a full stop while still in third gear (standard transmission) with the engine still running. She felt totally paralyzed. Her foot remained pressed on the accelerator pedal but the car would not move. She felt heat on her face, and a strong, pungent odor (like a "sweet skunk smell") filled the car.

The closest UFO was only about 20 feet away and 10 feet above the road. They appeared to be made of a smooth, glass-like substance and emitted the red glow uniformly from within. Four brighter red lights on the rear of the objects blinked slowly, about once every two seconds. Anmarie's face felt hot and flushed and her eyes watered. When another car approached from behind, the UFOs accelerated straight up, one at a time, and they moved away at low altitude toward the north west, disappearing in about 30 seconds. The AM radio immediately began playing and the CB radio came back on. The paralysis was gone. She arrived home some time after 8:00 p.m. and her mother noticed her flushed face, like a mild sunburn and a dazed look. Next day she had a mild rash or skin peeling around her eyes and nose, but the condition healed quickly. No aftereffects were found on the car, a 1970 Ford Maverick.

Source: *MUFON UFO Journal*, No. 134, March-April, 1979.

FEBRUARY 5, 1979; LAWITTA, TASMANIA

Features: Vehicle encounter, engulfment by light, impaired vision, E-M effects, amnesia, physical effects on car.

About 9:50 p.m. while driving home from Hamilton to Hobart, about 71 km, a man (name on file with Tasmanian UFO Investigation Centre) noticed that his car radio died out. Seconds later an intense white light enveloped the car (a Ford Cortina

71 TC station wagon) and he could not see beyond the hood. At this moment the headlights and engine both failed. His memory became fuzzy, and the next thing he recalled was continuing to drive along the Lyell Highway and reaching the intersection with the Midland Highway at Granton.

He was stopped by police for driving without headlights. He was unable to say who he was, where he lived, or where he was going and was taken to a hospital in a dazed condition and state of shock. When a nurse shone a light into his eyes, he reacted as if scared and some memory began to return. His car later was found to have a dead battery and low oil level, and low water in the radiator. The alternator cut-out switch and headlight wiring had to be replaced. It was not possible to determine whether there was an unaccounted for period of time.

Special significance: Details suggestive of possible abduction.

Source: *MUFON UFO Journal*, No. 142, December 1979.

FEBRUARY 8, 1979; LIVERPOOL CREEK, QUEENSLAND, AUSTRALIA

Features: Vehicle encounter, UFO on road, E-M effects associated with light flash.

About 9:00 p.m. a banana farmer (name on file with UFO Research-Queensland) was driving home from Innisfail to Mission Beach, N. Queensland when, about 1 km north of the Liverpool Creek bridge on the Bruce Highway, he noticed a dull white light sitting on the edge of the road. As he neared, he could see a dark, beehive shape behind the light. The light then rose vertically and when about 1 m off the road and about 10 m away, there was a blinding flash of light. All the car lights and the engine failed, so he put the car into neutral (automatic transmission) and coasted to a stop in a nearby truck rest area. As he started to light a cigarette, the headlights and dash lights came back on and the engine was started without difficulty. The man reported feeling as if he had just awakened from a nightmare. Later checks of the car found nothing wrong: battery leads were tight and free of corrosion. A magnetic signature check was performed on the car, compared to one of the same make and mileage, but no significant differences were found.

Source: *MUFON UFO Journal*, No. 142, December 1979.

JULY 25, 1979; CANOGA PARK, CALIFORNIA

Features: Vehicle encounter, time loss, abduction, physical exam.

Shari N., a housewife and cocktail waitress in her 30's, was driving the short distance home from work when she saw an object that she thought was a plane crashing. She arrived home unaccountably late.

Under later hypnosis she described getting out of the car and approaching the object. She recalled being examined while lying on her back; her back was hurting. She was bound around the stomach, and a being (not clearly described) probed her shoulder and stomach, inserted something in her leg, and dabbed her eyes. Finally she was returned to the car.

Source: Investigation report in MUFON files.

AUGUST 4, 1979; TORONTO, ONTARIO, CANADA

Features: Shadowy beings, blackout, abduction, body probings, physical traces, telepathy, space ride, physiological effects.

Sarah H., 14, was "drawn" to a field during a period of repeated UFO sightings and there saw an arrowhead-shaped UFO approach and four "shadowy" figures emerge. She blacked out. Later she recalled being on board the craft, and displayed prick marks on her hand. Physical traces were evident at the encounter site. Under hypnosis she described being on board, along with a man in his 40's who said he was from another

Canadian town. A normal earth cat was also observed on board, "temporarily" according to the beings, who communicated via telepathy. Sarah noted that her hands passed through what appeared to be normal matter. The seven beings were "transparent" and said they were "crystal" beings dependent on light. They told her they would return when she was 25. The beings took a blood sample from Sarah and, before returning her to the field, took her on a space ride during which she could see the earth from above, and some unidentified red place.

Source: Canadian UFO Research Network investigation report in MUFON files.

SEPTEMBER 21, 1979; SZTUM, POLAND

Features: Confrontation, engulfing "fog," abduction, perceptual anomalies, communication, sound, brilliant illumination, telepathy.

Miroslaw Goralski and Krzysztof Kobus had been working in Goralski's garden until 9:00 p.m. and were cleaning their tools, when a UFO (seen by one as a "ring" and by the other from a different angle as "two silver deltas connected by a cross") descended abruptly into the enclosure. Both men experienced a squeaking or high frequency sound in their heads. As they approached to investigate they were engulfed by a dense white "fog" and illuminated by bright light. They felt inertial effects as if rising at high speed. Kobus propped himself against a soft object like an "armchair," which later vanished and experienced a kaleidoscope of colors and odd sensations as if ideas were flowing into his brain from an external source.

Goralski addressed questions to supposed unseen entities and obtained partial answers in unspecified fashion (telepathy?). "What is matter?," he asked. The answer: "The most important attribute of matter is its ability to pervade through other matter." Goralski leaned over to the edge of the "fog" and could clearly see the town below. He, experienced a visual display like a "time channel," including people in costumes of bygone days. Suddenly they fell as if from a height of about 30 cm and landed back in the garden. Goralski ran home, arriving about 9:30 p.m. The witnesses were submitted to psychological testing, which showed normal personalities. Their lives were disrupted by the experience, which shocked and confused them.

Source: "Abduction Case in Poland," by Emilia Popik (editor, Gdansk, Poland), *MUFON UFO Journal*, No. 150, Aug. 1980.

APRIL 2, 1980; PUDASJARVI, FINLAND

Features: Vehicle encounter, abnormal "fog," car lights deflected, humanoids, physical exam on table, communication, time loss, physiological effects.

Aino Ivanoff, 52, was driving across a bridge at 1:15 a.m. when she entered a "strange fog" and her car headlights were deflected upwards. She braked the car to a stop, then saw a silvery domed UFO with portholes. She was taken inside and examined on a metallic table by three men wearing dark clothing. When she was returned to her car, the fog persisted and she had to drive most of the way home in it. She noticed that 2 hours were unaccounted for. After the incident she was extremely tired for a week, and found five small dots on her right shoulder. She was given an anti-war message and told that they (the beings) were unable to have children. Most of the story emerged under hypnosis.

Source: Quarterly Report 2/80, UFO Research of Finland, 17950 Kylama, Finland.

MAY 14, 1980; SIMPSON COUNTY, MISSISSIPPI

Features: Vehicle encounter, light beam, E-M effects.

Howard and Julia Pickrel, travelling from Dallas, Texas, were driving on U.S. 49 through Simpson County (between Jackson and Hattiesburg) about 3:30 a.m. when they saw a glowing disc high in the sky. "There was a beam of light (from the disc) making a spot of light about as long as a fourth of a city block and as wide as our car," Mrs. Pickrel said. As they drove through the light beam ". . . the (car) lights went on and off about seven or eight times. It was just like someone was turning them on and off. Then we drove out into the darkness, and the lights never flickered again."

Source: *Daily Herald*, Biloxi-Gulfport, Miss., May 14, 1980.

AUGUST 22, 1980; EAST TEXAS

Features: Vehicle encounter, E-M effects, levitation, wind, abduction, "fog" or "smoke," humanoids, physical exam on table, communication, translocation.

Megan Elliot (pseudonym), 20's, was visiting her mother when her 18-month-old daughter, Renee, became ill, crying and insisting on going home. Unable to ease her condition, Megan hurriedly climbed in her 1978 Honda Civic and started the 70-mile drive home along dark, lonely roads in the early a.m. After driving about 30 miles, Megan's radio became garbled, she heard a loud electrical noise, and the lights began to dim. Then the car was lifted off the road and she could see the tops of tall pine trees being blown as if in a windstorm. The car entered the flat metal bottom of an object through an opening into a circular, brightly lit room. A "voice" told her to get out of the car, but she refused; a small humanoid creature then approached, his feet enshrouded in "a dry-ice type fog," and removed the locked door of the car.

Megan and Renee were forced to go with the creature, who had a large head, no ears, no eyebrows, oval eyes without lashes, no body hair at all, broad flat nose, small slit-like mouth, and thumbless four-fingered hands. They were clamped down on tables in a room that also had "smoke" on the floor and, in the presence of two more humanoid beings, probed by various devices. Afterwards, they were detained and fed with various colored and shaped pellets, before being returned to the car and lowered back to the road. Megan found herself only about 5 miles from home, 25 miles closer than the point of abduction. Under later regressive hypnosis, Megan described extensive communication with the beings. She was able to recall intricate details of the interior of the apparent craft and of the humanoid beings.

Source: *MUFON UFO Journal*, No. 167, Jan. 1982.

SEPTEMBER 30, 1980; "WHITE ACRES," SALE, VICTORIA, S. AUSTRALIA

Features: Physiological effect, effects on watch, sound, heat, physical markings on ground, animal reactions, water disappearance.

At 1:00 a.m. George Blackwell, a station hand, awoke to a whistling sound, heard cattle bellowing and a horse running around in apparent panic. He went out to investigate and saw a silhouetted object approaching from the southwest about 2-3 meters above the ground, passing in front of and behind various landmarks. The object seemed to land in the vicinity of a concrete water tank. In the moonlight, he had seen that the UFO was about 8 meters in diameter, top-shaped and spinning, with blue and orange lights coming from it. (Compare to June 29, 1964, Lavonia, Ga.). Blackwell got on his motorcycle and rode toward the UFO, which remained visible on the ground close to the water tank, still emitting the whistling noise. When he was within about 50 meters of the UFO, he felt an odd sensation within his body which he could only describe as making him feel "like a plate of jelly."

At about 15 meters from the UFO, the noise was so loud he had to cover his ears with his hands as he stopped and watched. After a few minutes, there was a loud "bang" and a blast of heat and air, and the UFO rose and moved away to the east, becoming silent. A shower of debris fell from underneath it to the ground. At 1:50 a.m. he arrived back at home and noted that his watch had stopped at 1:10 a.m. He found that the watch worked normally if placed on the table, but stopped whenever he put it on his wrist. Next morning he found at the landing site a 46 cm wide black ring about 8.5

meters across. To the east was a scattering of debris, cow pads, and rocks. Investigators obtained soil and rock samples for analysis. Blackwell discovered that 10,000 gallons of water had disappeared from the tank.

Source: *MUFON UFO Journal*, No. 156, February 1981.

OCTOBER 23, 1980; MORENCI, ARIZONA

Features: Light beams, directedness, "impossible" nonaerodynamic maneuvers.

Randall Rogers and Larry Mortensen, employed by Phelps-Dodge Corporation at their copper smelting site, left their work area at 8:55 p.m. for a break, picking up three others en route to the lunch area. A large boomerang-shaped object was seen to approach slowly from the north at about 1,500-2,000 feet altitude and stop above the north smoke stack. After a minute or so it descended to about 700 to 1,000 feet. Shortly afterwards a brilliant beam of light was emitted from the foreward apex and shone directly down into the interior of the smoke stack. The beam went out, and the UFO moved slowly south, stopped above the south smoke stack, and a beam was emitted down into it. Again, the beam went out; the UFO started moving slowly south, then accelerated rapidly.

At this point one of the workers said he wished the object would come back so he could get a better look at it. Almost as if in response, the UFO abruptly reversed course and returned to the smelter area without turning, banking, or other change of attitude. The object was dull black in color, nonreflective, and one "wing" appeared to be shorter than the other. No seams or other surface markings were visible. On each "wing" were 8 bright reddish lights, 4 each on the leading and trailing edges. The lights were interconnected by a white tube of light; they remained steady at all times, not blinking or pulsating. No sound was heard. The UFO finally accelerated out of sight to the north. The weather was clear and a full moon had just risen.

The same or a similar object was observed again at 9:00 p.m. This time red lights were observed to emerge from it, speed away, and later return and merge with the boomerang-shaped UFO, which then sped away to the North.

Source: *APRO Bulletin*, v. 29, no. 7, Aug. 1981.

NOVEMBER 19, 1980; Nr. LONGMONT, COLORADO

Features: Light beam, sound, E-M effects, time loss, levitation, abduction, heavy "mist," odor, brilliant illumination, physical examination, communication/telepathy, "healing," physiological effects.

At 11:45 p.m., returning home to Longmont from Denver, "Michael" (pseudonym) an art teacher and his wife "Mary" saw an intense beam of blue light "lock onto" their car and heard a loud "swishing" sound. The car lights dimmed and the radio faded out, as they felt the car being lifted off the road. Next conscious memory was of continuing along the road, puzzled that it was 12:55 a.m. Next day Mary found an odd rectangular marking on her lower abdomen.

Under later hypnosis, Michael described the car being lifted up to a domed craft, apparently suspended in a dense cloud or "heavy mist." A strong odor, that he thought electrical in nature, pervaded the area. A gray-skinned being wearing shiny, gold-colored clothing led them into a brightly lighted area where they submitted him (and Mary, in a separate location) to physiological probings, nude on an examination table over which hovered a "floating light."

Michael felt his memory bank was being "drained away," later replaced along with some additional knowledge. The beings, who had elongated bald heads with narrow chins and four elongated fingers, seemed to be able to communicate without speaking. Finally they were let go, experiencing the sound, light beam, etc. in reverse sequence and the car placed back on the road going 55 m.p.h.

Mary, 2-months pregnant at the time, later contracted severe streptococcal pneumonia and there was fear for the baby, but though born prematurely at 7 months, the child was well-developed and normal. Michael had several large suspected cancerous melanomas on his legs before the incident; afterwards they were greatly reduced in size and discoloration.

Under deep hypnosis, Michael drew sketches of the beings and craft (included with the article). He thought the beings indicated to him that there are many co-existing dimensions. For various reasons, including her illness, Mary was not available for hypnosis, and Michael displayed psychological conflicts about the perceived experience, preventing further investigation.

Source: *International UFO Reporter*, Vol. 7, No. 5, Sept.-Oct., 1982.

DECEMBER 29, 1980; HUFFMAN, TEXAS

Features: Vehicle encounter, confrontation, heat, sound, severe physiological effects (radiation), mystery helicopters.

About 9:00 p.m., Betty Cash, 52, was driving her 1980 Cutlass Supreme from New Caney to Dayton, Texas, on Highway 1485. With her was a friend, Vicky Landrum, and Vicky's grandson Colby, 7. Suddenly a luminous, fiery-looking object resembling a vertically oriented ellipse descended over the road ahead, emitting a beeping noise that persisted throughout the sighting. Red-orange flames were emitted periodically from the UFO toward the road, with an audible "woosh." Afraid to drive beneath the UFO, Betty stopped the car and they opened the doors to stand by the car and watch. The glow was brilliant, and they could feel strong heat and hear a loud roaring noise. Colby became terrified, so Vicky took him back inside the car, but Betty remained outside for a longer period of time. Finally, the UFO rose and moved away to the southwest with a large number of helicopters (20 or more) now visible in pursuit of it.

The car was so hot that Betty turned on the air conditioner, though the evening was cool and the heater had been on previously. After dropping Vicky and Colby off, Betty continued home, feeling ill, arriving about 9:50 p.m. Numerous symptoms appeared almost immediately: swollen neck, head and facial blisters, swollen earlobes and eyelids. Later her eyes swelled shut and she experienced nausea, vomiting, and diarrhea. She also experienced severe hair loss. Betty was hospitalized for 15 days, and has been in and out of hospitals since.

Vicky and Colby experienced similar, but milder, symptoms. Colby's face was "sunburned" and both had stomach aches and diarrhea for several days. Vicky experienced some loss of hair and a sensation as if her scalp were "asleep." The fingernails on her left hand, which she had placed on top of the car during the sighting, showed odd line-like indentations across their width. Colby suffered severe psychological aftereffects.

Source: *MUFON UFO Journal*, No. 158, April 1981; "Cash-Landrum Case: The Issue of Government Responsibility," by John F. Schuessler, *MUFON 1986 UFO Symposium Proceedings* (Seguin, Tex.: MUFON, 1986).

JUNE 12, 1981; ALICE, TEXAS

Features: Vehicle encounter, E-M effects, loss of vehicle control, levitation, water evaporation.

Robert Gomez, a vacuum truck driver, was headed west on highway FR 665 toward Alice after finishing a job, leaving about 165 gallons of water in the tank and zero pressure. About 2:10 p.m. he saw a bright object in the sky that he first thought was an airplane, until it increased in brilliance and stopped in midair. The object was a domed disc, brilliant white, with a dark ring around the outer perimeter and a dark inner ring around its center. Gomez then felt the truck slowing down and pressed down on the accelerator; the exhaust stacks were blowing smoke, but the truck apparently was about a foot off the road. The AM radio stopped playing but the CB was still working, so he reported the sighting to his dispatcher. Afterwards, the UFO disappeared into clouds. Smoke was discovered coming out of the water tank valve, which now showed 55 pounds of pressure on the gauge. He opened the valve to drain the remaining water, but all that came out was steam.

Source: *MUFON UFO Journal,* No. 167, Jan. 1982.

JULY 31, 1981; LIEKSA, FINLAND

Features: Vehicle encounter (boat), paralysis, time loss, physiological effects.

Two 35-year-old vacationing men were steering their motorboat past Vaaraniemi Cape at 8:40 p.m., when they saw a black sphere in the sky with a large light and several smaller lights around it. The large light approached them and the men stopped the boat. Then a black object with two lights on it, and covered by "fog," flew to the stern of the boat. One of the men felt paralyzed and couldn't move his head, but the two men were able to talk with each other. Then the lights and object disappeared into the sky.

Afterwards the men realized that they were not sitting at the same positions in the boat as they had been at the start of the sighting. The boat was still near the cape despite strong water currents and wind. Looking at their watches, they discovered that it was 4:10 a.m. on the following morning. They could not account for the lost 7 hours. After the experience they suffered from shaking hands, nightmares, and a disrupted sense of balance. Two attempts to hypnotize the men were unsuccessful, and investigation continues.

Special significance: Features suggestive of a possible abduction.

Source: UFO Research of Finland, Kylama, third quarter report, 1981.

NOVEMBER 27, 1982; PALATINE, ILLINOIS

Features: Police witnesses, vehicle encounter, brilliant illumination, light beam.

Commander Michael McDonald of the Police Department was patrolling about 5:00 a.m. when a brilliant light (compared to a white phosphorous flare) illuminated the area around his car. Looking for the source, he saw a large white light with tinges of red moving slowly toward the south at an estimated 900 to 1,000 feet altitude.

After pulling over to watch for about 30-45 seconds from a parking lot, he drove south to follow the light. Two other officers, alerted by radio, also observed the light, which changed direction to the southeast. On permission of the Commander, the two gave chase at speeds up to 60-65 m.p.h., but the light increased its speed and outdistanced them.

A few minutes later, McDonald noted a bright light to the east and notified the other officers, who then observed a diffuse "domed disc" (edges fuzzy rather than sharp) which was seen to emit a beam of light toward the ground. The object then slowly descended behind the treeline of a forest preserve.

Visibility was 12-15 miles with scattered, broken cloud cover at 2,500 feet and high clouds at 8,000 feet. Wind was from the north at 8 m.p.h. Size of the object was calculated to be approximately 30 feet diameter.

Sighting was investigated by Mark Rodeghier and Mark Chesney of the Center for UFO Studies. Their files include the tape recording of police communications during the sighting.

Source: *International UFO Reporter*, Mar.-Apr., 1983.

MARCH 1985; Nr. SANTIAGO, CHILE

Features: Vehicle encounter, brilliant illumination, E-M effects, physiological effects.

A 45-year-old industrialist, driving on the highway between Aculeo Lake and Santiago about 9:30 p.m., reported anonymously to a leading Chilean UFO investigator that he was listening to the radio in his 1982 Mercedes Benz when he was "... suddenly surprised with a powerful light illuminating the road ... [and the car], shaking the vehicle in an unusual and strong way ... the radio began to buzz with interfering noise and the electrical system of the motor stopped."

Leaning out of his car window and looking up, he saw "... a huge object with a diameter of approximately 30 meters hovering over his car and illuminating it with a strong stream of light so brilliant and powerful that it caused pain to his eyes."

The encounter lasted 15 minutes, after which the radio functioned normally and the witness restarted his car and fled the scene.

Sources: *MUFON 1987 International UFO Symposium Proceedings*, p. 200-201

MAY 11, 1986; Nr. SEDONA, ARIZONA

Features: Aerial encounter.

Robert H. Henderson, a minister, and his wife, Nann, of Phoenix, Ariz., were flying north at 8,500 feet in their Cessna-172 at 4 p.m. in clear weather. In the vicinity of Verde Valley a flash of light ahead caught their attention. Then a very bright object was seen approaching nearly head-on. As Henderson prepared to take evasive action, the object — now seen to be wingless and resembling a "modified half-sphere, with the flat side down" — passed quickly to the left and below the airplane. The closure rate was estimated to be about 1,200 m.p.h.

Henderson went through a classic "escalation of hypotheses" (a term coined by J. Allen Hynek to describe the typical reaction of rational UFO witnesses attempting to account for their sighting in conventional terms). "My first thought was 'airplane' but it was moving too fast. Then I thought 'helicopter' and the same objection came to mind." No wings, no rotor, large size, brilliance. The object did not fit with anything familiar to his experience.

Appendix A

Source: *MUFON UFO Journal*, No. 222, Oct. 1986.

MAY 15, 1986; Nr. BELO HORIZONTE, BRAZIL

Features: Light beam, physiological effects, "voices" (sound).

Joaquim — a 70-year-old farm worker, watched as a UFO hovered about 50 paces away and approximately 10-15 meters above the ground for about 30 minutes. The object was flashing a beam of light around the terrain, and occasionally on him as he stood in a doorway. Due to the brilliance of the light, he shielded his face with his left arm. On one occasion the light struck his right eye; he later lost about 80% of the vision in that eye and his left arm was burned "like a sunburn."

Joaquim also said he "heard voices, but couldn't understand the language." When the UFO lifted off and went away, it hit some electric wires and broke one of them. Power company repairmen came out several days later to repair the wire.

Source: *MUFON UFO Journal*, No. 232, Aug. 1987

MAY 19, 1986; Nr. SAO PAULO AND RIO DE JANEIRO, BRAZIL

Features: Multiple independent sensors, radar-visual, military and civilian pilots, jet interceptor scrambles, cat-and-mouse pursuit.

Between 9:00 p.m. and midnight, the Brazilian integrated military air defense and civilian air traffic control system was flooded with radar UFO sightings and confirmatory reports by pilots. One of the early pilot witnesses was Ospires Silva, president of Petrobras (State oil conglomerate), in his private plane, along with his companion Alcir Pereira da Silva, an airline pilot.

As they were about to land at Sao Jose dos Campos Airport about 9:10 p.m., the control tower alerted them to radar-UFO targets. They looked and saw bright red or red-orange lights ". . . not at all like stars or planes." Aborting the landing, they attempted to pursue one of the objects, which blinked on and off, appearing in a new location each time as if changing position rapidly. After about 30 minutes, they gave up the chase and landed.

By this time the Air Defense/Air Traffic Control Center was on full alert, the radar screens showing numerous unidentified targets. Three F-5E fighter jets were scrambled from Santa Cruz AFB, near Sao Paulo, starting about 10:23 p.m. One of the pilots, Capt. Marcio Jordao, 29, was able to approach within 12 miles of an unidentified target, visible to him as a strong, constant light changing colors continuously from white to green. He broke off contact when the object moved away out to sea. Another, Lt. Kleber Caldas Marinho, 25, chased a very intense red light, which changed to white, then green, then red again. Running low on fuel, he had to return to base. Both ground and airborne radar were tracking the objects.

After the F-5E pilots made visual contact, more jets were scrambled from Anapolis AFB, Goias State, about 10:50 p.m. This second flight consisted of three Mirage III fighters equipped with Sidewinders and Matra missiles. One of the pilots, Capt. Armindo Souza Viriato de Freitas, 30, was vectored toward 10-13 unidentified targets at a distance of 20 miles. Radar controllers saw the objects surround his plane, six stationed on one side and seven on the other, and later following his plane at a distance of two miles. The targets made sharp turns beyond the capability of aircraft. Capt. Viriato tracked the objects on his radar at a distance of 12 miles, but only saw them visually once as they climbed vertically.

The Air Force Minister, Brig. Gen. Octavio Moreira Lima, made the events public at a press conference and allowed the pilots and radar officers to submit to news media questioning in Brasilia. (Their comments are summarized in the Granchi reference.) One of the air traffic controllers, Lt. Valdecir Fernando Coehlo, stated:

> "In my 14 years of experience as a radar operator, I never saw anything like this."

Appendix A

Note: The case bears a strong resemblance to the famous July 1952 radar-visual sightings and jet interceptor pursuit cases over Washington, D.C.

Sources: "UFOs Over Brazil," by Walt Andrus, and "More on Brazilian OVNIs," by Willy Smith, *MUFON UFO Journal*, No. 221, Sept. 1986; "UFO Alert in Brazil," by J. Antonio Huneeus, and "Brazilian Briefing," by Irene Granchi, *MUFON UFO Journal*, No. 223, Nov. 1986; "Brazilian Incident," by Willy Smith, *International UFO Reporter*, July-Aug. 1986.

AUGUST 1, 1986; BANKSONS LAKE, MICHIGAN

Features: Large object, brilliant lights, physiological effects (eye damage).

At about 10:30 p.m., John Long and Richard Jandura were fishing from a small boat on the lake in Van Buren County. What appeared to be the landing lights of a very large aircraft were observed approaching from the south-southeast at low altitude, as if about to land at Kalamazoo County Airport. The apparent craft, however, seemed to be too large for such a small airport.

The object appeared to be at very low altitude, perhaps 200-300 feet, and ". . . about as long as a football field [i.e., 100 yards]." A steady white light was emitted from the front, and three red lights blinked on the edges of the object. When it reached a point almost directly in front of them and over the water, the white light flashed brilliantly and went out. (Long's blood pressure seemed to rise at this point, and he became very emotionally upset, according to the investigator's report.)

There was no wind, the water was calm, and — they suddenly realized — no sound had been heard despite the large apparent size and seeming aircraft-like nature of the object. A wavy, "heat-ray-like" effect was noted between the flashing lights. After about 15 minutes, the object passed out of view

319

in the northwest in the general direction of South Haven on Lake Michigan, site of the Palisades nuclear power plant.

Long reported the event to various local, State, and Federal authorities. Next day he had "bloodshot and watery eyes," which cleared up after two days. Jandura also experienced "swelling and discoloration" of the left eye and his doctor prescribed antibiotics.

Source: *MUFON UFO Journal*, No. 222, Oct. 1986.

NOVEMBER 17, 1986; Nr. FORT YUKON, ALASKA

Features: Aerial confrontation, cockpit illumination, heat, radar-visual, E-M effects.

Capt. Kenju Terauchi, Co-Pilot Takanori Tamefuji, and Flight Engineer Yoshio Tsukuba of Japan Airlines flight no. 1628, a Boeing 747 frieghter en route to Anchorage from Iceland, were on a 215 degree heading (southwestward) over northeast Alaska at 35,000 ft. At 5:11 p.m. (local time) they noticed some lights about 30 degrees to the left and below.

Capt. Terauchi at first thought the lights were military planes from one of the nearby Air Force Bases, but then noticed that they appeared to be traveling along a parallel course to his plane and did not resemble normal aircraft. About 7 minutes later, the lights abruptly moved directly in front of the aircraft. "Most unexpectedly, two spaceships stopped in front of our face, shooting off lights [like 'numerous exhaust pipes']. The inside cockpit shined brightly and I felt warm in the face," Terauchi said.

The unidentified objects appeared as two rectangular clusters or arrays of light, one above the other, clearly visible from the Captain's left seat. After several minutes, the objects suddenly changed position and appeared side by side. The abrupt maneuvers again startled the experienced airmen. The two objects (or light arrays) also were "swinging" or "undulating" to left and right in unison, as if linked together.

After deciding that they were not observing conventional aircraft, the crew contacted the regional FAA air traffic control center by radio and requested identification of the unidentified "traffic" in their path. The FAA air traffic controllers could not account for the objects as any known aircraft, but initially did not confirm having any unexplained radar targets.

While the unidentified objects remained in full view of the B-747 crew, VHF radio communications (both transmitting and receiving) were garbled. The communication difficulties ceased when the two objects departed, moving away to the left of the aircraft. Two "flat" white lights continued to pace the aircraft.

About this time the FAA air traffic controllers contacted Elmendorf AFB to determine whether Air Force radar was tracking any UFOs. Capt. Terauchi also directed his airborne weather radar to the left, and it showed a large unidentified object within about 8 miles of the aircraft. FAA also reported an unidentified radar target trailing the plane, but this did not coincide with what the crew was observing visually.

Meanwhile, from the perspective of the Japan Airlines crew, the two sets of lights pacing their aircraft dropped back and were lost from view, both visually and on radar. The Air Force radar controller about this time reported sporadic unidentified radar targets near the B-747. At one point, radio communications back and forth between FAA and the Air Force confirmed the presence of a radar target "right in front of the [JAL 1628]." Comparing notes, civilian and military radar controllers both were detecting something unusual in the vicinity of JAL flight no. 1628.

About 5:30 p.m., as JAL flight no. 1628 was in the vicinity of Fairbanks, Alaska, Capt. Terauchi ". . . checked the pale white light behind us . . . [and then saw] a silhouette of a gigantic spaceship." Radio communications again became garbled at this point. The UFO was walnut-shaped (i.e., rounded and symmetrical above and below) with a central flange, and of apparently gigantic size. [This configuration has also been described as "Saturn-shaped."]

After sighting this gigantic object, the crew openly expressed fear for the first time and requested a sharp change of course. "It felt like a long time before we received permission," Capt. Terauchi said. At this time, radiocommunications again became garbled.

After making a change of course, "We checked our rear [and] there was still the ship following us." Increasingly fearful, the crew requested a change of altitude — a descent — to avoid the UFO ("We had to get away from that object"). Finally, after the B-747 executed a turn, the "spaceship" disappeared.

Source: "Fantastic Flight of JAL 1628," by Bruce Maccabee, *International UFO Reporter*, Mar.-Apr. 1987, special issue devoted entirely to this case (23 p.).

APPENDIX B:
SAMPLE OF
GOVERNMENT UFO DOCUMENTS

Note: Many documents have had passages deleted by the Government agency that released them to the public. These have been indicated in text with a bar. Ex: ████████████

OBJECT REPORT [CIA]

OBJECT REPORT

On 24 April 1949, at 3 miles north of Arrey, New Mexico, (107°
19½'W 32° 52½'N) 4 Navy enlisted men from White Sands Proving Ground
(Chief Akers, Davidson, Fitzsimmons and Moorman) and I saw a rapidly
moving object while making a pibal wind run. We had released a 350 gram
balloon at about 1020 MST and were following it with a standard ML-47
(David White) Theodolite. After the 1030 reading, Davidson took over
the theodolite, and Akers and I looked up to find the balloon with
naked eye. We thought we had the balloon when we saw a whitish spherical
object right along the direction the theodolite (45° elevation and 210°
azimuth) was pointing. The object was drifting east rapidly (5°/sec.
as estimated by stopwatch and width of fingers) but we had thought to
encounter similar winds on the balloon. When the difference in angle
between the theodolite and supposed balloon became apparent, I took
over the theodolite and found the true balloon still there, whereupon
I abandoned it and picked up the object after it came out of the sun.
(The computed bearing of sun was 127° azimuth and elevation 60°) The
object was moving too fast to crank the theodolite around, therefore one
of the men pointed the theodolite and I looked.

The object was an ellipsoid about 2½ : I slenderness ratio, length
about .02° subtended angle, and white in color, except for a light
yellow of one side as though it were in shadow. I could not get a hard
focus on the object due to the speed at which the angles changed. Therefor
I saw no good detail at all.

The Azimuth angle continued to decrease as the object continued on
a north heading, growing smaller in size. At around 20° - 25° Azimuth,
the Azimuth held constant and the elevation angle began increasing from
the 25° minimum to about 25°. The object then apparently disappeared
due to distance after a total time of observation of about 60 seconds.

On 24 April 1949, at 3 miles north of Arrey, New Mexico,
(107° 19½' W 30° 52½' N) 4 Navy enlisted men from White
Sands Proving Ground (Chief Akers, Davidson, Fitzsimmons
and Moorman) and I saw a rapidly moving object while making a pibal wind run. We had released a 350 gram balloon
at about 1020 MST and were following it with a standard
ML-47 (David White) Theodolite. After the 1030 reading,
Davidson took over the theodolite, and Akers and I looked
up to find the balloon with naked eye. We thought we had the
balloon when we saw a whitish spherical object right along
the direction the theodolite (45° elevation and 210° azimuth)
was pointing. The object was drifting east rapidly (5°/sec. as
estimated by stopwatch and width of fingers) but we had
thought to encounter similar winds on the balloon. When the
difference in angle between the theodolite and supposed balloon
became apparent, I took over the theodolite and found the true

balloon still there, whereupon I abandoned it and picked up the object after it came out of the sun. (The computed bearing of sun was 127° azimuth and elevation 60°) The object was moving too fast to crank the theodolite around, therefore one of the men pointed the theodolite and I looked.

The object was an ellipsoid about 2½:1 slenderness ratio, length about .02° subtended angle, and white in color, except for a light yellow of one side as though it were in shadow. I could not get a hard focus on the object due to the speed at which the angles changed. Therefore I saw no good detail at all.

The Azimuth angle continued to decrease as the object continued on a north heading, growing smaller in size. At around 20°-25° Azimuth, the Azimuth held constant and the elevation angle began increasing from the 25° minimum to about 29°. The object then apparently disappeared due to distance after a total time of observation of about 60 seconds.

The object was not a balloon and was some distance away. Assuming escape velocity, a track was figured which put the elevation about the station of about 300,000 feet over the observed period. If this is true, the flight would have probably gone over the White Sands Proving Ground, Holloman Air Force Base and Los Alamos.

We made another pibal wind run 15 minutes later. This balloon burst after an 88 minute flight of 93,000 feet only 13 miles due south of us. Therefore this object could not have been a free balloon moving at such angular speed below 90,000 feet.

Information is desired if this was some new or experimental aircraft or for any explanation whatsoever.

NOTE:
No clouds in sky, no haze.
No noise, very quite in area
(no cars, planes or other
(engines running)
No trail, no exhaust visible.
No odor.

/s/ C.B. Moore
C.B. Moore
General Mills Aeronautical Research
2010 E. Hennepin Avenue
Minneapolis, 13, Minnesota
Geneva 0371 X 385

FBI MEMO ON CRASHED "SAUCERS"

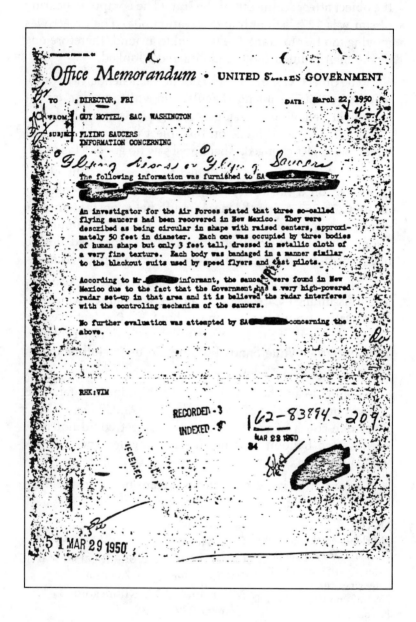

Office Memorandum • UNITED STATES GOVERNMENT

TO : DIRECTOR, FBI   DATE: March 22, 1950

FROM : GUY HOTTEL, SAC, WASHINGTON

SUBJECT: FLYING SAUCERS
         INFORMATION CONCERNING

The following information was furnished to SA ████████ by

An investigator for the Air Forces stated that three so-called
flying saucers had been recovered in New Mexico. They were
described as being circular in shape with raised centers, approximately 50 feet in diameter. Each one was occupied by three bodies
of human shape but only 3 feet tall, dressed in metallic cloth of
a very fine texture. Each body was bandaged in a manner similar
to the blackout suits used by speed flyers and test pilots.

According to Mr. ████████ informant, the saucers were found in New
Mexico due to the fact that the Government has a very high-powered
radar set-up in that area and it is believed the radar interferes
with the controling mechanism of the saucers.

No further evaluation was attempted by SA ████████ concerning the
above.

RHK:VIM

RECORDED - 3
INDEXED - 5

162-83894 - 209

MAR 23 1950

51 MAR 29 1950

TO: DIRECTOR, FBI   **DATE: March 22, 1950**

FROM: GUY HOTTEL, SAC, WASHINGTON

SUBJECT: FLYING SAUCERS
              INFORMATION CONCERNING

Flying Discs or Flying Saucers [handwritten]

The following information was furnished to SA ███████████

An investigator for the Air Force stated that three so-called fly-ing saucers had been recovered in New Mexico. They were described as being circular in shape with raised centers, ap-proximately 50 feet in diameter. Each one was occupied by three bodies of human shape but only 3 feet tall, dressed in metallic cloth of a very fine texture. Each body was bandaged in a manner similar to the blackout suits used by speed flyers and test pilots.

According to Mr. ███████ informant, the saucers were found in New Mexico due to the fact that the Government has a very high-powered radar set-up in that area and it is believed the radar interferes with the controling mechanism of the saucers.

No further evaluation was attempted by SA ███████ con-cerning the above.

STAFF MESSAGE DIVISION
INCOMING CLASSIFIED MESSAGE

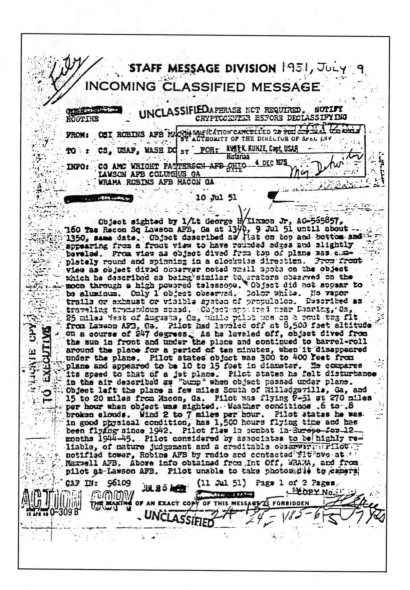

STAFF MESSAGE DIVISION 1951, JULY 9

INCOMING CLASSIFIED MESSAGE

UNCLASSIFIED APERASE NOT REQUIRED. NOTIFY
ROUTINE CRYPTOCENTER BEFORE DECLASSIFYING

CLASSIFICATION CANCELLED TO YOU CENTRAL CROSS
BY ACTHORITY OF THE DIRECTOR OF SEC INV

FROM: OSI ROBINS AFB MACON

TO : CS, USAF, WASH DC BY FOR: KUBEK KUNZE Capt USAF
Historian

INFO: CO AMC WRIGHT PATTERSON AFB OHIO 4 DEC 1975
LAWSON AFB COLUMBUS GA
WRAMA ROBINS AFB MACON GA

10 Jul 51

Object sighted by 1/Lt George H Kinmon Jr, AO-555857,
160 Tac Recon Sq Lawson AFB, Ga at 1340, 9 Jul 51 until about
1350, same date. Object described as flat on top and bottom and
appearing from a front view to have rounded edges and slightly
beveled. From view as object dived from top of plane was completely round and spinning in a clockwise direction. From front
view as object dived observer noted small spots on the object
which he described as being similar to craters observed on the
moon through a high powered telescope. Object did not appear to
be aluminum. Only 1 object observed. Color white. No vapor
trails or exhaust or visible system of propulsion. Described as
traveling tremendous speed. Object appeared near Dearing, Ga,
25 miles West of Augusta, Ga, while pilot was on a routing flt
from Lawson AFB, Ga. Pilot had leveled off at 8,500 feet altitude
on a course of 247 degrees. As he leveled off, object dived from
the sun in front and under the plane and continued to barrel-roll
around the plane for a period of ten minutes, when it disappeared
under the plane. Pilot states object was 300 to 400 feet from
plane and appeared to be 10 to 15 feet in diameter. He compares
its speed to that of a jet plane. Pilot states he felt disturbance
in the air described as "bump" when object passed under plane.
Object left the plane a few miles South of Milladgeville, Ga, and
15 to 20 miles from Macon, Ga. Pilot was flying P-51 at 270 miles
per hour when object was sighted. Weather conditions .6 to .8
broken clouds. Wind 2 to 7 miles per hour. Pilot states he was
in good physical condition, has 1,500 hours flying time and has
been flying since 1942. Pilot flew in combat in Europe for 12
months 1944-45. Pilot considered by associates to be highly reliable, of mature judgement and a creditable observer. Pilot
notified tower, Robins AFB by radio and contacted flt ovc at
Maxwell AFB. Above info obtained from Int Off, WRAMA, and from
pilot at Lawson AFB. Pilot unable to take photosub to camera

CAP IN: 96109   JUL 25   (11 Jul 51) Page 1 of 2 Pages.

COPY No.

THE MAKING OF AN EXACT COPY OF THIS MESSAGE IS FORBIDDEN

ACTION COPY

O-309 B

UNCLASSIFIED

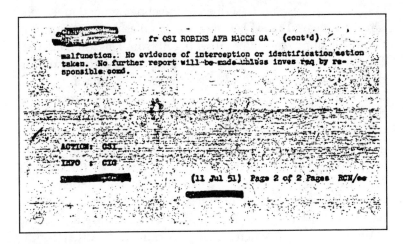

fr OSI ROBINS AFB MACON GA   (cont'd)

malfunction. No evidence of interception or identification action taken. No further report will be made unless inves req by responsible ecmd.

ACTION: OSI

INFO : CIG

(11 Jul 51)   Page 2 of 2 Pages   RCH/ee

UNCLASSIFIED

ROUTINE

FROM: OSI ROBINS AFB MACON

TO: CS, USAF, WASH DC   FOR: KURT K. KUNZE,
                                                Capt, USAF,
                                                Historian

INFO: CO AMC WRIGHT PATTERSON AFB OHIO
           LAWSON AFB COLUMBUS GA
           WRAMA ROBINS AFB MACON GA.

10 Jul 51

Object sighted by 1/Lt George H. Kinmon Jr., AO-565857, 160 Tac Recon Sq Lawson AFB, Ga at 1340, 9 Jul 51 until about 1350, same date. Object described as flat on top and bottom and appearing from a front view to have rounded edges and slightly beveled. From view as object dived from top of plane was completely round and spinning in a clockwise direction. From front view as object dived observer noted small spots on the object which he described as being similar to craters observed on the moon through a high powered telescope. Object did not appear to be aluminum. Only 1 object observed. Color white. No vapor trails or exhaust or visible system of propulsion. Described as traveling tremendous speed. Object appeared near Dearing, Ga, 25 miles West of Augusta, Ga, while pilot was on a routine tng flt from Lawson AFB, Ga. Pilot had leveled off at 8,500 feet altitude on a course of 247 degrees. As he leveled off, object dived from the sun in front and under the plane and continued to barrel-roll around the plane for a period of ten minutes, when it disappeared under the plane. Pilot states object was 300 to 400 feet from plane and appeared to be 10 to 15 feet in diameter. He compares its speed to that of a jet plane. Pilot states he felt disturbance in the air described as "bump" when object passed under plane. Object left the plane a few miles South of Milledgeville, Ga, and 15 to 20 miles from Macon, Ga. Pilot was flying F-51 at 270 miles per hour when object was sighted. Weather conditions .6 to .8 broken clouds. Wind 2 to 7 miles per hour. Pilot states he was in good physical condition, has 1,500 hours flying time and has been flying since 1942. Pilot flew in combat in Europe for 12 months 1944-45. Pilot considered by associates to be highly reliable, of mature judgement and a creditable observer. Pilot notified tower, Robins AFB by radio and contacted flt svc at Maxwell AFB. Above info obtained from Int Off, WRAMA, and from pilot at Lawson AFB. Pilot unable to take photos due to camera malfunction. No evidence of interception or identification action taken. No further report will be made unless inves req by responsible comd.

Appendix B

SPOT INTELLIGENCE REPORT 23 JUL 1952

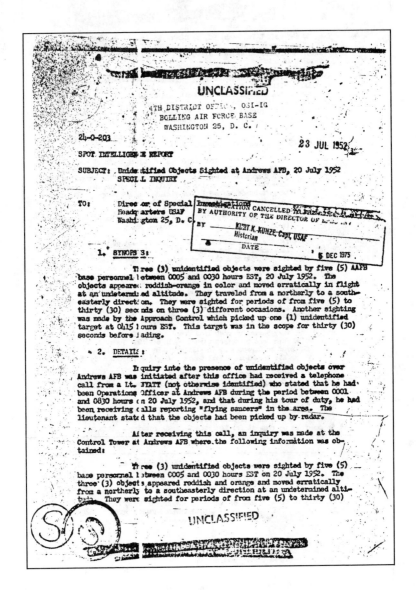

UNCLASSIFIED

4TH DISTRICT OFFICE, OSI-IG
BOLLING AIR FORCE BASE
WASHINGTON 25, D. C.

24-0-203

23 JUL 1952

SPOT INTELLIGENCE REPORT

SUBJECT: Unidentified Objects Sighted at Andrews AFB, 20 July 1952
SPECIAL INQUIRY

TO: Director of Special Investigations
Headquarters USAF
Washington 25, D. C.

INVESTIGATION CANCELLED
BY AUTHORITY OF THE DIRECTOR OF ...
BY
KURT K. KUNZE, Capt, USAF
Historian
DATE 5 DEC 1975

1. SYNOPSIS:

Three (3) unidentified objects were sighted by five (5) AAFB base personnel between 0005 and 0030 hours EST, 20 July 1952. The objects appeared reddish-orange in color and moved erratically in flight at an undetermined altitude. They traveled from a northerly to a south-easterly direction. They were sighted for periods of from five (5) to thirty (30) seconds on three (3) different occasions. Another sighting was made by the Approach Control which picked up one (1) unidentified target at 0415 hours EST. This target was in the scope for thirty (30) seconds before fading.

2. DETAILS:

Inquiry into the presence of unidentified objects over Andrews AFB was initiated after this office had received a telephone call from a Lt. WYATT (not otherwise identified) who stated that he had been Operations Officer at Andrews AFB during the period between 0001 and 0830 hours on 20 July 1952, and that during his tour of duty, he had been receiving calls reporting "flying sancers" in the area. The lieutenant stated that the objects had been picked up by radar.

After receiving this call, an inquiry was made at the Control Tower at Andrews AFB where the following information was obtained:

Three (3) unidentified objects were sighted by five (5) base personnel between 0005 and 0030 hours EST on 20 July 1952. The three (3) objects appeared reddish and orange and moved erratically from a northerly to a southeasterly direction at an undetermined altitude. They were sighted for periods of from five (5) to thirty (30)

UNCLASSIFIED

331

Ltr, DO #4, OSI, BAFB, Wash, DC, to Dir of Sp Invest, Hq USAF, Wash, DC, File 21-0-203, dtd _____, SPOT INTELLIGENCE REPORT, Subj: Unidentified Objects Sighted at Andrews AFB, 20 July 1952, SPECIAL INQUIRY

seconds on three (3) occasions by _____ Civilians, WILLIAM B. BRADY, A/1C, JOHN P. IZZO, T/Sgt. (all of whom are assigned to the control tower at AAFB), and Capt. HARRY W. REDDING, AC-818935, Airdrome Officer on duty at the time. At 0415 hours EST, the Approach Control picked up one (1) unidentified target which remained on the scope for thirty (30) seconds and then disappeared.

The following is a copy of the AACS Control Tower Log, 1909th AACS Squadron, dated 20 July 1952:

"0005 Phone call advsg that there was an object south of ADW. A/1C BRADY looked south and saw a orange object that appeared for just a moment then disapeared. The party on the phone saw the same thing. Wash Center also calling to advise they have five targets unidentified in the vicinity of ADW Range. TWR personnel used to observe from roof of the TWR.
"0120 While watching from the TWR roof Mr. DeBoves, T/Sgt IZZO and myself, Capt H. W. REDDING, observed what appeared to be two falling stars but they had an orange hue and a tail and were traveling at a fast pace.
"0125 T/Sgt and Mr. DeBoves also saw a third object that appeared like the first two objects (appeared like a falling star).
"0235 ADW A/O making a full report including the report by the party on the phone. Wash Center received a call from Capital Airlines plane that he saw three objects near HERNDON and reported that they were like nothing he had ever seen. He also reported three more between HRN and Martinsburg. Wash Center first saw these targets around 2340 and then about ten minutes later they moved toward ADW.
"0330 Wash Center advised the targets seemed to move more frequently when there were aircraft moving. As daylight was approaching they seemed to move less frequently.
"0530 Wash Center advised target north of ADW. Tower could not see it.
"TWX sent to Director of Intelligence, Hq USAF, Washington 25, D. C.
Air Technical Intell Center, Wright-Patterson AFB, Ohio
ATTN: ATIAA-26
Commanding General, Ent AFB, Colorado Springs, Colo.
Commanding Officer, Headquarters Command, USAF, Bolling AFB."

3. ACTION:

No investigation of this matter was conducted by this office inasmuch as no request for investigation was received. This matter was

---

DO #4, OSI, BAFB, Wash, DC, to Dir of Sp Invest, Hq USAF, Wash, File 24-0-203, dtd _____, SPOT INTELLIGENCE REPORT, Subj: Unidentified Objects Sighted at Andrews AFB, 20 July 1952, SPECIAL INQUIRY

coordinated with Capt. BENJAMIN BERKOW, Director of Intelligence, Headquarters Command, Bolling Air Force Base, who stated that his office would handle the required investigation.

DONALD B. WHITE
Colonel, USAF
District Commander

Appendix B

4TH DISTRICT OFFICE, OSI-IG
BOLLING AIR FORCE BASE
WASHINGTON 25, D.C.

24-0-203

SPOT INTELLIGENCE REPORT   23 JUL 1952

SUBJECT: Unidentified Objects Sighted at Andrews AFB,
         20 July 1952
         SPECIAL INQUIRY

TO: Director of Special Investigations
         Headquarters USAF
         Washington 25, D.C.

1. <u>SYNOPSIS</u>:

Three (3) unidentified objects were sighted by five (5) AAFB base personnel between 0005 and 0030 hours EST, 20 July 1952. The objects appeared reddish-orange in color and moved erratically in flight at an undetermined altitude. They traveled from a northerly to a south-easterly direction. They were sighted for periods of from five (5) to thirty (30) seconds on three (3) different occasions. Another sighting was made by the Approach Control which picked up one (1) unidentified target at 0415 hours EST. This target was in the scope for thirty (30) seconds before fading.

2. <u>DETAILS</u>:

Inquiry into the presence of unidentified objects over Andrews AFB was initiated after this office had received a telephone call from a Lt. HYATT (not otherwise identified) who stated that he had been Operations Officer at Andrews AFB during the period between 0001 and 0830 hours on 20 July 1952, and that during his tour of duty, he had been receiving calls reporting "flying saucers" in the area. The lieutenant stated that the objects had been picked up by radar.

After receiving this call, an inquiry was made at the Control Tower at Andrews AFB where the following information was obtained:

Three (3) unidentified objects were sighted by five (5) base personnel between 0005 and 0030 hours EST on 20 July 1952. The three (3) objects appeared reddish and orange and moved erratically from a northerly to a southeasterly direction at an undetermined altitude. They were sighted for periods of from five (5) to thirty (30) seconds on three (3) occasions ▮▮▮▮ Civilians, WILLIAM B. BRADY, A/1C, JOHN P. IZZO, T/Sgt. (all of whom are assigned to the control tower at AAFB), and Capt. HARRY W. REDDING, AO-818935, Airdrome Officer on duty at the time. At 0415 hours EST, the Approach Control picked up one (1) unidentified target which remained on the scope for thirty (30) seconds and then disappeared.

The following is a copy of the AACS Control Tower Log, 1909th AACS Squadron, dated 20 July 1952:

"0005 Phone call advsg that there was an object south of ADW. A/1C BRADY looked south and saw a orange object that appeared for just a moment then disapeared. The party on the phone saw the same thing. Wash Center also calling to advise they have five targets unindentified in the vicinity of ADW Range. TWR personnel used to observe from roof of the TWR.

"0120 While watching from the TWR roof Mr. DeBoves, T/Sgt IZZO and myself, Capt H.W. REDDING, observed what appeared to be two falling stars but they had an orange hue and a tail and were traveling at a fast pace.

"0125 T/Sgt and Mr. DeBoves also saw a third object that appeared like the first two objects (appeared like a falling star).

"0235 ADW A/O making a full report including the report by the party on the phone. Wash Center received a call from Capital Airlines plane that he saw three objects near HERNDON and reported that they were like nothing he had ever seen. He also reported three more between HRN and Martinsburg. Wash Center first saw these targets around 2340 and then about ten minutes later they moved toward ADW.

"0330 Wash Center advised the targets seemed to move more frequently when there were aircraft moving. As daylight was approaching they seemed to move less frequently.

"0530 Wash Center advised target north of ADW. Tower could not see it, TWX sent to Director of Intelligence, Hq USAF, Washington 25, D.C. Air Technical Intell Center, Wright-Patterson AFB, Ohio
ATTN: ATIAA-26
Commanding General, Ent AFB, Colorado Springs, Colo.
Commanding Officer, Headquarters Command, USAF, Bolling AFB."

3. <u>ACTION</u>:

No investigation of this matter was conducted by this office inasmuch as no request for investigation was received. This matter was coordinated with Capt. BENJAMIN BERKOW, Director of Intelligence, Headquarters Command, Bolling Air Force Base, who stated that his office could handle the required investigation.

> DONALD B. WHITE
> Colonel, USAF
> District Commander

MEMORANDUM FOR:
DIRECTOR OF CENTRAL INTELLIGENCE [1952]

MEMORANDUM FOR: Director of Central Intelligence

THRU : Deputy Director for Intelligence

SUBJECT : Unidentified Flying Objects

1. On 20 August, the DCI, after a briefing by OSI on the above subject, directed the preparation of an NSCID for submission to the Council stating the need for investigation and directing agencies concerned to cooperate in such investigations.

2. In attempting to draft such a directive and the supporting staff studies, it became apparent to DD/I, Acting AD/SI and AD/IC that the problem was largely a research and development problem, and it was decided by DD/I to attempt to initiate action through P&DB. A conference was held between DI/USAF, Chairman of P&DB, DD/I, Acting AD/SI and AD/IC at which time it was decided that Dr. Whitman, Chairman of P&DB, would investigate the possibility of undertaking research and development studies through Air Force agencies.

MEMORANDUM FOR: Director of Central Intelligence

THRU: Deputy Director for Intelligence

SUBJECT: Unidentified Flying Objects

1. On 20 August, the DCI, after a briefing by OSI on the above subject, directed the preparation of an NSCID for submission to the Council stating the need for investigation and directing agencies concerned to cooperate in such investigations.

2. In attempting to draft such a directive and the supporting staff studies, it became apparent to DD/I, Acting AD/SI and AD/IC that the problem was largely a research and development problem, and it was decided by DD/I to attempt to initiate action through P&DB. A conference was held between DI/USAF, Chairman of P&DB, DD/I, Acting AD/SI and AD/IC at which time it was decided that Dr. Whitman, Chairman of P&DB, would investigate the possibility of undertaking research and development studies through Air Force agencies.

3. On approximately 6 November, we were advised by Chairman, P&DB, that inquiries in the Air Staff did not disclose "undue concern" over this matter, but that it had been referred to the Air Defense Command for considerations. No further word has been received from P&DB.

4. Recent reports reaching CIA indicated that further action was desirable and another briefing by the cognizant A-2 and ATIC personnel was held on 25 November. At this time, the reports of incidents convince us that there is something going on that must have immediate attention. The details of some of these incidents have been discussed by AD/SI with DDS. Sightings of unexplained flying objects at great altitudes and travelling at high speeds in the vicinity of major U.S. defense installations are of such nature that they are not attributable to natural phenomena or known types of aerial vehicles.

5. OSI is proceeding to the establishment of a consulting group of sufficient competence and stature to review this matter and convince the responsible authorities in the community that immediate research and development on this subject must be undertaken. This can be done expeditiously under the aegis of CANIS.

6. Attached hereto is a draft memorandum to the NSC and a simple draft NS Directive establishing this matter as a priority project throughout the intelligence and the defense research and development community.

H. MARSHALL CHADWELL
Assistant Director
Scientific Intelligence

Attachments:
Draft memo to NSC with
draft directive

UNUSUAL UFOB REPORT

CIA   JUL 1 2 1955

Acting Assistant Director for
  Scientific Intelligence

Chief, Physics & Electronics Division, SI

Unusual UFOB Report

    1. The attached copy of a cable is a preliminary
report from Pepperrell Air Force Base, Newfoundland
reporting on what appears to be an unusual "unidentified
flying object" sighting.

    2. Essentially, the "object" was apparently simultaneously
observed by a tanker aircraft (KC 97) pilot (visually) and by
a ground radar (type unknown) site (electronically). While
such dual (visual and electronic) sightings of UFOBs are
reported from time to time, this particular report is somewhat unique in that:

       a. the "pilot of Archie 29 maintained visual contacts
with object calling direction changes of object to (radar) site
by radio. Direction changes correlated exactly with those
painted on scope by controller."

       b. In previous cases the dual (visual and electronic)
sightings are mostly of a few minutes duration at most. This
one was observed by radar, at least, for 49 minutes.

    3. It is reasonable to believe that more information will
be available on this when complete report (AF Form 112) is
issued.

                                              TODOS M. ODARENKO

Attachment.

cc: ASD/SI
     GED/SI
     SS/SI

CIA   July 12 1955
Acting Assistant Director for
  Scientific Intelligence

Chief, Physics & Electronics Division, SI

Unusual UFOB Report

1. The attached copy of a cable is a preliminary report from Pepperrell Air Force Base, Newfoundland reporting on what appears to be an unusual "unidentified flying object" sighting.

2. Essentially, the "object" was apparently simultaneously observed by a tanker aircraft (KC 97) pilot (visually) and by a ground radar (type unknown) site (electronically). While such dual (visual and electronic sightings of UFOBs are reported from time to time, this particular report is somewhat unique in that:

a. the "pilot of Archie 29 maintained visual contacts with object calling direction changes of object to (radar) site by radio. Direction changes correlated exactly with those painted on scope by controller."

b. In previous cases the dual (visual and electronic) sightings are mostly of a few minutes duration at most. This one was observed by radar, at least, for 49 minutes.

3. It is reasonable to believe that more information will be available on this when complete report (AF Form ll2) is issued.

                                         TODOS M. ODARENKO

Attachment.

cc: ASD/SI
    GMD/SI
    SS/SI

UNINVITED GUESTS

SUBJECT: AFB PENETRATION

N M C C
THE NATIONAL MILITARY COMMAND CENTER
WASHINGTON, D.C. 20301

THE JOINT STAFF

29 October 1975
0605 EST

MEMORANDUM FOR RECORD

Subject: AFB Penetration

1. At 290200 EST AFOC informed NMCC that an unidentified helicopter, possibly two, had been sighted flying low over Loring AFB Maine, in proximity to a weapons storage area.

— 2. An Army National Guard helo was called in to assist in locating the unidentified helo(s).

— 3. NORAD was informed of the incident by SAC, requested and recieved authority from Canadian officials to proceed into Canadian airspace if necessary to locate the intruder.

— 4. At 0404 SAC Command Center informed NMCC that the army helo assisting on the scene had not sighted the unidentified helo(s).

5. A similar incident was reported at Loring the evening of 28 October 1975.

C. D. ROBERTS, JR.
Brigadier General, USMC
Deputy Director for
Operations (NMCC)

NMCC
THE NATIONAL MILITARY COMMAND CENTER
WASHINGTON, D.C. 20301

THE JOINT STAFF

29 October 1975
0605 EST

MEMORANDUM FOR RECORD

Subject: AFB Penetration

1. At 290200 EST AFOC informed NMCC that an unidentified helicopter, possibly two, had been sighted flying low over Loring AFB Maine, in proximity to a weapons storage area.

2. An Army National Guard helo was called in to assist in locating the unidentified helo(s).

3. NORAD was informed of the incident by SAC, requested and received authority from Canadian officials to proceed into Canadian airspace if necessary to locate the intruder.

4. At 0404 SAC Command Center informed NMCC that the army helo assisting on the scene had not sighted the unidentified helo(s).

5. A similar incident was reported at Loring the evening of 28 October 1975.

C. D. ROBERTS, JR.
Brigadier General, USMC
Deputy Director for
Operations (NMCC)

Distribution:
CJCS (5)	CSA
DJS (3)	CNO
J-30	CSAF
J-31	CMC
J-32	CH, WWMCCS OPS & EVAL DIV
J-32A	DDO (NMCC)
J-33	ADDO (NMCC)
J-34	CCOC (NMCC)
J-35	DIA REP FOR NMIC
J-38	NSA REP
PA REP	CIA REP
NWSB	WEST HEM DESK

SUBJECT: REPORT OF UFO — CANNON AFB NM

N M C C
THE NATIONAL MILITARY COMMAND CENTER
WASHINGTON, D.C. 20301

THE JOINT STAFF

21 Janaury 1976
0630 EST

MEMORANDUM FOR RECORD

Subject: Report of UFO - Cannon AFB NM

Reference: AFOC Phonecon 21055 EST Jan 76

The following information was received from the Air Force
Operations Center at 0555 EST:

"Two UFOs are reported near the flight line at Cannon AFB,
New Mexico. Security Police observing them reported the UFOs
to be 25 yards in diameter, gold or silver in color with blue
light on top, hole in the middle and red light on bottom. Air
Force is checking with radar. Additicnally, checking weather
inversion data."

J.B. MORIN
Rear Admiral, USN
Deputy Director for
Operations, NMCC

NMCC
THE NATIONAL MILITARY COMMAND CENTER
WASHINGTON, D.C. 20301

THE JOINT STAFF   21 January 1976
                                         0630 EST

MEMORANDUM FOR RECORD

SUBJECT: Report of UFO — Cannon AFB NM

Reference: AFOC Phonecon 21055 EST Jan 76

The following information was received from the Air Force Operations Center at 0555 EST:

"Two UFOs are reported near the flight line at Cannon AFB, New Mexico. Security Police observing them reported the UFOs to be 25 yards in diameter, gold or silver in color with blue light on top, hole in the middle and red light on bottom. Air Force is checking with radar. Additionally, checking weather inversion data."

> J.B. MORIN
> Rear Admiral, USN
> Deputy Director for
> Operations, NMCC

SUBJECT:
REPORTS OF UNIDENTIFIED FLYING OBJECTS (UFOs)

N M C C

THE NATIONAL MILITARY COMMAND CENTER
WASHINGTON, D.C. 20301

30 July 1976
0345 EDT

THE JOINT STAFF

MEMORANDUM FOR RECORD

Subject: Reports of Unidentified Flying Objects (UFOs)

1. At approximately 0345 EDT, the ANMCC called to indicate
they had received several reports of UFO's in the vicinity
of Fort Ritchie. The following events summarize the reports
(times are approximate).

    a. 0130 - Civilians reported a UFO sighting near
Mt. Airy, Md. This information was obtained via a call
from the National Aeronautics Board (?) to the Fort
Ritchie Military Police.

    b. 0255 - Two separate patrols from Site R reported
sighting 3 oblong objects with a reddish tint, moving
east to west. Personnel were located at separate locations
on top of the mountain at Site R.

    c. 0300 - Desk Sgt at Site R went to the top of the
Site R mountain and observed a UFO over the ammo storage
area at 100-200 yards altitude.

    d. 0345 - An Army Police Sgt on the way to work at
Site R reported sighting a UFO in the vicinity of Site R.

2. ANMCC was requested to have each individual write a
statement on the sightings. One individual stated the object
was about the size of a 2 1/2 ton truck.

3. Based on a JCS memorandum, subject: Temperature Inversion
Analysis, dated 13 November 1975, the NMCC contacted the Air
Force Global Weather Central. The Duty Officer, LTC OVERBY,
reported that the Dulles International Airport observations
showed two temperature inversions existed at the time of the

alleged sightings. The first extended from the surface to
1,000 feet absolute and the second existed between 27,000
and 30,000 feet, absolute. He also said the atmosphere
between 12,000 and 20,000 feet was heavily saturated with
moisture. A hard copy message will follow.

L. J. Le Blanc Jr.
L. J. LEBLANC, Jr.
Brigadier General, USMC
Deputy Director for
Operations, NMCC

Appendix B

NMCC
THE NATIONAL MILITARY COMMAND CENTER
WASHINGTON, D.C. 20301

THE JOINT STAFF   30 July 1976
                                                   0545 EDT

MEMORANDUM FOR RECORD

SUBJECT: Reports of Unidentified Flying Objects (UFOs)

1. At approximately 0345 EDT, the ANMCC called to indicate they had received several reports of UFO's in the vicinity of Fort Ritchie. The following events summarize the reports (times are approximate.

    a. 0130 — Civilians reported a UFO sighting near Mt. Airy, Md. This information was obtained via a call from the National Aeronautics Board (?) to the Fort Ritchie Military Police.

    b. 0255 — Two separate patrols from Site R reported sighting 3 oblong objects with a reddish tint, moving east to west. Personnel were located at separate locations on top of the mountain at Site R.

    c. 0300 — Desk Sgt at Site R went to the top of the Site R mountain and observed a UFO over the ammo storage area at 100-200 yards altitude.

    d. 0345 — An Army Police Sgt on the way to work at Site R reported sighting a UFO in the vicinity of Site R.

2. ANMCC was requested to have each individual write a statement on the sightings. One individual stated the object was about the size of a 2-1/2 ton truck.

3. Based on a JCS memorandum, subject: Temperature Inversion Analysis, dated 13 November 1975, the NMCC contacted the Air Force Global Weather Central. The Duty Officer, LTC OVERBY, reported that the Dulles International Airport observations showed two temperature inversions existed at the time

of the alleged sightings. The first extended from the surface to 1,000 feet absolute and the second existed between 27,000 and 30,000 feet, absolute. He also said the atmosphere between 12,000 and 20,000 feet was heavily saturated with moisture. A hard copy message will follow.

L.J. LEBLANC, Jr.
Brigadier General, USMC
Deputy Director for
Operations, NMCC

DISTRIBUTION:
J-30
J-31
J-32
J-33
DDO
ADDO
CCOC
WHEM Desk
ASD/PA Rep

Appendix B

COMPLAINT FORM:
ALLEGED SIGHTINGS OF UNIDENTIFIED AERIAL LIGHTS
IN RESTRICTED TEST RANGE

COMPLAINT FORM		Hq 1 V 0 S

	ADMINISTRATIVE DATA	

TITLE
KIRTLAND AFB, NM, 8 Aug – 3 Sep 80, Alleged Sigthings of Unidentified Aerial Lights in Restricted Test Range.

DATE 2 – 9 Sept 80 **TIME** 1200

PLACE AFOSI Det 1700, Kirtland AFB, NM

HOW RECEIVED
X IN PERSON | TELEPHONICALLY | IN WRITING

SOURCE AND EVALUATION
MAJOR ERNEST E. EDWARDS

RESIDENCE OR BUSINESS ADDRESS
Commander, 1608 SPS, Manzano
Kirtland AFB, NM

PHONE 4-7516

CR **44** APPLIES

II	SUMMARY OF INFORMATION	

REMARKS

1. On 2 Sept 80, SOURCE related on 8 Aug 80, three Security Policemen assigned to 1608 SPS, KAFB, NM, on duty inside the Manzano Weapons Storage Area sighted an unidentified light in the air that traveled from North to South over the Coyote Canyon area of the Department of Defense Restricted Test Range on KAFB, NM. The Security Policemen identified as: SSGT STEPHEN FERENZ, Area Supervisor, AIC MARTIN W. RIST and AMN ANTHONY D. FRAZIER, were later interviewed separately by SOURCE and all three related the same statement; At approximately 2350hrs., while on duty in Charlie Sector, East Side of Manzano, the three observed a very bright light in the sky approximately 3 miles North-North East of their position. The light traveled with great speed and stopped suddenly in the sky over Coyote Canyon. The three first thought the object was a helicopter, however, after observing the strange aerial maneuvers (stop and go), they felt a helicopter couldn't have performed such skills. The light landed in the Coyote Canyon area. Sometime later, three witnessed the light take off and leave proceeding straight up at a hight speed and disappear.

2. Central Security Control (CSC) inside Manzano, contacted Sandia Security, who conducts frequent building checks on two alarmed structures in the area. They advised that a patrol was already in the area and would investigate.

3. On 11 Aug 80, RUSS CURTIS, Sandia Security, advised that on 9 Aug 80, a Sandia Security Guard, (who wishes his name not be divulged for fear of harassment), related the following: At approximately 0020hrs., he was driving East on the Coyote Canyon access road on a routine building check of an alarmed structure . As he approached the structure he observed a bright light near the ground behind the structure. He also observed an object he first thought was a helicopter. But after driving closer, he observed a round disk shaped object. He attempted to radio for a back up patrol but his radio would not work. As he approached the object on foot armed with a shotgun, the object took off in a vertical direction at a high rate of speed. The guard was a former helicopter mechanic in the U.S. Army and stated the object he observed was not a helicopter.

4. SOURCE advised on 22 Aug 80, three other security policemen observed the same

DATE FORWARDED HQ AFOSI
Hq 1 V 0 S   10 Sep 80

AFOSI FORM 88 ATTACHED ☐ YES ☐ NO

DATE 8 Sept 80 **TYPED OR PRINTED NAME OF SPECIAL AGENT** RICHARD C. DOTY, SA

SIGNATURE Richard C. Doty

DISTRICT FILE NO. 80178 93-C/29

DCII RESULTS

NEGATIVE √ | POSITIVE (See Attached)

AFOSI FORM 1 JUN 76   PREVIOUS EDITION WILL BE USED

347

aerial phenomena described by the first three. Again the object landed in Coyote Canyon. They did not see the object take off.

5. Coyote Canyon is part of a large restricted test range used by the Air Force Weapons Laboratory, Sandia Laboratories, Defense Nuclear Agency and the Department of Energy. The range was formerly patrolled by Sandia Security, however, they only conduct building checks there now.

6. On 10 Aug 80, a New Mexico State Patrolman sighted an aerial object land in the Manzano's between Belen and Albuquerque, NM. The Patrolman reported the sighting to the Kirtland AFB Command Post, who later referred the patrolman to the AFOSI Dist 17. AFOSI Dist 17 advised the patrolman to make a report through his own agency. On 11 Aug 80, the Kirtland Public Information office advised the patrolman the USAF no longer investigates such sightings unless they occur on an USAF base.

7. WRITER contacted all the agencies who utilized the test range and it was learned no aerial tests are conducted in the Coyote Canyon area. Only ground tests are conducted.

8. On 8 Sept 80, WRITER learned from Sandia Security that another Security Guard observed a object land near an alarmed structure sometime during the first week of August, but did not report it until just recently for fear of harassment.

9. The two alarmed structures located within the area contains HQ CR 44 material.

COMPLAINT FORM 2 - 9 Sept 80   H91V05
ADMINISTRATIVE DATA

Title:
KIRTLAND AFB, NM, 8 Aug - 3 Sep 80,
Alleged Sightings of Unidentified
Aerial Lights in Restricted Test Range.
Date: 2-9 Sept 80
Time: 1200
Place: AFOSI Det 1700, Kirtland AFB, NM
Source and Evaluation: MAJOR ERNEST E. EDWARDS
Residence or Business Address:
Commander, 1608 SPS, Manzano, Kirtland AFB, NM
Phone: 4-7516
CR __44__ APPLIES
SUMMARY OF INFORMATION
Remarks:

1. On 2 Sept 80, SOURCE related on 8 Aug 80, three Security Policeman assigned to 1608 SPS, KAFB, NM, on duty inside the Manzano Weapons Storage Area sighted an uniden-

tified light in the air that traveled from North to South over the Coyote Canyon area of the Department of Defense Restricted Test Range on KAFB, NM. The Security Policemen identified as: SSGT STEPHEN FERENZ, Area Supervisor, AIC MARTIN W. RIST and AMN ANTHONY D. FRAZIER, were later interviewed separately by SOURCE and all three related the same statement: At approximately 2350 hrs., while on duty in Charlie Sector, East Side of Manzano, the three observed a very bright light in the sky approximately 3 miles North-North East of their position. The light traveled with great speed and stopped suddenly in the sky over Coyote Canyon. The three first thought the object was a helicopter, however, after observing the strange aerial maneuvers (stop and go), they felt a helicopter couldn't have performed such skills. The light landed in the Coyote Canyon area. Sometime later, three witnessed the light take off and leave proceeding straight up at a high speed and disappear.

2.   Central Security Control (CSC) inside Manzano, contacted Sandia Security, who conducts frequent building checks on two alarmed structures in the area. They advised that a patrol was already in the area and would investigate.

3.   ON 11 Aug 80, RUSS CURTIS, Sandia Security, advised that on 9 Aug 80, a Sandia Security Guard, (who wishes his name not be divulged for fear of harassment), related the following: At approximately 0020 hrs., he was driving east on the Coyote Canyon access road on a routine building check of an alarmed structure. As he approached the structure he observed a bright light near the ground behind the structure. He also observed an object he first thought was a helicopter. But after driving closer, he observed a round disk shaped object. He attempted to radio for a back up patrol but his radio would not work. As he approached the object on foot armed with a shotgun, the object took off in a vertical direction at a high rate of speed. The guard was a former helicopter mechanic in the U.S. Army and stated the object he observed was not a helicopter.

4. SOURCE advised on 22 Aug 80, three other security policemen observed the same aerial phenomena described by the first three. Again the object landed in Coyote Canyon. They did not see the object take off.

5. Coyote Canyon is part of a large restricted test range used by the Air Force Weapons Laboratory, Sandia Laboratories, Defense Nuclear Agency and the Department of Energy. The range was formerly patrolled by Sandia Security, however, they only conduct building checks there now.

6. On 10 Aug 80, a New Mexico State Patrolman sighted an aerial object land in the Manzano's between Belen and Albuquerque, NM. The Patrolman reported the sighting to the Kirtland AFB Command Post, who later referred the patrolman to the AFOSI Dist 17. AFOSI Dist 17 advised the patrolman to make a report through his own agency. On 11 Aug 80, the Kirtland Public Information office advised the patrolman the USAF no longer investigates such sightings unless they occur on a USAF base.

7. WRITER contacted all the agencies who utilized the test range and it was learned no aerial tests are conducted in the Coyote Canyon area. Only ground tests are conducted.

8. On 8 Sept 80, WRITER learned from Sandia Security that another Security Guard observed a object land near an alarmed structure sometime during the first week of August, but did not report it until just recently for fear of harassment.

9. The two alarmed structures located within the contains HQ CR 44 material.

Date forwarded HQ AFOSI: H91V05 10 Sep 80
Date: Sept 80
Typed or printed name of special agent: RICHARD C. DOTY, SA
District file no.: 8017D93-0/29
Signature:

Appendix B

CIA LETTER TO AUTHOR, 21 DECEMBER 1987

Central Intelligence Agency

Washington, D.C. 20505

Mr. Richard H. Hall   21 December 1987
4418 39th Street
Brentwood, MD   20722

Dear Mr. Hall:

This is in response to your letter of 8 April 1986 in which
you appeal the determination made by this Agency with regard to
your 5 June 1985 Privacy Act request for records pertaining to
yourself. In our decision letter of 3 April 1986, you were
informed that there were no documents available to you under
the Privacy Act of 1974. In response to your appeal,
responsive documents were located and reviewed as described
below.

Your appeal has been presented to the Central Intelligence
Agency Information Review Committee and has been considered
under the provisions of both the Freedom of Information Act
(FOIA) and the Privacy Act (PA). Pursuant to the authority
delegated under paragraph 1900.51(a) of Chapter XIX, Title 32
of the Code of Federal Regulations, Mr. Carroll L. Hauver,
Inspector General, and Mr. Clair E. George, Deputy Director for
Operations, have reviewed the responsive documents which are
listed below, the determinations made with respect to them, and
the propriety of the application of the FOIA and PA exemptions
asserted with respect to these documents.

Mr. Hauver has reviewed documents numbered 1 through 5, and
Mr. George has reviewed documents 6 through 16. A description
of each document, the determinations made with respect to each,
and the basis for exempting any of these materials from the
disclosure requirements of the FOIA and PA follow.

Document Numbers and Descriptions	Determinations	Exemption Basis FOIA	PA
1. Form 610, w/att., 12 September 1973	Release in part	(b)(3)	(j)(1)
2. Letter, 28 August 1973	Release in part	(b)(3)	(j)(1)

351

3.	Journal, 20 August 1973	Release in part	(b)(3), (b)(6)	(j)(1) (b)
4.	Journal, 26 September 1966	Release in part	(b)(1), (b)(3), (b)(6)	(j)(1), (k)(1), (b)
5.	Journal, 7 June 1977	Release in part	(b)(6)	(b)

[Note: Non-relevant Congressional material has been deleted from documents 3, 4, and 5.]

6.	Letter, 16 May 1973	Release in full		
7.	Letter, 19 June 1973	Release in full		
8.	Letter, 8 August 1973	Release in full		
9.	Memorandum, 25 January 1965	Release in part	(b)(1), (b)(3)	(j)(1), (k)(1)
10.	Routing Sheet, 29 June 1973	Release in part	(b)(3)	(j)(1)
11.	Memorandum, 14 August 1973	Release in part	(b)(1), (b)(3)	(j)(1), (k)(1)
12.	File Cover Sheet, undated	Deny in entirety	(b)(3)	(j)(1)
13.	Form 180, 21 January 1965	Deny in entirety	(b)(1), (b)(3)	(j)(1), (k)(1)
14.	Memorandum, 10 February 1965	Deny in entirety	(b)(1), (b)(3)	(j)(1), (k)(1)
15.	Form 25, 2 March 1965	Deny in entirety	(b)(1), (b)(3)	(j)(1), (k)(1)
16.	Form 1124a, 24 March 1965	Deny in entirety	(b)(1), (b)(3)	(j)(1), (k)(1)

2

Exemption (b)(1) encompasses matters which are specifically authorized under criteria established by the appropriate Executive order to be kept secret in the interest of national defense or foreign policy and which are, in fact, currently and properly classified.

Exemption (b)(3) pertains to information exempt from disclosure by statute. The relevant statutes are subsection 102(d)(3) of the National Security Act of 1947, as amended, 50 U.S.C. §403(d)(3), which makes the Director of Central Intelligence responsible for protecting intelligence sources and methods from unauthorized disclosure and section 6 of the Central Intelligence Agency Act of 1949, as amended, 50 U.S.C. §403g, which exempts from the disclosure requirement information pertaining to the organization, functions, names, official titles, salaries, or numbers of personnel employed by the Agency.

Exemption (b)(6) applies to information the disclosure of which would constitute a clearly unwarranted invasion of the privacy of an individual other than the requester.

Information withheld on the basis of exemption (j)(1) concerns intelligence sources and methods encompassed by those portions of systems of records which the Director of Central Intelligence has determined to be exempt from access by individuals pursuant to the authority granted by subsection (j)(1) and regulations promulgated thereunder (32 C.F.R. 1901.61).

Information withheld on the basis of exemption (k)(1) in this instance encompasses those portions of all systems of records which the Director of Central Intelligence has determined to be exempt from access by individuals pursuant to the authority granted by subsection (k)(1) and regulations promulgated thereunder (32 C.F.R. 1901.71). The information is properly classified under the terms of the appropriate Executive order and subject to the provisions of the Freedom of Information Act, 5 U.S.C. §552 (b)(1).

Subsection (b) has been applied to justify the withholding of information on individuals other than yourself, the release of which would constitute an unwarranted invasion of their privacy.

In view of your specific interest in any "paper trail" concerning yourself, please be advised that the denied documents are internal Agency documents concerning the matter mentioned in paragraph 6 of document number 9 and contain no information regarding you other than basic biographic data.

3

Copies of documents 1 through 11 as they may be released are enclosed.

In accordance with the provisions of the FOIA and the PA, you have the right to seek judicial review of the above determinations in a United States district court.

We appreciate your patience while your appeal was being considered.

Sincerely,

William F. Donnelly
Chairman
Information Review Committee

Enclosures

CIA MEMO ON NICAP AND RICHARD HALL

UNITED STATES GOVERNMENT

Memorandum

-72-65

TO : Chief, Contact Division   DATE: 25 January 1965
     Attn:

FROM : Chief,

SUBJECT: National Investigation Committee on Aerial Phenomena (NICAP) Case

    1. This confirms ███████ conversation 19 January 1965, at which time various samples and reports on UFO sightings procured from NICAP were given to ████████ for transmittal to OSI. The information was desired by OSI to assist them in the preparation of a paper for ████████ on UFO's.

    2. In accordance with ████████ request, we met on 19 January 1965 with Mr. Richard Harris Hall, Acting Director of NICAP. Though Major William Kehoe, founder of NICAP, is still listed as Director of the organization, we gather that he is present on the premises at 1536 Connecticut Avenue, N. W., only infrequently.

    3. The material which was given to us on loan by Mr. Hall is representative of the type of information available at NICAP. Their past and present correspondence from all over the US relative to UFO sightings is voluminous. They have slack periods, as was the case in December 1964, thus there were no "Investigators" reports immediately available for the month of December. NICAP has active Committees scattered throughout the US. Investigators active with these committees call upon the sources of reported UFO sightings to obtain first hand, eye witness accounts of the sightings. A printed form, prepared by the Air Force for NICAP's use, is utilized during the interview, and submitted to NICAP headquarters along with the source's eye witness account as told to the investigator. It was our understanding that copies of these reports go directly to various Air Force bases. There apparently is a strong feeling on the part of NICAP officials, i.e., Kehoe and Hall, that the Air Force tends to downgrade the importance of UFO sightings because they(the Air Force) does not care to have too much made of the sightings by the US press. We were told by Mr. Hall that there have been instances where the Air Force has attempted to intimidate witnesses and get them to sign false statements relative to UFO sightings.

APPROVED FOR RELEASE
Date   NOV 1987

REVIEWED FOR RELEASE
Date *19 Aug 86*

W/S-72-65
25 January 1965
Case ▓▓▓▓▓

4. The most recent UFO sighting of considerable interest to NICAP was the series of pick-ups of UFO's on the radar screen of the Patuxent Naval Air Station between 1500 and 1530 on 19 December 1964. This incident was reported in the press as a single sighting, a UFO approaching Patuxent at speeds up to 3800 miles per hour. The Air Force a day or so later stated in the press that the blip was caused by faulty radar equipment. Actually, according to Hall, who talked with an unidentified person close to the situation, there were three separate sightings:

(a) Two UFO's about 10 miles apart, southeast of Patuxent, approaching at a high rate of speed, disappeared from the screen;

(b) A single UFO picked up 39 miles southeast of Patuxent, altitude estimated somewhere between three thousand and 25 thousand feet, approaching base at estimated speed of six thousand miles per hour. UFO lost from screen about 10 miles out;

(c) A single UFO eight miles northeast of Patuxent, approaching at high rate of speed, made 160° turn, and dropped off the screen.

The Federal Aviation Agency (FAA) station at Salisbury, Maryland, was con▓▓▓ to determine if any reported UFO's; a radio operator had received message from a US Coast Guard ship reporting "visual objects sighted" in same locale at approximately the same time of day. Hall did give us the name of one of the radar operators at Patuxent--a Chief Pinkerton.

5. There was another UFO sighting reported in the area by the Washington Post within the last week or 10 days. Several men watching from the windows of the old Munitions Building on Constitution Avenue watched several UFO's on the horizon traveling at high rates of speed. They have promised to fill out NICAP's sighting questionnaire, which Hall says we are welcome to see when available.

6. ▓▓▓▓▓▓ informed us that she is requesting a security clearance on Mr. Hall predicated upon biographic information provided by ▓▓▓▓▓▓▓

APPROVED FOR RELEASE
Date ▓ ▓ NOV 1987

UNITED STATES GOVERNMENT
MEMORANDUM

████-72-65

TO: Chief, Contact Division
        Attn: ████████████

FROM: Chief, ████████████   DATE: 25 January 1965

SUBJECT: National Investigation Committee on Aerial
           Phenomena (NICAP) Case ████████

1. This confirms ████████ conversation 19 January 1965, at which time various samples and reports on UFO sightings procured from NICAP were given to ████████ for transmittal to OSI. The information was desired by OSI to assist them in the preparation of a paper for ████████ on UFO's.

2. In accordance with ████████ request, we met on 19 January 1965 with Mr. Richard Harris Hall, Acting Director of NICAP. Though Major William Kehoe, founder of NICAP, is still listed as Director of the organization, we gather that he is present on the premises at 1536 Connecticut Avenue, N.W., only infrequently.

3. The material which was given to us on loan by Mr. Hall is representative of the type of information available at NICAP. Their past and present correspondence from all over the US relative to UFO sightings is voluminous. They have slack periods, as was the case in December 1964, thus there were no "Investigators" reports immediately available for the month of December. NICAP has active Committees scattered throughout the US. Investigators active with these committees call upon the sources of reported UFO sightings to obtain first hand, eye witness accounts of the sightings. A printed form, prepared by the Air Force for NICAP's use, is utilized during the interview, and submitted to NICAP headquarters along with the source's eye witness account as told to the investigator. It

was our understanding that copies of these reports go directly to various Air Force bases. There apparently is a strong feeling on the part of NICAP officials, i.e., Kehoe and Hall, that the Air Force tends to downgrade the importance of UFO sightings because they (the Air Force) does not care to have too much made of the sightings by the US press. We were told by Mr. Hall that there have been instances where the Air Force has attempted to intimidate witnesses and get them to sign false statements relative to UFO sightings.

4. The most recent UFO sighting of considerable interest to NICAP was the series of pick-ups of UFO's on the radar screen of the Patuxent Navel Air Station between 1500 and 1530 on 19 December 1964. This incident was reported in the press as a single sighting, a UFO approaching Patuxent at speeds up to 3800 miles per hour. The Air Force a day or so later stated in the press that the blip was caused by faulty radar equipment. Actually, according to Hall, who talked with an unidentified person close to the situation, there were three separate sightings:

(a) Two UFO's about 10 miles apart, southeast of Patuxent, approaching at a high rate of speed, disappeared from the screen;

(b) A single UFO picked up 39 miles southeast of Patuxent, altitude estimated somewhere between three thousand and 25 thousand feet, approaching base at estimated speed of six thousand miles per hour. UFO lost from screen about 10 miles out;

(c) A single UFO eight miles northeast of Patuxent, approaching at high rate of speed, made 160° turn, and dropped off the screen.

The Federal Aviation Agency (FAA) station at Salisbury, Maryland, was contacted to determine if any reported UFO's; a radio operator had received a message from a US Coast Guard ship reporting "visual objects sighted" in same locale at approximately the same time of day. Hall did give us the name of one of the radar operators at Patuxent — A Chief Pinkerton.

5. There was another UFO sighting reported in the area by the Washington Post within the last week or 10 days. Several men watching from the windows of the old Munitions Building on Constitution Avenue watched several UFO's on the horizon traveling at high rates of speed. They have promised to fill out NICAP's sighting questionnaire, which Hall says we are welcome to see when available.

6. ██████████ informed us that she is requesting a security clearance on Mr. Hall predicated upon biographic information provided by ██████████ .

APPROVED FOR RELEASE
Date _____ NOV 1987 _____

358

Appendix B

CLASSIFIED "VITAL INTELLIGENCE SIGHTING" REPORT TO AIR DEFENSE COMMAND

```
                  ≈                    ≈

EMERGENCY
26 JULY 1953
D44
Y 260555Z
FM PERRIN AFB TEX
TO JEDEN/COMDR ADC ENT AFB COLO
JWFDL/COMDR CTAF RANDOLPH AFB TEX
BEPW/SEC DEF WASHINGOTN DC
/ZEN/CG 4TH ARMY FT SAM HOUSTON TEX
CIRVIS 3346N 9632W  GROUND OBSERVED SEVEN UNIDENTIFIED FLYING OBJECTS
WITH ONE BRIGHT RED LIGHT ON EACH OBJECT HOVERING AT ESTIMATED
ALTITUDES FROM FIVE TO EIGHT THOUSAND FEET.  VISUALLY OBSERVED FROM
PERRIN TOWER AND CITIZENS OF DENISON AND SHERMAN TEXAS.  NO LATERAL
MOVEMENT WAS OBSERVED.  FORMATION WAS IN GROUPS OF THREE WITH ONE
TRAILING AND THEN COMING TOGETHER TO FORM THE LETTER ZEBRA.  FORMATION
THEN CIRCLED WHILE GAINING ALTITUDE AND FADED FROM SIGHT ONE AT A TIME.
NO AIR TO AIR CONTACT MADE.  NO RADAR CONTACT MADE BY PERRIN RADAR.
VISUAL CONTACT WAS MAINTAINED FROM 2139C TO 2155C.  VISIBILITY
UNLIMITED WITH CLEAR SKY CONDITION.

//NOTE: THIS MSG HAS BEEN RELAYED O CIA BY ELECTRICAL MEANS//


DIST   03/32...ARMY/AF...ACTION
       002...05...202...WECDEF...CIA...CG...DIRNSA...50...JCS/SITROOM
       CNO/OOD

DLVY NR  242...WS/WLL

BEPN      BEPJC      BEPS
```

E M E R G E N C Y
26 JULY 1953

D44
Y 260555Z
FM PERRIN AFB TEX
TO JEDEN/COMDR ADC ENT AFB COLO
JWFDL/COMDR CTAF RANDOLPH AFB TEX
BEPW/SEC DEF WASHINGTON, D.C.
/ZEN/CG 4TH ARMY FT SAM HOUSTON TEX

CIRVIS 3346N 9632W GROUND OBSERVED SEVEN UN-
IDENTIFIED FLYING OBJECTS WITH ONE BRIGHT RED
LIGHT ON EACH OBJECT HOVERING AT ESTIMATED
ALTITUDES FROM FIVE TO EIGHT THOUSAND FEET.
VISUALLY OBSERVED FROM PERRIN TOWER AND CIT-
IZENS OF DENISON AND SHERMAN TEXAS. NO LAT-
ERAL MOVEMENT WAS OBSERVED. FORMATION WAS
IN GROUPS OF THREE WITH ONE TRAILING AND THEN
COMING TOGETHER TO FORM THE LETTER ZEBRA.
FORMATION THEN CIRCLED WHILE GAINING ALTI-
TUDE AND FADED FROM SIGHT ONE AT A TIME. NO
AIR TO AIR CONTACT MADE. NO RADAR CONTACT
MADE BY PERRIN RADAR. VISUAL CONTACT WAS
MAINTAINED FROM 2139C TO 2155C. VISIBILITY UN-
LIMITED WITH CLEAR SKY CONDITION.

//NOTE: THIS MSG HAS BEEN RELAYED TO CIA BY ELEC-
TRICAL MEANS//

DIST   03/32 ... ARMY/AF ... ACTION
       002 ... 05 ... 202 ... WECDEF ... CIA ... CG
       ... DIRNSA ... 50 ... JCS/SITROOM
       CNO/OOD

DLVY NR 242 ... WS/WLL

B E P N   B E P J C   B E P S

Appendix B

SUBJECT: AIR SPACE VIOLATION
AT OAK RIDGE, TENNESSEE

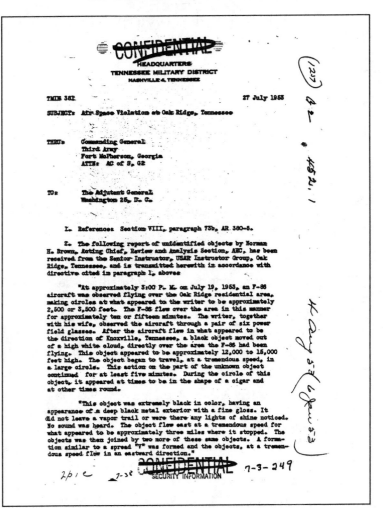

361

~~CONFIDENTIAL~~

HEADQUARTERS
TENNESSEE MILITARY DISTRICT
NASHVILLE 4, TENNESSEE

TMIN 381   27 July 1953

SUBJECT: Air Space Violation at Oak Ridge, Tennessee

THRU: Commanding General
       Third Army
       Fort McPherson, Georgia
       ATTN: AC of S. G2

TO: The Adjutant General
        Washington 25 D.C.

1. Reference: Section VIII, paragraph 73b, AR 380-5.

2. The following report of unidentified objects by Norman H. Brown, Acting Chief, Review and Analysis Section, AEC, has been received from the Senior Instructor, USAR Instructor Group, Oak Ridge, Tennessee, and is transmitted herewith in accordance with directive cited in paragraph 1, above:

"At approximately 3:00 P.M. on July 19, 1953, an F-86 aircraft was observed flying over the Oak Ridge residential area, making circles at what appeared to the writer to be approximately 2,500 or 3,500 feet. The F-86 flew over the area in this manner for approximately ten or fifteen minutes. The writer, together with his wife, observed the aircraft through a pair of six power field glasses. After the aircraft flew in what appeared to be the direction of Knoxville, Tennessee, a black object moved out of a high white cloud, directly over the area the F-86 had been flying. This object began to travel, at a tremendous speed, in a large circle. This action on the part of the unknown object continued for at least five minutes. During the circle of this object, it appeared at times to be in the shape of a cigar and at other times round.

"This object was extremely black in color, having an appearance of a deep black metal exterior with a fine gloss. It did not leave a vapor trail or were there any lights of shine noticed. No sound was heard. The object flew east at a tremendous speed for what appeared to be approximately three miles where it stopped. The object was then joined by two more of these same objects. A formation similar to a spread "V" was formed and the objects, at a tremendous speed flew in an eastward direction.

3. Further information will be reported as received.

FOR THE CHIEF:

Captain, ASC
Asst. Adjutant

SECURITY INFORMATION

APPENDIX C:
MJ-12 DOCUMENTS

BRIEFING DOCUMENT: OPERATION MAJESTIC 12
PREPARED FOR PRESIDENT-ELECT
DWIGHT D. EISENHOWER
18 NOVEMBER 1952

NATIONAL SECURITY INFORMATION

* * * * * * * * * * * *
* TOP SECRET *
* * * * * * * * * * * *

EYES ONLY   COPY ONE OF ONE.

BRIEFING DOCUMENT: OPERATION MAJESTIC 12

PREPARED FOR PRESIDENT-ELECT DWIGHT D. EISENHOWER: (EYES ONLY)

18 NOVEMBER, 1952

WARNING: This is a ████████████████ document containing compartmentalized information essential to the national security of the United States. ███████████████ to the material herein is strictly limited to those possessing Majestic-12 clearance level. Reproduction in any form or the taking of written or mechanically transcribed notes is strictly forbidden.

T52-EXEMPT (E)

~~EYES ONLY~~
• ~~TOP SECRET~~ •

~~EYES ONLY~~   COPY ONE OF ONE.

SUBJECT: OPERATION MAJESTIC-12 PRELIMINARY BRIEFING FOR
     PRESIDENT-ELECT EISENHOWER.

DOCUMENT PREPARED 18 NOVEMBER, 1952.

BRIEFING OFFICER: ADM. ROSCOE H. HILLENKOETTER (MJ-1)

NOTE: This document has been prepared as a preliminary briefing
only. It should be regarded as introductory to a full operations
briefing intended to follow.

OPERATION MAJESTIC-12 is a TOP SECRET Research and Development/
Intelligence operation responsible directly and only to the
President of the United States. Operations of the project are
carried out under control of the Majestic-12 (Majic-12) Group
which was established by special classified executive order of
President Truman on 24 September, 1947, upon recommendation by
Dr. Vannevar Bush and Secretary James Forrestal. (See Attachment
"A".) Members of the Majestic-12 Group were designated as follows:

          Adm. Roscoe H. Hillenkoetter
          Dr. Vannevar Bush
          Secy. James V. Forrestal*
          Gen. Nathan F. Twining
          Gen. Hoyt S. Vandenberg
          Dr. Detlev Bronk
          Dr. Jerome Hunsaker
          Mr. Sidney W. Souers
          Mr. Gordon Gray
          Dr. Donald Menzel
          Gen. Robert M. Montague
          Dr. Lloyd V. Berkner

The death of Secretary Forrestal on 22 May, 1949, created
a vacancy which remained unfilled until 01 August, 1950, upon
which date Gen. Walter B. Smith was designated as permanent
replacement.

T52-EXEMPT (E)

~~EYES ONLY~~   COPY <u>ONE</u> OF <u>ONE</u>.

On 24 June, 1947, a civilian pilot flying over the Cascade
Mountains in the State of Washington observed nine flying
disc-shaped aircraft traveling in formation at a high rate
of speed. Although this was not the first known sighting
of such objects, it was the first to gain widespread attention
in the public media. Hundreds of reports of sightings of
similar objects followed. Many of these came from highly
credible military and civilian sources. These reports resulted in independent efforts by several different elements
of the military to ascertain the nature and purpose of these
objects in the interests of national defense. A number of
witnesses were interviewed and there were several unsuccessful
attempts to utilize aircraft in efforts to pursue reported
discs in flight. Public reaction bordered on near hysteria
at times.

In spite of these efforts, little of substance was learned
about the objects until a local rancher reported that one
had crashed in a remote region of New Mexico located approximately seventy-five miles northwest of Roswell Army Air
Base (now Walker Field).

On 07 July, 1947, a secret operation was begun to assure
recovery of the wreckage of this object for scientific study.
During the course of this operation, aerial reconnaissance
discovered that four small human-like beings had apparently
ejected from the craft at some point before it exploded.
These had fallen to earth about two miles east of the wreckage
site. All four were dead and badly decomposed due to action
by predators and exposure to the elements during the approximately one week time period which had elapsed before their
discovery. A special scientific team took charge of removing
these bodies for study. (See Attachment "C".) The wreckage
of the craft was also removed to several different locations.
(See Attachment "B".) Civilian and military witnesses in
the area were debriefed, and news reporters were given the
effective cover story that the object had been a misguided
weather research balloon.

COPY <u>ONE</u> OF <u>ONE</u>.

A covert analytical effort organized by Gen. Twining and
Dr. Bush acting on the direct orders of the President, resulted in a preliminary concensus (19 September, 1947) that
the disc was most likely a short range reconnaissance craft.
This conclusion was based for the most part on the craft's
size and the apparent lack of any identifiable provisioning.
(See Attachment "D".) A similar analysis of the four dead
occupants was arranged by Dr. Bronk. It was the tentative
conclusion of this group (30 November, 1947) that although
these creatures are human-like in appearance, the biological
and evolutionary processes responsible for their development
has apparently been quite different from those observed or
postulated in homo-sapiens. Dr. Bronk's team has suggested
the term "Extra-terrestrial Biological Entities", or "EBEs",
be adopted as the standard term of reference for these
creatures until such time as a more definitive designation
can be agreed upon.

Since it is virtually certain that these craft do not originate in any country on earth, considerable speculation has
centered around what their point of origin might be and how
they get here. Mars was and remains a possibility, although
some scientists, most notably Dr. Menzel, consider it more
likely that we are dealing with beings from another solar
system entirely.

Numerous examples of what appear to be a form of writing
were found in the wreckage. Efforts to decipher these have
remained largely unsuccessful. (See Attachment "E".)
Equally unsuccessful have been efforts to determine the
method of propulsion or the nature.or method of transmission
of the power source involved. Research along these lines
has been complicated by the complete absence of identifiable
wings, propellers, jets, or other conventional methods of
propulsion and guidance, as well as a total lack of metallic
wiring, vacuum tubes, or similar recognizable electronic
components. (See Attachment "F".) It is assumed that the
propulsion unit was completely destroyed by the explosion
which caused the crash.

T52-EXEMPT (E)

369

COPY <u>ONE</u> OF <u>ONE</u>.

A need for as much additional information as possible about
these craft, their performance characteristics and their
purpose led to the undertaking known as U.S. Air Force Project
SIGN in December, 1947. In order to preserve security, liason
between SIGN and Majestic-12 was limited to two individuals
within the Intelligence Division of Air Materiel Command whose
role was to pass along certain types of information through
channels. SIGN evolved into Project GRUDGE in December, 1948.
The operation is currently being conducted under the code name
BLUE BOOK, with liason maintained through the Air Force officer
who is head of the project.

On 06 December, 1950, a second object, probably of similar
origin, impacted the earth at high speed in the El Indio -
Guerrero area of the Texas - Mexican boder after following
a long trajectory through the atmosphere. By the time a
search team arrived, what remained of the object had been almost
totally incinerated. Such material as could be recovered was
transported to the A.E.C. facility at Sandia, New Mexico, for
study.

Implications for the National Security are of continuing importance in that the motives and ultimate intentions of these
visitors remain completely unknown. In addition, a significant
upsurge in the surveillance activity of these craft beginning
in May and continuing through the autumn of this year has caused
considerable concern that new developments may be imminent.
It is for these reasons, as well as the obvious international
and technological considerations and the ultimate need to
avoid a public panic at all costs, that the Majestic-12 Group
remains of the unanimous opinion that imposition of the
strictest security precautions should continue without interruption into the new administration. At the same time, contingency plan MJ-1949-04P/78 (Top Secret - Eyes Only) should
be held in continued readiness should the need to make a
public announcement present itself. (See Attachment "G".)

~~~~ ONLY

COPY <u>ONE</u> OF <u>ONE</u>.

ENUMERATION OF ATTACHMENTS:

•ATTACHMENT "A"........Special Classified Executive
                       Order #092447. (TS/EO)

•ATTACHMENT "B"........Operation Majestic-12 Status
                       Report #1, Part A. 30 NOV '47.
                       (TS-MAJIC/EO)

•ATTACHMENT "C"........Operation Majestic-12 Status
                       Report #1, Part B. 30 NOV '47.
                       (TS-MAJIC/EO)

•ATTACHMENT "D"........Operation Majestic-12 Preliminary
                       Analytical Report. 19 SEP '47.
                       (TS-MAJIC/EO)

•ATTACHMENT "E"........Operation Majestic-12 Blue Team
                       Report #5. 30 JUN '52.
                       (TS-MAJIC/EO)

•ATTACHMENT "F"........Operation Majestic-12 Status
                       Report #2. 31 JAN '48.
                       (TS-MAJIC/EO)

•ATTACHMENT "G"........Operation Majestic-12 Contingency
                       Plan MJ-1949-04P/78: 31 JAN '49.
                       (TS-MAJIC/EO)

•ATTACHMENT "H"........Operation Majestic-12, Maps and
                       Photographs Folio (Extractions).
                       (TS-MAJIC/EO)

T52-EXEMPT (E)

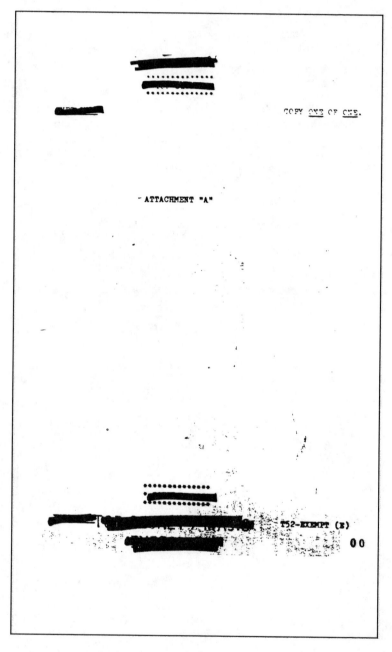

COPY ONE OF ONE.

ATTACHMENT "A"

T52-EXEMPT (B)

00

THE WHITE HOUSE
WASHINGTON

September 24, 1947.

MEMORANDUM FOR THE SECRETARY OF DEFENSE

Dear Secretary Forrestal:

As per our recent conversation on this matter, you are hereby authorized to proceed with all due speed and caution upon your undertaking. Hereafter this matter shall be referred to only as Operation Majestic Twelve.

It continues to be my feeling that any future considerations relative to the ultimate disposition of this matter should rest solely with the Office of the President following appropriate discussions with yourself, Dr. Bush and the Director of Central Intelligence.

COPY <u>ONE</u> OF <u>ONE</u>.

BRIEFING DOCUMENT: OPERATION MAJESTIC 12
PREPARED FOR PRESIDENT-ELECT
DWIGHT D. EISENHOWER: ▬▬▬▬
18 NOVEMBER, 1952

WARNING: This is a ▬▬▬▬▬ document containing compartmentalized information essential to the national security of the United States. ▬▬▬▬▬ the material herein is strictly limited to those possessing Majestic-12 clearance level. Reproduction in any form or the taking of written or mechanically transcribed notes is strictly forbidden.

SUBJECT: OPERATION MAJESTIC-12 PRELIMINARY BRIEFING FOR PRESIDENT-ELECT EISENHOWER.

DOCUMENT PREPARED 18 NOVEMBER, 1952.

BRIEFING OFFICER: ADM. ROSCOE H. HILLENKOETTER (MJ-1)

NOTE: This document has been prepared as a preliminary briefing only. It should be regarded as introductory to a full operations briefing intended to follow.

OPERATION MAJESTIC-12 is a TOP SECRET Research and Development/Intelligence operation responsible directly and only to the President of the United States. Operations of the project are carried out under control of the Majestic-12 (Majic-12) Group which was established by special classified executive order of President Truman on 24 September, 1947, upon recommendation by Dr. Vannevar Bush and Secretary James Forrestal. (See Attachment "A". Members of the Majestic-12 Group were designated as follows:

> Adm. Roscoe H. Hillenkoetter
> Dr. Vannevar Bush
> Secy. James V. Forrestal
> Gen. Nathan F. Twining
> Gen. Hoyt S. Vandenberg
> Dr. Detlev Bronk
> Dr. Jerome Hunsaker
> Mr. Sidney W. Souers
> Mr. Gordon Gray
> Dr. Donald Menzel
> Gen. Robert M. Montague
> Dr. Lloyd V. Berkner

The death of Secretary Forrestal on 22 May, 1949, created a vacancy which remained unfilled until 01 August, 1950, upon which date Gen. Walter B. Smith was designated as permanent replacement.

On 24 June, 1947, a civilian pilot flying over the Cascade Mountains in the State of Washington observed nine flying disc-shaped aircraft traveling in formation at a high rate of speed. Although this was not the first known sighting of such objects, it was the first to gain widespread attention in the public media. Hundreds of reports of sightings of similar objects followed. Many of these came from highly credible military and civilian sources. These reports resulted in independent efforts by several different elements of the military to ascertain the nature and purpose of these objects in the interests of national defense. A number of witnesses were interviewed and there were several unsuccessful attempts to utilize aircraft in efforts to pursue reported discs in flight. Public reaction bordered on near hysteria at times.

In spite of these efforts, little of substance was learned about the objects until a local rancher reported that one had crashed in a remote region of New Mexico located approximately seventy-five miles northwest of Roswell Army Air Base (now Walker Field).

On 07 July, 1947, a secret operation was begun to assure recovery of the wreckage of this object for scientific study. During the course of this operation, aerial reconnaissance discovered that four small human-like beings had apparently ejected from the craft at some point before it exploded. These had fallen to earth about two miles east of the wreckage site. All four were dead and badly decomposed due to action by predators and exposure to the elements during the approximately one week time period which had elapsed before their discovery. A special scientific team took charge of removing these bodies for study. (See Attachment "C".) The wreckage of the craft was also removed to several different locations. (See Attachment "B".) Civilian and military witnesses in the area were debriefed, and news reporters were given the effective cover story that the object had been a misguided weather research balloon.

A covert analytical effort organized by Gen. Twining and Dr. Bush acting on the direct orders of the President, resulted in a preliminary concensus (19 September, 1947) that the disc was most likely a short range reconnaissance craft. This conclusion was based for the most part on the craft's size and the apparent lack of any identifiable provisioning. (See Attachment "D".) A similar analysis of the four dead occupants was arranged by Dr. Bronk. It was the tentative conclusion of this group (30 November, 1947) that although these creatures are human-like in appearance, the biological and evolutionary processes responsible for their development has apparently been quite different from those observed or postulated in homo-sapiens. Dr. Bronk's team has suggested the term "Extra-terrestrial Biological Entities", or "EBEs", be adopted as the standard term of reference for these creatures until such time as a more definitive designation can be agreed upon.

376

Since it is virtually certain that these craft do not originate in any country on earth, considerable speculation has centered around what their point of origin might be and how they get here. Mars was and remains a possibility, although some scientists, most notably Dr. Menzel, consider it more likely that we are dealing with beings from another solar system entirely.

Numerous examples of what appear to be a form of writing were found in the wreckage. Efforts to decipher these have remained largely unsuccessful. (See Attachment "E".) Equally unsuccessful have been efforts to determine the method of propulsion or the nature or method of transmission of the power source involved. Research along these lines has been complicated by the complete absence of identifiable wings, propellers, jets, or other conventional methods of propulsion and guidance, as well as a total lack of metallic wiring, vacuum tubes, or similar recognizable electronic components. (See Attachment "F".) It is assumed that the propulsion unit was completely destroyed by the explosion which caused the crash.

A need for as much additional information as possible about these craft, their performance characteristics and their purpose led to the undertaking known as U.S. Air Force Project SIGN in December, 1947. In order to preserve security, liason between SIGN and Majestic-12 was limited to two individuals within the Intelligence Division of Air Materiel Command whose role was to pass along certain types of information through channels. SIGN evolved into Project GRUDGE in December, 1948. The operation is currently being conducted under the code name BLUE BOOK, with liason maintained through the Air Force officer who is head of the project.

On 06 December, 1950, a second object, probably of similar origin, impacted the earth at high speed in the El Indio-Guerrero area of the Texas-Mexican border after following a long trajectory through the atmosphere. By the time a search team arrived, what remained of the object had been almost totally incinerated. Such material as could be recovered was transported to the A.E.C. facility at Sandia, New Mexico, for study.

Implications for the National Security are of continuing importance in that the motives and ultimate intentions of these visitors remain completely unknown. In addition, a significant upsurge in the surveillance activity of these craft beginning in May and continuing through the autumn of this year has caused considerable concern that new developments may be imminent. It is for these reasons, as well as the obvious international and technological considerations and the ultimate need to avoid a public panic at all costs, that the Majestic-12 Group remains of the unanimous opinion that imposition of the strictest security precautions should continue without interruption into the new administration. At the same time, contingency plan MJ-1949-O4P/78 (Top Secret-Eyes Only) should be held in continued readiness should the need to make a public announcement present itself. (See Attachment "G".)

ENUMERATION OF ATTACHMENTS:

*ATTACHMENT "A" ..Special Classified Executive Order #092447. (TS/EO)

*ATTACHMENT "B" ..Operation Majestic-12 Status Report #1, Part A. 30 NOV '47. (TS-MAJIC/EO)

*ATTACHMENT "C" ..Operation Majestic-12 Status Report #1, Part B. 30 NOV '47. (TS-MAJIC/EO)

*ATTACHMENT "D" ..Operation Majestic-12 Preliminary Analytical Report. 19 SEP '47. (TS-MAJIC/EO)

*ATTACHMENT "E" ..Operation Majestic-12 Blue Team Report #5. 30 JUN '52. (TS-MAJIC/EO)

*ATTACHMENT "F"....Operation Majestic-12 Status Report #2. 31 JAN '48. (TS-MAJIC/EO)

*ATTACHMENT "G" ..Operation Majestic-12 Contingency
Plan MJ-1949-O4P/78: 31 JAN '49.
(TS-MAJIC/EO)

*ATTACHMENT "H" ..Operation Majestic-12, Maps and
Photographs Folio (Extractions).
(TS-MAJIC/EO)

*ATTACHMENT "A"
~~TOP SECRET~~
~~EYES ONLY~~
THE WHITE HOUSE
WASHINGTON

September 24, 1947.

MEMORANDUM FOR THE SECRETARY OF DEFENSE

Dear Secretary Forrestral:

As per our recent conversation on this matter, you are
hereby authorized to proceed with all due speed and caution
upon your undertaking. Hereafter this matter shall be referred to only as Operation Majestic Twelve.

It continues to be my feeling that any future considerations relative to the ultimate disposition of this matter should
rest solely with the Office of the President following appropriate
discussions with yourself, Dr. Bush and the Director of Central Intelligence.

/s/ Harry S Truman

APPENDIX D:
ACRONYMS & ABBREVIATIONS

AAAS: American Association for the Advancement of Science.

AFB: Air Force Base.

AIAA: American Institute of Aeronautics and Astronautics.

APRO: Aerial Phenomena Research Organization (Tucson, Ariz.)

CE I, II, III: Close encounters of the First, Second, and Third Kind (defined by Dr. J. Allen Hynek in *The UFO Experience: A Scientific Inquiry*, Regnery, 1972).

CIA: Central Intelligence Agency.

CUFOS: J. Allen Hynek Center for UFO Studies (Chicago, Ill.)

DOD: Department of Defense.

E-M: Electromagnetic (effects on vehicles and electrical systems during UFO sightings).

ETH: Extraterrestrial hypothesis to explain UFOs.

ETI(s): Extraterrestrial intelligence(s).

FBI: Federal Bureau of Investigation.

FOIA: Freedom of Information Act (which establishes ground rules for and expedites citizen access to Government documents).

HUMCAT: Humanoid Catalogue (computer catalogue of data on entities reported in association with UFOs).

ICBM: Intercontinental Ballistic Missile.

IEEE: Institute of Electrical and Electronics Engineers.

MUFON: Mutual UFO Network (Seguin, Tex.).

MJ-12: Majestic-12; purported group of scientists and military leaders controlling Government studies of crashed UFOs.

NICAP: National Investigations Committee on Aerial Phenomena (formerly in Washington, D.C.; files now incorporated into Center for UFO Studies, Chicago, Ill.)

NORAD: North American Air Defense Command.

NSA: National Security Agency.

OPEC: Organization of Petroleum Exporting Countries.

UFOCAT: UFO Catalogue (computer catalogue of data on UFO sightings operated by CUFOS).

USAF: U.S. Air Force.

AURORA PRESS

Aurora Press is devoted to pioneering books that catalyze personal growth, balance and transformation. Aurora makes available in a digestible format, an innovative synthesis of ancient wisdom with twentieth century resources, integrating esoteric knowledge and daily life.

Recent titles include:

COMING HOME
Deborah Duda

CRYSTAL ENLIGHTENMENT
Katrina Raphaell

CRYSTAL HEALING
Katrina Raphaell

SILVER DENTAL FILLINGS • THE TOXIC TIMEBOMB
Sam Ziff

AWAKEN HEALING ENERGY THROUGH THE TAO
Mantak Chia

TAOIST SECRETS OF LOVE
Mantak Chia

THE LUNATION CYCLE
Dane Rudhyar

SELF HEALING, YOGA AND DESTINY
Elisabeth Haich

For a complete catalog write:

AURORA PRESS
P.O. BOX 573
SANTA FE NEW MEXICO 87504
(505) 989-9804